# Hidden Heritage

THE S. MARK TAPER FOUNDATION

IMPRINT IN JEWISH STUDIES

BY THIS ENDOWMENT

THE S. MARK TAPER FOUNDATION SUPPORTS

THE APPRECIATION AND UNDERSTANDING

OF THE RICHNESS AND DIVERSITY OF

JEWISH LIFE AND CULTURE

# Hidden Heritage

*The Legacy of the Crypto-Jews*

Janet Liebman Jacobs

UNIVERSITY OF CALIFORNIA PRESS
*Berkeley · Los Angeles · London*

The publisher gratefully acknowledges the generous contribution to this book provided by the Jewish Studies Endowment of the University of California Press Associates, which is supported by a major gift from the S. Mark Taper Foundation.

University of California Press
Berkeley and Los Angeles, California

University of California Press, Ltd.
London, England



Library of Congress Cataloging-in-Publication Data
Jacobs, Janet Liebman.
Hidden heritage : the legecy of the Crypto-Jews / Janet Liebman Jacobs.
p. cm.
Includes bibliographical references (p. ) and index.
ISBN 0–520-23346-8 (Cloth : alk. paper)—ISBN 0–520-23517-7 (Paper : alk. paper)
1. Marranos—United States—History. 2. Jews—United States—History. 3. Marranos—Religious life. 4. Marranos—Social life and customs. 5. Jews—Identity. 6. United States—Ethnic relations. I. Title.

E184.36.E84 J33 2002
305.892'4073—dc21 2002000857

Manufactured in the United States of America
10 09 08 07 06 05 04 03 02
10 9 8 7 6 5 4 3 2 1

The paper used in this publication is both acid-free and totally chlorine-free (TCF). It meets the minimum requirements of ANSI/NISO Z39.48–1992 (R 1997) *(Permanence of Paper)*.∞

*In memory of my father, Jesse,*
*my grandmother, Bettie, and*
*my great-grandmother, Tillie Canella*

# Contents

# Acknowledgments

This book would not have been possible without the generosity and participation of the crypto-Jewish descendants who so willingly gave of their time and of themselves over many years of study and research. Because of the difficulties and challenges posed by the process of recovering ethnic origins, I am particularly grateful to the participants who gave me their trust and who allowed me to enter into a world of family secrets, remembered ancestors, and personal soul searching. I am indebted especially to Carmen Epstein, whose wonderful restaurant, Mamacita's, provided a starting point from which to begin my study of crypto-Jewish culture and the recovery of Jewish ancestry.

As my research progressed, many people, all along the way, offered advice and help. Among those to whom I am most grateful are Max Costillo, Magda Hinojosa, Stanley Hordes, David Kazzaz, Kathe MacLaren, Otto Maduro, Joan Markowitz, Anita Rodriguez, Catherine Lucero Sedillo, and Harriet Silverman. I would also like to acknowledge and remember, with gratitude, Bertha Muske, whose insights and perspectives greatly contributed to my research.

I would not have succeeded in completing this book without the dedication of colleagues and friends who generously gave of their time in reading and commenting on either all or major portions of the manuscript. I would like to thank Ira Becker, Lynn Davidman, Robert Ferry, Deborah Flick, David Gitlitz, Donna Goldstein, Steven Kepnes, and Diane Jonte-Pace. Each of these readers offered critical insights and suggestions that vastly improved the quality of the analysis. I would also like to thank Cheryl Townsend Gilkes and Ruth Wallace for their helpful comments, and Andrew Glassco for his help with translation. I gratefully acknowledge the interest of my colleague Paul Shankman, who continually sent along information on crypto-Jewish studies and events.

I am grateful for the research support provided by the Association for the Sociology of Religion, the Memorial Foundation for Jewish Culture, and the University of Colorado Impart Program. I would also like to thank Melissa Amado and the Bloom Southwest Jewish Archives for providing research assistance and materials in the early stages of the project. Amanda Arthur, Kris Gilmore, and Heili Lehr were an invaluable help with the references and bibliography, while Jeanie Lusby and Anna Vayr graciously offered the staff support of the Women's Studies Program at the University of Colorado. I am especially grateful to my editor, Reed Malcolm, for his patience and support, and to David Gill and Mimi Kusch for their vigorous editorial assistance.

Finally, I would like to express deep appreciation to my cousin, Aileen Wissner, who gave me the gift of my Sephardic ancestors, and to my family, Gary, Jamie, and Michael, whose love and support followed me throughout my research and fieldwork into the changing landscape of crypto-Jewish descent.

I'm crossing the Bridges of Memory now
to the land of my ancestral home; there's the house
of the fortune teller, her name I remember:

Estrella Ben Roya, a storyteller.
She told the villagers' futures, then
passed on her powers to me. What

would you like to know? I'll tell you.
It lives in my heart's memory.

Brenda Serotte, from "Crossing the Bridge of Sighs,"
*Poems and Ladino Translations*

INTRODUCTION

# Crypto-Jewish Descent

## *An Ethnographic Study in Historical Perspective*

The year 1992 marked the five-hundred-year anniversary of the expulsion of the Jews from Spain. With the commemoration of this critical juncture in European Jewish life, the memory of the Inquisition and its abuses became the subject of scholarly publications, conferences, symposia, and reports in the popular press.[1] Through the acknowledgment of this painful period in the history of Spanish Jewry, the significance of the Sephardic (Spanish Jewish)[2] diaspora was brought to public consciousness in the United States, providing a historical lens through which to consider the origins of antisemitism in medieval Europe. Central to the 1992 commemoration discourse was the role that crypto-Judaism (the secret practice of the Jewish religion) played in preserving Jewish rites and beliefs both before and after the Sephardic diaspora. In the scholarly proceedings as well as the media coverage, crypto-Judaism was remembered as one means by which medieval Jews coped with the demands of forced conversion: outwardly they became Christian while secretly they concealed their Jewish practices and beliefs.

During the 1992 commemoration, the history of the crypto-Jews was frequently highlighted in public presentations. The unique place that the crypto-Jews assumed in the remembrance dialogue can in part be explained by the discovery in the twentieth century of a surviving crypto-Jewish culture in areas of the United States and Latin America where crypto-Jews had settled during the Spanish and Portuguese colonial period. Commemoration ceremonies, lectures, and media programming frequently featured firsthand accounts of modern descendants of the Spanish and Portuguese crypto-Jews whose Christian families had maintained some semblance of Jewish rituals since the sixteenth and seventeenth centuries. In 1992 and then again in 1996, when the expulsion of the Jews from Portugal was memorialized, descendants of the colonial crypto-Jews found themselves at the center of a Sephardic revivalism in the United States, as reports of secret prayers and hidden Sabbath customs were circulated in both the secular and religious press.[3] More often than not, these reports spoke of mothers and grandmothers who, concealed behind curtained windows and closed doors, performed hidden rituals that had been in their families for centuries. As the images of surviving medieval practices captured the public's imagination, a new body of scholarship on both the historical and modern aspects of crypto-Jewish culture began to appear in the literature on Sephardic Jews.

Intrigued by the reports of surviving crypto-Judaism, I began my research into contemporary crypto-Jewish culture in 1993. Initially, my goal was to investigate the role of women in the preservation of Jewish culture. Living in close proximity to the regions where many crypto-Jewish descendants resided, I became interested in the survival of remnant forms of crypto-Judaism and especially in the maintenance of Jewish-based customs by women within the Latina/o Catholic household.[4] As I pursued this study of gender and cultural persistence, I was flooded with my own memories of childhood stories of the secret Jews of Spain. In my 1950s Sunday school education, this medieval phenomenon had been briefly and somewhat dramatically presented as tales of Christian converts who secretly lit Sabbath candles and privately prayed in the darkest caverns of their homes. The name by which these secret Jews were then known was "Marrano," a word that in my childhood recollections carried with it its own distinct imagery of danger in the face of religious constancy. By 1993, however, the term was no longer in common use, its meaning attributed to the word for swine or pig.[5] Even so, it was the 1950s image of the medieval Marranos that framed my childhood reminiscences of the secret Spanish Jews.

As I recalled the stories of the mysterious Marrano culture, I also remembered that my father had once told me that his mother was a Spanish Jew. Yet when I tried to reconstruct this information, I realized that everything I knew about my Jewish heritage was linked to the Ashkenazic (Austrian and Eastern European) culture of my maternal grandparents and paternal grandfather. Although I became increasingly convinced of my own "secret" Sephardic ancestry, I received little confermation for this belief until a few months before my father's death. It was the fall of 1995. Preparations for the Portuguese quincentenary (five-hundred-year anniversary of the expulsion) were already under way. I was visiting with my father, who, although quite ill, suddenly began to talk about the Golden Age of Sephardic Judaism, when Spanish Jewish thinkers proliferated in Muslim Spain.[6] I thought that my father must have seen the stories on the Portuguese quincentenary in the Jewish press, and I assumed that these reports had rekindled his sudden interest in Sephardic history. Abruptly, however, his conversation shifted from Sephardic art and culture to the loss of his mother in childhood. Quite unexpectedly, he explained, as if for the first time, that his mother was a Spanish Jew and that there were Marranos in her family. "You know," he said, "the Marranos, the secret Jews, they're our ancestors too."

My father then went on to describe a family genealogy that traced my grandmother's Spanish ancestors to a prominent sixteenth-century Marrano family whose exile from Spain took them first to Portugal and then to the Ottoman Empire.[7] Once in Turkey, where Jews were welcomed, my ancestors apparently returned to Judaism, a religion they maintained with orthodoxy through later immigrations to Eastern Europe and the United States. As I listened to my father's account of this somewhat hidden ancestral history, I could not help but recall the deathbed revelations described by the crypto-Jewish descendants with whom I had spoken. As the descendants' parents or elderly family members neared death, they would frequently reveal for the first time a family history that linked their heritage to crypto-Jewish origins. My father's sudden willingness to talk about his Spanish ancestry provided an almost eerie parallel to the deathbed disclosures described by these descendants.

The knowledge of my Sephardic ancestry created a more personal connection to the descendant community, and, as a result, I found myself rethinking the goals of the research. In addition to the study of gender and cultural preservation, I expanded my project to include an investigation into the effects of hidden ancestry on the construction of religious and ethnic identity. In particular, I sought to explore how the descendants of medieval crypto-Jews responded to the discovery of their Jewish heritage and to the secrecy that surrounds this ancestral history. I therefore began my inquiry with a study of the history of the Iberian crypto-Jews. To help contextualize the more contemporary phenomenon, a brief historical overview of the development of crypto-Judaism is presented below.

## HISTORICAL ANTECEDENTS TO THE CONTEMPORARY CRYPTO-JEWISH PHENOMENON

The beginnings of Sephardic crypto-Judaism are found in fourteenth-century Spain when, as a result of political and social changes, attacks against the centuries-old Spanish Jewish community became pervasive. Fueled both by economic conditions and ecclesiastical antisemitism, violence against the Jews began in 1391 in Seville and quickly spread to Ciudad Real and Burgos before reaching Valencia.[8] Within the year, Jewish communities in Toledo, Barcelona, Gerona, and Aragon bore the effects of mob-incited violence as homes were burned, businesses looted, synagogues destroyed, and Jews murdered. As the religious persecution escalated, large numbers of Jews acquiesced to the demands of forced conversion, while others voluntarily chose to become Christian. The result of these events was the creation of a disparate and varied convert population whose differing approaches to Christian assimilation transformed the religious culture of medieval Spain. Amid the diverse reactions to the widespread policies of forced conversion was a strategy of resistance that came to be known as crypto-Judaism. This practice, which was adopted by a portion of the Jewish converts, involved the clandestine observance of Judaism among individuals and families who had undergone conversion but who secretly remained faithful to Jewish beliefs and traditions.[9]

The historical scholarship on this period of Sephardic history suggests that crypto-Judaism was one of a number of conversion responses adopted by the besieged Jews of Spain. The historians David Gitlitz and José Faur identify at least four types of converts that emerged from the anti-Jewish pogroms. According to these scholars, the convert population included true converts who became faithful to Christianity; partial converts who vacillated between Judaism and Christianity or attempted a syncretic accommodation of the two religions; crypto-Jewish converts who, to the extent possible, remained faithful to Judaism; and atheistic converts who rejected both Christianity and Judaism in light of the continued religious persecution and violence. While all these categories of converts were classified as New Christians *(cristianos nuevos)* by Church authorities, it was the crypto-Jews who came under the greatest scrutiny, since their continued adherence to Judaism was viewed as heresy by the medieval church.[10]

After this period of intensified conversions, the tensions between competing Jewish and Christian belief systems grew more fervent as rabbis sought to defend the principles of Judaism in the face of the Church's escalating attempts to obtain and sustain converts. During this time of religious upheaval, the Church held religious debates that focused on the Messiah and the acceptance of Jesus as the son of God. In these debates, the most ardent proponents of the Christian viewpoint were frequently theologians who had previously converted to Christianity. As these religious polemics further demoralized the Spanish Jews, the Church grew more emphatic about the dangers that Judaism posed for Christian society. Fears about the continued proliferation of crypto-Judaism led to a campaign to establish an Inquisition in Spain that, according to Church officials, would at last rid the country of the Jewish "plague of heresy."[11] In 1478, at the request of King Ferdinand and Queen Isabella, the pope granted the Spanish monarchy the authority to appoint inquisitors in Castile, a papal decision that initiated the centuries-long Spanish Inquisition. From the outset, the Inquisition was intended to eliminate the heresy of crypto-Judaism. The Holy Office thus took as its mission the discovery and punishment of those converts who continued to engage in the practices of Judaism and who were therefore guilty of the crime of "Judaizing."[12]

Between 1481 and 1488, 750 men and women in Seville were burned at the stake for Judaizing, and at least five thousand others were punished for acts of Jewish heresy.[13] In support of the extreme measures taken by the Church, the sixteenth-century historian and priest Andres Bernáldez reported that the harsh actions of the Inquisition had been necessitated by the rapid spread of crypto-Judaism among the converts of Seville, Cordova, Toledo, and Segovia. The following passage from his writings served to justify the actions of the Holy Office:

> All of them were Jews, and clung to their hope, like the Israelites in Eygpt, who suffered many blows at the hands of the Egyptians and yet believed that God would lead them out from the midst of them, as He did with a mighty hand and an outstretched arm. So, too, the *conversos* looked upon the Christians as Egyptians or worse, and believed that God had them in His keeping and preserved them as by a miracle. They held steadfastly to their faith that God would guide and remember them and bring them out from the midst of the Christians and lead them to the Holy and Promised Land. The Inquisition proposed to destroy their belief and the believers. "The fire has been kindled, and it will burn until not one of them is left alive."[14]

To facilitate the prosecution and punishment of Jewish heretics, the Church developed a systematic approach to the identification of crypto-

Jews by creating the Edicts of Grace, documents so named because they offered a grace period to anyone who willingly confessed their heretical practices. In an early-twentieth-century history of the Inquisition, Henry Charles Lea highlights the dramatic and often fearful conditions under which the Edicts of Grace (later called the Edicts of Faith) were disseminated at public meetings and at church services. Lea's characterization of these proceedings captures the gravity of the Edict ceremonies and the frightening sermons that would sometimes accompany a grace period during which few had confessed to the sin of Judaizing:

> The clergy marched in procession; the cross was covered with black and two flaming torches were on the altar, where the priests stood in profound silence during the reading of the curse:—"We excommunicate and anathematize, in the name of the Father and the Son and of the Holy Ghost, in form of law, all apostate heretics from our holy Catholic faith, their fautors and concealers who do not reveal them, and we curse them that they may be accursed as members of the devil and separated from the bosom and Unity of the holy Mother Church. . . . May all the curses and plagues of Egypt which befell King Pharaoh come upon them because they disobey the commandments of God."[15]

With the widespread dissemination of the Edicts, the responsibility for identifying and reporting heresy fell to neighbors, friends, servants, and other family members whose own souls were at stake if they failed to report the sins of the Judaizers with whom they interacted. By describing in detail the blasphemous rites, beliefs, and practices of the unfaithful, the Edicts emphasized the special importance that rituals played in the observance of hidden Judaism. A Church document dating from the seventeenth century thus included the following criteria for the identification of crypto-Jewish heresy:

> To wit: if any of you has seen or heard say that any person or persons have kept any Sabbaths in honor or observance of the Law of Moses, putting on clean personal linen and their best or festival clothing, placing clean linen on their tables and throwing clean sheets on their beds in honor of the Sabbath, not kindling a fire or doing any work on those days, beginning on Friday afternoon. Or who have porged or deveined the meat they are preparing to eat, soaking it in water to remove the blood, or who have removed the sciatic vein from a leg of mutton or any other animal. . . . Or who have fasted on the Great Fast which is called the Fast of Pardon, going barefoot on that day . . . or who fast the Fast of Queen Esther, or the fast of Rebeaso, which they call the Loss of the Holy Temple, or other Jewish fasts during the week, such as Mondays or Thursdays. . . . Or who celebrate the Festival of unleavened bread, beginning by eating lettuce, celery or other bitter herbs on those days. Or who observe the

> Festival of Booths, putting up huts of green branches, eating there and hosting their friends and exchanging food. Or the Festival of the Little Lights, lighting them one by one until there are ten, and then putting them out again, praying Jewish prayers on those occasions.[16]

At the same time that the Edicts were intended to alert the citizenry to the nature and type of heresy committed by the crypto-Jews, the detailed documents also cataloged a wide range of Jewish customs and religious practices. Thus, as Gitlitz points out, they offered an incomparable source of information that, ironically, may have been of great value to the crypto-Jewish communities whose knowledge of Judaism lessened with each succeeding generation of converts. In this regard, the Edicts would have been of particular importance after the Jews were expelled from Spain. Until that time, the crypto-Jewish adherents had access to the knowledge, books, and artifacts that were maintained by observant Spanish Jews, a population of the Sephardim who throughout the fifteenth century had resisted pressure to convert.[17] With the expulsion of this religious minority, access to Jewish sources became harder to obtain. Under these conditions, the Edicts were especially informative, as their codification of Jewish rites and beliefs filled the void left by the destruction of traditional Sephardic culture. Gitlitz therefore convincingly argues that over time the pronouncements of the Inquisition helped to sustain a set of rituals, beliefs, and customs that contributed to the ongoing development of crypto-Jewish culture.[18]

Although the exact number of crypto-Jewish adherents is unknown, the statistics on the accused Judaizers tried by the Inquisition vary greatly, with estimates ranging from twenty-five thousand to fifty thousand.[19] Within this broad range of accused heretics, it is difficult to determine who in fact actually practiced crypto-Judaism and who became faithful Christian converts. Because of the extreme conditions under which confessions were obtained by the Inquisition, historians disagree on both the scope of the crypto-Jewish phenomenon and on the nature of the religious culture that came to be associated with the observance of hidden Judaism. Scholars such as Gitlitz and Yosef Yerushalmi, for example, argue that a distinct crypto-Jewish culture developed during the medieval and premodern periods, while others such as Benzion Netanyahu maintain that most forced converts and their immediate descendants assimilated to Christianity, leaving all aspects of their Jewish faith behind.[20] Within this somewhat contentious field of study, a strong case has been made for the existence of a crypto-Jewish subculture that not only proliferated in Spain but also spread to other parts of the Iberian peninsula with the emigration of Spanish Jews into Portugal at the end of the fifteenth century.

The Spanish exiles in Portugal were, for the most part, observant Jews who were expelled from Spain on the premise that they perpetuated heresy through their influence on the convert communities. In return for payment, King John II of Portugal offered asylum and religious freedom to the practicing Spanish Jews. Soon after they arrived in Portugal, however, he enacted a series of repressive measures that gave the Jews a choice between conversion and slavery, while forcibly taking Jewish children from their parents. King John's successor, Manuel I, at first appeared to be more tolerant of the Jewish exiles but later changed his position after his betrothal to the daughter of King Ferdinand and Queen Isabella. In compliance with the Spanish royalty's demand for the expulsion of the Jews from Portugal, Manuel issued an expulsion order in 1496. Fearing the loss of a productive and economically viable Jewish population, he replaced this order with a demand for conversion that prohibited Jewish emigration and that once again led to the seizure of Jewish children for the purpose of forced baptism. Faced with these extreme conditions of religious coercion, the Jews in Portugal resisted Christian assimilation by forming an extensive crypto-Jewish network. The persistence of crypto-Judaism in Portugal led in 1540 to the establishment of the Inquisition in Portugal, where crypto-Judaism had taken on a more fervent character than now existed in Spain.[21]

Some thirty years after the Inquisition was initiated in Portugal, tribunals were established in the colonies of the Americas, first in Peru and then in Mexico City (New Spain), two colonial territories to which the crypto-Jews had begun to emigrate. During the sixteenth and seventeenth centuries, crypto-Jewish immigration to the colonies appears to have been fairly extensive.[22] In addition to Peru and New Spain, areas of Brazil, Colombia, Venezuela, Argentina, Uruguay, and Paraguay were settled by crypto-Jewish converts.[23] In accordance with the objectives of the European Holy Office, the Inquisitional investigations in the colonized regions were intended to rout out and punish heresy, particularly among crypto-Jews who had emigrated to the colonies.[24] The effect of the Inquisition on the sixteenth-century Mexican crypto-Jewish community was especially devastating, since many prominent crypto-Jews were imprisoned and persecuted, including members of the renowned and powerful Carvajal family.[25] Following the trials of the 1580s and 1590s, which led to the imprisonment and death of many of those who had been accused of Judaizing, the crypto-Jewish community ceased to exist as an identifiable culture in Mexico City. Consequently, the Holy Office reduced its activities dramatically during the next fifty years.[26]

By 1640, however, crypto-Judaism had once again resurfaced in the Mexican territories, as crypto-Jewish colonists from Spain and Portugal began arriving in New Spain in the early seventeenth century. These colonists brought with them knowledge of Judaism that they had obtained from their commercial travels in Holland, Italy, and Greece, countries where the practice of traditional Judaism had not been prohibited. Through their exposure to Jewish life and custom, the seventeenth-century crypto-Jewish settlers helped to reestablish a crypto-Jewish culture in Mexico City that contributed to a revitalization of crypto-Judaism among the preexisting sixteenth-century convert populations. Stanley Hordes's research on this period of crypto-Jewish revitalization suggests that an identifiable crypto-Jewish community reemerged in Mexico City, establishing itself in a section of the city that was curiously close to the headquarters of the Holy Office. In his account of this burgeoning crypto-Jewish culture, Hordes describes a somewhat insular community that primarily married and traded among themselves. Within this community, religious observance appears to have been an important source of shared culture, especially among women, as rituals of fasting, mourning, and the Sabbath were practiced together.[27]

With the rise in crypto-Jewish activity in the seventeenth century and the simultaneous development of tensions between Spain and Portugal, the Church resumed its effort to eradicate Jewish heresy in Mexico. Between 1640 and 1650 an increased number of tribunals were held in which those accused of Judaizing were imprisoned and sentenced to death. After this reintensification of the Inquisition in Mexico City, the history of crypto-Judaism in New Spain becomes less clear, since the decline in the Holy Office's activities after 1650 led to a decrease in the documentation of crypto-Jewish observance. One school of thought suggests that, with the resurgence of the Inquisition, surviving crypto-Jewish populations sought refuge in the frontier region of Nuevo Leon and the borderlands that today comprise the Southwest of the United States, areas that may have been settled by earlier generations of crypto-Jews who were in search of a "secure haven."[28] Other scholars maintain that economic opportunities rather than religious persecution led to emigration into these territories by converts who may or may not have been practicing crypto-Jews.[29] Current research on twentieth-century remnant populations suggests that, in the aftermath of the seventeenth-century persecutions, crypto-Judaism in New Spain, including the frontier regions, persisted in fragmentary forms among families who retained at least some remnant customs and beliefs that were Jewish in origin. Within this family-centered realm of cultural persistence, women in particular continued to reproduce the ritual life of their forebears as they had in earlier centuries in Spain and Portugal.

As a significant cultural phenomenon, the history of crypto-Judaism and its survival into the twentieth century suggests a pattern of ethnic masking and cultural persistence that in varying degrees can be found throughout the history of European Jewry. For centuries and in diverse geographic and nationalist settings, Jews were considered outsiders, living on the periphery of the "other's" culture while struggling with the tensions of religious compromise, cultural adaptation, and ethnic pretense. Because Jews could often "pass" as members of the dominant culture, the strategy of blending became one of many means by which Jews sought to protect themselves in host cultures throughout the world. The crypto-Jews of medieval Spain represent one of the earliest and most drastic examples of this form of extreme Jewish assimilation. Using secrecy and subterfuge as weapons against cultural annihilation, they survived by acquiescing to the uncompromising demands of religious conversion. Such behaviors cannot be understood apart from the larger issues surrounding antisemitism, religious persecution, and the dangers associated with Jewish ethnicity, issues that remain salient for the twentieth-century descendants of the medieval and early-modern converts.

## CRYPTO-JEWISH STUDIES IN THE TWENTIETH CENTURY AND THE CURRENT RESEARCH PROJECT

As the historical overview suggests, knowledge of medieval and premodern crypto-Jews is primarily derived from the examination of Inquisition records and the testimony of those accused of Judaizing. As a database for the study of historical crypto-Judaism, these documents, which were scrupulously maintained by the Church, have proven to be a rich source of information on the religious practices and inner lives of the crypto-Jewish adherents. From the early work of Lea to the more contemporary research of Gitlitz and Levine Melammed, the trial records of the Inquisition have served as a starting point from which to begin the investigation into crypto-Judaism as it existed in earlier centuries. For scholars of twentieth-century remnant culture, however, the task of documenting and verifying crypto-Jewish survival has been more difficult, especially because the end of the Inquisition brought an end to the detailed record keeping on hidden religious practices. As a result, scholars in the field of twentieth-century crypto-Jewish studies have had to rely on sources other than Church records to substantiate the continued existence of crypto-Jewish culture in contemporary society.

For historians, the Church material helped to reveal the plethora of Jewish rites that formed the body of crypto-Jewish observance.[30] By comparison, investigations into the twentieth-century phenomenon have been less systematized and more anecdotal. The first published account of the twentieth-century phenomenon was, in fact, a report written by a Polish Jewish engineer, Samuel Schwarz, who, in his travels through Portugal, had come across a community of crypto-Jewish descendants in the hill town of Belmonte.[31] In the 1920s, Schwarz wrote up his observations of Jewish-based rituals and prayers as they were still being practiced in this remote community. Schwarz's report, while not that of a traditional scholar, was nonetheless accepted as the first real evidence of the survival of remnant crypto-Jewish culture in twentieth-century Europe.

It would be many years later before similar claims would be made for descendant populations living in Latin America and the Southwest of the United States, most notably in Arizona, Colorado, New Mexico, and Texas. Since the 1980s, data on remnant crypto-Jewish culture in the Americas have been primarily gathered through contemporary ethnographies (and a few historical accounts) focusing on the survival of modern crypto-Jewish practices and beliefs.[32] As distinguished from the archival research on historical crypto-Jews, contemporary studies for the most part rely on participant observation, oral histories, and family narratives that attest to the presence and survival of Jewish-based rituals and customs that, in some regions of the Americas, may have been sustained through intermarriage among Latina/o Christian families with Jewish ancestry.[33] Descendant narratives and ethnographic accounts have thus replaced Inquisition documents as the primary source of scholarship on the survival of crypto-Jewish culture.

This shift in approach has resulted in the development of controversies and tensions surrounding research into remnant forms of crypto-Judaism. As the research expanded into the late twentieth century, descendants' claims to Jewish origins were often challenged, while their narratives of cultural survival were frequently met with skepticism, particularly as the popular press tended to romanticize the family culture portrayed in the descendants' recollections. Among scholars, ancestral crypto-Jewish heritage soon became an area of contested identity, sparking debates between those who accepted the plausibility of the survival of remnant crypto-Jewish practices and beliefs and those who challenged the claims of modern descendants. As groups of individuals in Mexico, Brazil, and the United States have continued to identify themselves as descendants with crypto-Jewish ancestry,[34] questions of credibility and historical accuracy remain significant for contemporary investigations into the modern-day phenomenon. Within the most recent studies of modern descent, scholars in the fields of anthropology, Jewish studies, and history have focused on the documentation of present-day claims of crypto-Jewish survival, methods of research, and the legitimacy of "true" colonial links.[35]

Keenly aware of the questions surrounding descendant credibility and the significance of ancestral origins, I carefully considered the criteria that I would use to define the parameters of my own study of this unique and contested cultural phenomenon. Based on the existing research in the field and my preliminary investigations into remnant crypto-Jewish culture, I developed three indicators of crypto-Jewish heritage that guided my research process. These were the existence of Jewish-based rituals in the family of origin, the existence of Inquisition records bearing Jewish family names, and the oral transmission of Jewish ancestry by family members. According to these criteria, I included in the project descendants from diverse cultural and geographic backgrounds whose narratives and life histories revealed the presence of crypto-Jewish ancestry in their family backgrounds. Using the ethnographic methods of in-depth interviews and participant observation, I collected data on twentieth-century crypto-Jewish descendants during a period of five years. In that time, I recorded life-history narratives of fifty individuals—twenty-five women and twenty-five men—the majority of whom reported that they had two or more indicators of crypto-Jewish descent as elaborated above.

Among the participants, eighteen of the respondents' families emigrated to the United States from Mexico and other countries of Latin America where crypto-Jews had settled during the colonial period. These countries include Cuba, Venezuela, and Uruguay. The remaining sample population consists of individuals descended from crypto-Jews whose families settled in what is now the Southwest of the United States in the sixteenth, seventeenth, and eighteenth centuries. I obtained participants for the study primarily through referrals from three organizations: the

Society for Crypto-Judaic Studies, the Hispano Crypto-Jewish Research Center, and the Society of Hispanic Historical and Ancestral Research.

The Society for Crypto-Judaic Studies, which was founded more than a decade ago, is a research network that brings together both scholars and nonacademics working in the field of crypto-Judaism. The society holds annual meetings to discuss recent developments in this area of study and publishes a newsletter, *Halapid,* numerous times a year. The Hispano Crypto-Jewish Research Center is at the University of Denver and was established to provide information on the culture, history, and heritage of crypto-Jews and their descendants. While the Society for Crypto-Judaic Studies and the Hispano Crypto-Jewish Research Center focus exclusively on crypto-Judaism, the Society of Hispanic Historical and Ancestral Research is a genealogy organization that sponsors cultural events and annual meetings on Hispanic ancestry and identity in the Americas. In addition to using these three organizations, I also found respondents through individual contacts and "snowball" sampling, whereby descendants provided referrals to other individuals who are of crypto-Jewish background.

Within the population of descendants that comprise this study, the majority of participants were raised as Latina/o Catholics, although in six cases, the respondent's family had converted from Catholicism to Protestantism. While most of the participants had some Christian background, the level of commitment to Christianity varied greatly among the respondents, with some having been raised in very religious families and others in families in which religion had been relatively unimportant. With regard to current religious affiliation, forty of the respondents identify as Jews. Of these forty, twenty-eight respondents have adopted an exclusively Jewish belief system, while twelve hold both Jewish and Christian beliefs. The remainder of the sample (ten respondents) acknowledge Jewish ancestry but remain religiously identified with Christianity.

Other differences that emerge among the descendants include variations in age, ethnic background, education, and occupation. The ages of the respondents range from thirty-three to seventy-two. Close to half the descendants reported that their ethnic heritage included Native American ancestry, while the remainder of the descendants characterized their ethnic backgrounds as Spanish European. A small portion of the descendants have a high school education and work in fields such as child care, dressmaking, and domestic labor. A larger number have attended college, and, of these, a sizable percentage holds advanced degrees in law, medicine, education, administration, and theology. Two participants have studied for the priesthood, and one is now an ordained clergyman.

Overall, the descendants who comprise the sample population represent a diverse group of individuals, including teachers, artists, administrators, and service providers. The participants are of mixed ethnicity and race, and their economic circumstances represent working-, middle-, and, in a few instances, upper-class backgrounds. Some of the descendants are recent immigrants to the United States, while others come from families who have lived in North America for centuries. Despite these vast differences, this varied group of individuals has in common a belief in a shared history of Spanish Jewish persecution and a desire to recover an ancestral past that is spiritually and ethnically rooted in Jewish tradition and culture. Thus, the participants represent a specific population of modern descendants for whom Sephardic ancestry has great meaning and for whom the recovery of Sephardic roots has transformed their understanding of themselves as members of a multiethnic and multireligious culture.

## FIELDWORK WITHIN A CULTURE OF SECRECY

My fieldwork with the descendants involved a broad range of experiences that took me to California, Arizona, New Mexico, Colorado, Texas, and Kansas. In each of these areas, descendants welcomed me into their homes, their places of work, and their religious life. I interviewed respondents in suburban housing developments, urban settings, and religious communities. I spent time on Indian reservations and in business and medical offices. Through recording narratives and oral histories, I gathered data on the descendant's upbringing, family history, and his or her discovery and integration of Jewish ancestry. In many cases, I found the interviews to be emotionally charged experiences in which participants would often share photographs of family members to whom they felt deeply attached and through whom they had traced their connection to Spanish Jewish ancestry. The relatives they spoke of included mothers, aunts, grandmothers, and, on a few occasions, fathers and grandfathers. Three of the descendants brought me to cemeteries where they pointed out family gravestones bearing a six-pointed star or a menorah-like candelabra, proof, they said, of their crypto-Jewish origins and of the crypto-Jewish presence in that region of the country. The participants offered me pictures, books, family genealogies, self-published autobiographies, and copies of Inquisition records that they had painstakingly reproduced in Madrid and Mexico City. These materials not only contributed to the database of the study but also provided evidence of the importance that these descendants place on their crypto-Jewish heritage.

Those participants who had converted to Judaism invited me into their synagogues. I attended Reform, Conservative, and Orthodox congregations that had become home to the crypto-Jewish descendants. I observed the excitement and commitment that these converts brought to their newly found Jewish faith, and I spoke with rabbis both inside and outside these congregations. In addition to this fieldwork, I attended conferences that were held by the Society for Crypto-Judaic Studies and the Society of Hispanic Historical and Ancestral Research. Panel presentations at these meetings included first-person accounts by descendants who were currently exploring their Sephardic heritage. Like the respondents whom I interviewed, these descendants frequently spoke of a "missing family piece" that had led them to search for their Jewish ancestry. The conference narratives added to the ethnographic material that the more personalized interviews provided.

The most difficult and poignant moments in my research were those in which descendants revealed that they knew they were Jewish because of the presence of a genetically transmitted disease in the family. In one case, a woman explained that her mother had recently been diagnosed with a rare nervous system disorder that is found primarily among Sephardic Jews. In another interview, a male descendant tearfully recounted the death of two of his children from a Sephardic-linked respiratory disease that had been incorrectly diagnosed in the South American country where he was then living. These two respondents brought an entirely different perspective to the meaning of lost ethnicity and the search for Sephardic roots.

Because of the emotional content of the narratives, I found the literature on feminist ethnography especially helpful as I negotiated the boundaries between the descendants and myself, boundaries that were influenced by our shared history of a "hidden" Sephardic past.[36] In reviewing the feminist discourse on empathy in the research setting, I became acutely aware of how the interview process created an openness and intimacy with the descendants that deepened my understanding of the personal transformations that accompany the recovery of Jewish origins.[37] Both the men and women who participated in the study were eager to end the silence about their Sephardic heritage, and thus as their narratives unfolded, they revealed a great deal about themselves and their concerns for the future. In some cases, the interviews served to relieve anxieties and tensions that had developed around issues of self-doubt and family secrecy. For these descendants, participation in the project provided an emotional release as they spoke of both the confusion and sadness that had been engendered by their discovery of hidden Jewish ancestry.

Throughout the interviews, a number of participants expressed concerns about exposure. As my research progressed, it became clear to me that the descendants felt vulnerable to charges of false claims by rabbinic authorities and by other scholars in this field.[38] Further, a good many of the participants had risked the antipathy of family members who were far from comfortable with the public disclosure of what had become their family's contested Jewish identity. While some families were in agreement on the acceptance of a Jewish lineage, others were in conflict over the discovery of Jewish ancestry, since siblings and parents had very different responses to the possibility of a Jewish heritage. In a few instances, descendants in the same family converted to Judaism after sharing research findings on their family's Jewish past with one another. This approach differed greatly from other family experiences in which a descendant's siblings, when presented with the genealogical and familial evidence, refused to talk about crypto-Jewish heritage, preferring instead to "let the past be the past." There were also reports of family members who expressed anger and dismay at the sibling or adult child who spoke of these private family matters to outsiders.

On two occasions, a descendant assured me that a relative that he or she knew would be delighted to participate in the project. When I called to set up an interview, however, the relative refused to talk with me, maintaining that he or she knew nothing about Jews in the family. In one memorable case, a descendant openly spoke of her Jewish lineage and offered to talk to her elderly mother, who had frequently spoken of their Jewish ancestry. Within a few weeks of our first meeting, I received two letters from the descendant. One asked that I not use her name in connection with any information that she had already given me. The other letter explained that interviewing her mother would not be useful "after all" because she now denied "ever having said anything to us about having any Jewish ancestors." These experiences convinced me that the secrecy surrounding Sephardic ancestry was not merely a vestige of the past. The vulnerability expressed by the descendants and the conflicts that continued to affect familial relationships were constant reminders of the ongoing tensions that influenced individuals of crypto-Jewish descent.[39] Because of these concerns about exposure and family tensions, I conducted the study under conditions of anonymity, which I have maintained throughout the writing of this book.

## THEORETICAL PERSPECTIVES AND THEMATIC CONTENT

From the outset, my research was designed to develop a theory of cultural persistence that addressed the role of women in the preservation of endangered ethnic and religious traditions. Throughout the analysis, this theoretical contribution is brought to bear on the interpretation of data and is elaborated through the principles of feminist theory and ethnic identity formation. In addition, I have included a variety of other theoretical approaches in the study, since the analysis of hidden ethnicity addresses a wide array of experiences relating to the study of secrecy, ethnic anxiety, and the effects of internalized racism on marginalized groups. Here theories of Jewish assimilation are developed that specifically address the interrelationship among gender, antisemitism, and histories of ethnic and religious victimization.

Among the many significant social and political theorists who laid the groundwork for this research are Georg Simmel and Frantz Fanon. Simmel, a nineteenth-century German Jewish sociologist, provided a framework for understanding the role of secrecy in culture and the social isolation of the ethnic stranger. Fanon, a twentieth-century African Caribbean psychiatrist and political theorist, offered a social-psychological context for exploring the impact of racial and ethnic prejudice on individuals who choose assimilation as their defense against the threat of physical as well as psychological violence. Taken together, the theoretical framework for the study includes feminist, social, psychoanalytic, and postcolonial perspectives, since each of these approaches contributes to an interdisciplinary understanding of hidden ancestry and the transformation of religious and ethnic identity.

Throughout this analytic treatment of modern crypto-Jewish experience, certain themes emerge from the narratives and oral histories of the descendants. Among the most important of these themes is the role of women as bearers of culture, a finding that resonates with the experience of other colonized and oppressed groups whose cultural survival relied on the creativity and persistence of women. Thus, the analysis contributes to an understanding of the relationship among gender, colonization, and the maintenance of religious culture. A second theme that emerges from the data is the effect of marginalization on ethnically diverse individuals who reside in cultural environments that place a high value on religious and ethnic homogeneity. Here, the study of crypto-Judaism helps to illuminate the impact of difference and stigma, illustrating the ways in which the longing for connection becomes a fundamental part of the human condition. Third, this book demonstrates the diverse and complex ways in which the category of "Jew" operates both in contemporary Western thought and in the social relations of Western society. This aspect of the analysis illustrates how the discovery of Jewish ancestry profoundly and deeply transforms a person's sense of self in a world where Jewishness has meant both difference and danger.

Further, this research reveals the ways in which the construction of ethnic and religious identity transcends time and geographic space. Because of the nature of the crypto-Jewish diaspora and the lingering effects of religious persecution on the consciousness of the descendants, the analysis moves back and forth between the historical reality of crypto-Jewish life and the contemporary manifestations of a Sephardic legacy in Latina/o culture. Accordingly, it traverses the boundary between history and modernity in a reexamination of the meaning of ancestral ties.

Within this interweaving of history and ethnography, the links between the past and present become illuminated in narratives and oral histories that contain traces of cultural and religious memory. Beginning with chapter 1, the book focuses on the persisting fears of antisemitism, situating the contemporary manifestations of crypto-Jewish heritage within a culture of secrecy and fear that continues to inform the adoption of a Jewish identity among Latinas/os in modern society. This perspective on the reproduction of crypto-Judaism over time provides a context for assessing the survival of hidden rituals and practices that is elaborated in chapter 2, in which the analysis of ritual preservation draws particular attention to the role that women play in the maintenance of Jewish-origin beliefs and customs.

The chapters on antisemitism and cultural persistence provide a foreground for the discussion of religious and ethnic identity that comprises the remainder of the book. Using the principles of object relations and psychoanalytic theory, chapter 3 explores the development of the spiritual self-in-relation. This theoretical treatment of identity formation lays the groundwork for the analyses in chapters 4 and 5, which focus on spiritual transformation among modern descendants. In chapter 4 the postcolonial construction of syncretic belief systems is explored among a small number of individuals who have chosen to blend their preexisting Christian faith with Jewish theology.

Chapter 5 then examines conversion to Judaism among a larger population of descendants who have reconstructed their religious worldview through the adoption of an exclusively Jewish spiritual perspective. Taken together, chapters 3, 4, and 5 provide insight into the transformation of religious consciousness among a group of individuals who are struggling with the challenges and possibilities of a multiethnic heritage. Chapter 6 then extends the discussion on self-transformation into the realm of social identity, and the construction of Jewish ethnicity is considered from the standpoint of ethnic alliances and the desire for ancestral connection. Finally, the conclusion considers the effects of cultural loss on the changing gender dynamics of religious persistence and the future transmission of Jewish heritage among the modern descendant population.

CHAPTER 1

# Secrecy, Antisemitism, and the Dangers of Jewishness

One of the most intriguing aspects of modern crypto-Judaism is the survival of a culture of secrecy that is evident in the patterns of silence and disclosure that characterize twentieth-century families with crypto-Jewish ancestors. The social and political value of secrecy as a response to danger was first studied by the nineteenth-century German social theorist Georg Simmel. In his work on the role that secrets play in social life, Simmel praised the secret as one of humankind's "greatest achievements":

> The secret in this sense, the hiding of realities by negative or positive means, is one of man's greatest achievements. In comparison with the childish stage in which every conception is expressed at once, and every undertaking is accessible to the eyes of all, the secret produces an immense enlargement of life: numerous contents of life cannot even emerge in the presence of full publicity. The secret offers, so to speak, the possibility of a second world alongside the manifest world; and the latter is decisively influenced by the former.[1]

Simmel goes on to argue that the "second world" created by secrecy is intended to protect those who act in secret by making their actions and behaviors invisible.[2] Simmel's observations provide an apt description of the role that secrecy played in the historical development of crypto-Judaism, where concealment of beliefs and practices was directly related to survival, and norms of silence and confidence were shared by members of medieval families and communities who sought to sustain, without injury, their prohibited way of life.

Simmel's theory of secrecy in social life lays the groundwork for the study of concealment in modern descendant families in which fears surrounding the discovery of Jewish ethnicity remain strong. The tendency toward protectiveness that continues to characterize the remnant culture of twentieth-century crypto-Judaism is reminiscent of the social dynamics of secrecy as first conceptualized by Simmel. At the same time, however, the study of modern crypto-Jewish life expands Simmel's analysis of secrecy into the larger arena of hidden ethnicity and the reproduction of fear-based behavior across generations of families who, while formerly part of a persecuted group, now live in relative security and safety. The persistence of secrecy among modern crypto-Jewish descendants illustrates the sociopsychological impact of historical oppression on individuals whose fears of antisemitism continued to re-create a culture of secrecy and concealment among families who bear traces of Jewish ancestry.

Antisemitism, then, both as a cultural ideology and as a violent form of oppression, provides the historical and social lens through which to view and understand the present-day tensions surrounding Jewish ethnicity within Latina/o families in the Americas. Through an examination of the social construction of Jewishness in European culture and the internalization of antisemitic ideologies by people with Jewish heritage, it is possible to obtain a better understanding of the persistence of secrecy in families with roots in crypto-Judaism. Beginning with an interrogation into the concept of the Jew in medieval European Christian society, this chapter will examine the "trauma" of Jewishness that lies at the heart of the crypto-Jewish phenomenon and the reproduction of secrecy over time and across generations.

## MEDIEVAL CHRISTIANITY AND THE PROMULGATION OF ANTISEMITISM

Studies of the origins of European antisemitism have focused on the cultural construction of the Jew as evil and racially impure.[3] In the theological discourse of the early Church, Jews were portrayed as a carnal people who were punished by God because of their responsibility for the crucifixion. From the first century on, the Jews were held accountable for the death of Christ, a heinous crime of deicide that came to define the Jewish people's relationship to Christianity.[4] As antipathy against the Jews was fostered throughout the Middle Ages, the notion of Jewish evil became rooted in the "*adversos Judaeos* tradition," an interpretive framework whereby passages from the Hebrew Bible (the Old Testament) were used by the Church to discredit and vilify the Jews.[5] According to theologian Rosemary Radford Ruether, "the Jew, theologically, is portrayed as the demonic unbeliever whose trail of perfidity and apostasy leads naturally to the killing of Christ and divine reprobation in history."[6] In this Christian-centered depiction of Jewish ethnicity and religion, Jewish rituals were often designated as the site of Jewish deviance and depravity. This racial and religious prejudice was especially evident in the proliferation of the legend of blood libel that came to be associated with Jewish heresy in the medieval period.[7] This legend maintained that Jews consumed the blood of Christians, especially young boys, in the practice of harmful Jewish magic. Rites of human sacrifice were thought to take place particularly at Easter when Jews reenacted the Crucifixion and baked Passover matzo (unleavened bread) made with the blood of a Christian child. In a fascinating study of Jews and Christians in European history, Claudine Fabre-Vassas discusses the canonization of boys who were presumed to be victims of Jewish rituals. Among the Christian martyrs was Simon, a French child who, according to the Benedictines, was a torture victim of Jewish murderers:

> In 1472, on the Wednesday of the Holy Week, Jews from the city of Trent, had asked one of their own named Tobie who practiced medicine to obtain a Christian child as a victim. The latter took advantage of the moment when the Christians gathered in their church for the Tenebrae service to entice a small child named Simon or Simeon, aged two years and several months, to follow him. . . . Meanwhile, on the night of Holy Thursday to Holy Friday, the Jews took the child to a vestibule contiguous to their synagogue. An old man named Moses took him on his knees: a kerchief was placed over the victim's head, while the wretches made various incisions on his little body and collected the blood that flowed from them in a basin. During this time some held his legs and others took his arms and spread them in the form of a cross. He was then placed on his feet, and two tormenters held him in this position as the others pierced his body with awls and chisels.[8]

Similar stories of murder and mutilation were well known in medieval Spain. The most celebrated of these cases involved accusations against a small group of converts and working-class Jews in the town of La Guardia, an area of Toledo that was believed to be an enclave of crypto-Jewish observance. In 1490 a suspected crypto-Jew was arrested for the murder and mutilation of a three-year-old boy. Tortured by the Inquisition, he admitted to taking part in the crime and named others as his accomplices. According to the charges, a conspiracy of Jews and crypto-Jews engaged in a ceremony of ritual murder that was intended to bring an end to the Inquisition and the rule of Christians over Jews through the practice of magic and sorcery. After a prolonged trial that was overseen by the Inquisitor General, Torquemada, the converts confessed to crucifying a young boy, cutting out his heart, and using his body as a host during the Jewish Passover. The condemned were then burned at the stake as a warning to others who might engage in such murderous practices. While historians found no proof of the crime, not even a child's body as evidence, the charges of murder and sacrifice in the La Guardia case resonated with the blood libel folklore that stigmatized both Jews and suspected crypto-Jews in Spain and France.[9]

In the decades immediately preceding the La Guardia arrests, the Spanish construction of the Jew as evil had found its greatest expression in the influence and writings of Alfonso de Espina, a fifteenth-century Franciscan monk who was confessor to Henry IV. It was Espina who first introduced the charge of ritual murder to Spain with accusations against a group of Jews in Tavara who were charged with the crucifixion of a Christian child.[10] Soon after the trial of the Tavara Jews, Espina completed his famed polemical work, *Fortalitium Fidei,* in which he described in detail the sins and crimes of the Jewish heretics and the blasphemous nature of the Jewish belief system. Among other forms of criminality, Espina's book spoke of the Jews' desecration of the host and their attempt at poisoning the king. One story in particular legitimized the death of the Jews through a parable of Jewish heresy that valorized the act of genocide as the "final solution" to the Jewish problem.[11] The story of the crypto-Jews that Espina disseminated recounted the alleged history of the Jews in England and the extreme measures that were taken to rid the kingdom of the destructive Jewish presence:

> Seeking to appease the wrath of God, who had visited war, famine and plague upon his country, the king of England decided to compel all the Jews in his realm to embrace Christianity. But the wrath of God was not appeased thereby, and the sufferings of the people increased. When the king asked the clergy to interpret the matter for him, they replied that it was due only to the heinousness of the converted Jews, who continued to sin even as they had done before they became Christians. They had occupied all the posts—"of pen and of rod"—in the kingdom, and enslaved the Christians. God then put wisdom into the heart of the king, and he rid his kingdom of these serpents, in the following manner. He pitched two

> tents on the sea-shore. In one tent he placed a scroll of the Law, and in the other a cross. Then he sat between the two tents on the royal throne, and courteously summoned the converted Jews to indicate the religion they would rather choose. All the Jews, with their womenfolk and children, then ran joyfully into the tent where the Torah was. As they came into the tent, they were slaughtered one by one and their bodies were flung into the sea. "Thus the land was purged and an end was put to its affliction."[12]

Espina's works brought together much of the antisemitic rhetoric of the Middle Ages, and his writings helped to promulgate the injurious beliefs that were already strong in northern Europe. Among these beliefs were that Jews were responsible for the plague, that they poisoned wells, that they worshiped Satan, and that they desecrated the sacred objects of Christianity.[13] As Espina's writings reveal, the crypto-Jews were particularly vulnerable to such accusations, since they sought to deceive the Church through their professed belief in Christ while in reality holding fast to the traditions and beliefs of their heretical ancestors. These negative attitudes toward crypto-Jews were further reinforced through the institutionalization of blood laws that linked Jewish evil to racial impurity. The *limpieza de sangre* (blood purity) statutes, which first appeared in the mid–fifteenth century, distinguished between New Christians and Old Christians. The goal of these laws was to establish a blood tie to Jewish ancestry that would render all converts the "offspring of perversion" and therefore unfit to own land, to hold public office, or to become clergy. The first blood law *(Sentencia-Estatuto),* established in Toledo in 1449, was especially significant in creating a link between conversion and the persistence of an ideology of the racially inferior Jew:[14]

> We declare the so called *conversos,* offspring of perverse Jewish ancestors, must be held by law to be infamous and ignominious, unfit, and unworthy to hold any public office or any benefice within the city of Toledo, or land within its jurisdiction, or to be commissioners for oaths or notaries, or to have authority over the true Christians of the Holy Catholic Church.[15]

The medieval Spanish construction of the Jew as racially, morally, and religiously unfit laid the foundation for the promulgation of diverse forms of antisemitism that influenced the formation of Latin American colonial culture from the sixteenth to the nineteenth century, when, after almost three hundred years, the Inquisition finally ended.[16] The cessation of the activities of the Holy Office, however, did not immediately put an end to antisemitism. Throughout the twentieth century, charges of deicide continued to stigmatize Jews, while social and political conditions in Latin America contributed to the vilification of the Jew as the greedy and wealthy exploiter of the poor in countries where economic depression and poverty had become widespread.[17] In the 1930s in Mexico, antisemitism became intertwined with fears of foreigners, who were blamed for labor unrest and the persistence of poverty. This form of cultural scapegoating was linked to Nazi ideology and the racialization of the Jews as a particularly dangerous immigrant group that was responsible for the economic crisis enveloping the country. Bringing together the anticommunist rhetoric of the far right with charges of heresy, tabloid newspapers in Mexico spoke of the Jewish problem of assimilation and the dangers that Jews posed for the survival of Christianity:

> Among the demolishers [of Christian culture] there are some of Jewish affiliation by blood, even though born in their country of residence. In Europe and the United States, it is also the Jews who direct the universal anti-religious movement. . . . The atavistic hate toward Christ has not lessened through the generations, in nearly two thousand years since the death of the Just One, sacrificed by the damned race.[18]

Thus, even as the memory of the Inquisition receded in the cultural consciousness of Latin American life, medieval constructs of the evil and harmful Jew continued to be pervasive, as Judith Elkin, a well-known scholar in Latin American Jewish studies, writes:

> An observer of Latin American life is nonplused by the medieval notions about Jews that circulate in Spanish-speaking lands. While liberals with whom foreign academics are most likely to come into contact receive Jews warmly, even affectionately, nativists encysted at the core of national life denounce Jews as guilty of deicide and as subversives. . . . The disjuncture between the commonplace of Latin American Jewish life and the golem mythology that enshrouds it is bizarre. Why do so many Latin Americans prefer anachronistic myths to the inoffensive reality of Latin American Jewish life?[19]

Against this backdrop of historically, religiously, and politically constructed antisemitism, the descendants of crypto-Jewish families in the Americas continued to inhabit a vulnerable social location, since the remnants of their ancestral religion and ethnicity were perceived as a constant source of potential danger. Within the framework of twentieth-century Latina/o culture, the danger of Jewishness, and thus discovery, was believed to be imminent in a wide range of social and political realities, from the rise of Nazism and the Holocaust to outbreaks of antisemitism in Latin America and the United States.[20] As the narratives of the descendants reveal, fear of discovery continued to inform family life, particularly in Mexico and the southwestern United States, where tensions surrounding Jewish origins remained especially strong.

## THE LEGACY OF PERSECUTION AND THE FORMATION OF MODERN CRYPTO-JUDAISM

Fundamental to the secrecy that surrounds crypto-Jewish heritage is the pervasive fear of violence against the Jews, a fear that was transmitted especially to those descendants who were raised in Mexico, where the memory of the Inquisition stands alongside the specter of the Holocaust, as each of these periods of violent antisemitism frame Jewish history. A narrative of a woman, now in her fifties, provides insight into a family culture in which Jewish ancestry was both a source of pride and an ongoing cause for familial tensions. This descendant was raised in an extended family in which both her mother and grandmother played a significant role in her upbringing. In keeping with the cultural norms of Latina family life,[21] it was primarily the women in her family who provided a tie to crypto-Judaism through the transmission of stories and ancestral history that spoke of divine covenants and death by fire:

> My grandmother would tell me stories about the Hebrews, why they are special and why we mustn't practice on the outside because it was like a covenant; you know we had to practice very secretly, because God had decided that we had to keep contact between him and us. She would say, "Remember we are Hebrew, and even though our husbands are Christians and our children, we still pass down that we are Hebrews to our children because we have a covenant, a very personal and sacred relationship with God." Now, she would explain about Catholicism coming along, and there was this fear that we always had. My grandmother also told us other stories. "There had been times when they burned you alive," she would tell us. "You just have to be careful. Never tell." And it was very real to us. A hundred years ago my grandmother was married, and she saw things that people do, that if you practiced another religion in a small village, then they burn your house down. So my grandmother really pounded into my head that I had to be really careful.

Growing up with the knowledge of her hidden Hebrew ancestry, this respondent experienced fears of both exclusion and death:

> My mother told me that the most important thing was that we were descendants of Abraham and we had to keep the Sabbath. But that was not something we could trust others to know. If other people found out, they would call us "sabististas," which was Saturday-morning worshipers.

. . . I always had this fear. I was thinking, "Oh, my God. What if they find out? What if they find out that I belong to another sect, that I have another belief?" They might kill me or something. And my friends did know that we were kind of different. And they used to accuse us, my sisters and brothers, of worshiping in another sect.

As family narratives kept alive the memory of Jewish suffering and the need for secrecy, the advent of the Holocaust reinforced the fear that the dangers of Jewishness were neither imagined nor historical. According to a number of descendants, the genocide of World War II, coupled with the periodic resurgence of antisemitic attacks on Jews or suspected Jews living in Latin America and the Southwest of the United States, renewed the desire for secrecy and denial among surviving crypto-Jewish populations. As one respondent explained:

Whatever might have been more out in the open went underground after the war. It was hidden after that just like in the old days because of the way the Jews were being treated in Germany and what was going on over there. I think that silenced people like my great-aunt who now tells me she knows we are Jewish, even has proof in a trunk with papers and a Bible, but refused to talk about it because her husband had been in the war, had been to Germany and saw what happened.

A fifty-two-year-old descendant from Venezuela similarly explained that his family had remained silent about their ancestral ethnicity because of fears generated by the Holocaust. Here he describes how he first learned of his Jewish background while a fifteen-year-old student in a Catholic school in Caracas:

One of the university chaplains invited me for lunch, and in the middle of lunch he told me that my name is Sephardic Jewish, a Sephardic name from the Iberian peninsula. He told me that my family was chased out of the Iberian peninsula in the fifteenth century, that they migrated to Holland and from Holland they went with the Dutch colonists to America. The official version that I had been told by my father (and which I never questioned because there was no reason to question it) was that this was not our real family name. That we were originally a Dutch family whose name was so complicated that when the family came in the eighteenth century to Venezuela, the customs officials couldn't spell it so they decided to simplify things and that's how we got our present name. . . . When this priest told me this about my family, I immediately thought, "That wasn't what my dad told me." And then I started asking, why did my father lie to us? And then I realized of course it was 1945, I was born in 1945. My dad had been in the United States one year earlier, the world was at war, and Jews were being slaughtered everywhere. It was bad to be a Jew in 1945, so he probably decided better to erase any connections

> with Judaism until this whole thing clears up. So when I approached him in 1960, fifteen years later, I suppose it was clear to him that there was no immediate danger for Jews so he said yes, we are originally Sephardic.

As a consequence of the persistent threat of violence against the Jews, a deep-seated ethnic anxiety appears to have survived among modern descendants of the crypto-Jews, even in families where remnant Jewish customs were still practiced and ancestral Jewish beliefs acknowledged. Such ethnic anxiety found its expression in the creation and maintenance of family cultures that, through silence and secrecy, conveyed a sense of difference, isolation, and danger to succeeding generations. A forty-nine-year-old woman who emigrated to the United States from Mexico offered this perspective on the underlying fears and tensions that informed her family life in Mexico as a young child:

> We survived because we kept it all inside the family—we tell no one and never discuss our private lives with those outside. Beginning with the Romans, starting with our exile, there has been an obsession to destroy the Jews. It is so ingrained in us who come from the *anusim*—who is friend and who is foe, who you trust and who you don't. That is our obsession. You know we have survived six hundred years because we have fought it, our annihilation.

The fear of discovery and annihilation expressed in this narrative was echoed by other descendants from both Latin America and the United States who internalized strong feelings of ethnic anxiety that originated in a consciousness of Jewish victimization. A descendant in his sixties living in New Mexico thus spoke of the psychological impact of living in two worlds, the public world of Christianity and the private world of secret Jewishness that his family inhabited:

> The history of persecution really affects you. When I was seeking to become a priest, I was interviewed by a psychiatrist who said I seemed like two people. And I said to him, why should this be so unusual—when you have experienced the fear of the Inquisition and then centuries of betrayal, you learn to live in two different worlds, you become two different people, the Christian and the hated Jew. Everybody hates the Jews.

As this account painfully reveals, the secrecy surrounding Jewish ancestry was strongly linked to perceived fear and hatred of the Jews. Descendants from a wide variety of Latina/o cultures were especially sensitive to the charge that Jews were responsible for the death of Christ, a particularly harmful expression of antisemitism that, according to the respondents, reinforced an antipathy against the Jews that characterized the Latina/o Catholic culture in which many of the respondents had been raised. A descendant now in his sixties described the culpability he felt for the death of God when, as a young boy, he learned of his "family secret" from the nuns at school:

> I asked my mother, I said, "The sister said we are Jews." And my mother's eyes filled with tears, and she said, "Go ask your grandfather." And I went out back where my grandfather was and I asked him, "Are we Jews?" and he said, "*Si, somos Judeos*" [Yes, we are Jews], and we have a very old history that we can trace back to the year 70. And I was very angry and upset. This experience was very traumatic for me. It was a time when we were still taught that the Jews killed Christ, and now I was being told that I was a Jew. It was very hard.

A similar identification with Jewish deicide was recounted by a descendant from Colorado who attended grade school in Denver in the 1960s:

> We lived in a Hispanic neighborhood, and the kids said the Jews were the killers of Christ and that they started wars. When they said things like that, I knew they were talking about me—my mother. I was about ten at the time so I asked my mom, "If we're Jewish, how come I don't know anything about Jews?" She answered me in Spanish. She said that I knew what I had to know. I think she was trying to protect me.

The tendency toward secrecy and protective assimilation found among crypto-Jewish descendants is not unique to this ethnic group but is characteristic of other diasporic Jewish cultures that, throughout history, have been forced to acculturate to ensure safety and survival. The descendant families thus continued to maintain and support accommodationist strategies that in some respects were similar to those practiced by other Jewish populations living throughout Europe. Accordingly, it may be helpful to consider the history of "passing" (extreme assimilationism) that has informed European and American Jewish life more universally in order to place the secrecy of the crypto-Jews in a larger perspective of ethnic deidentification.

## INTERNALIZED ANTISEMITISM AND ASSIMILATION AS RESPONSES TO THE DANGERS OF JEWISHNESS

Studies of Eastern European Jewry in pre-Holocaust Europe document the extent to which passing became a strategy for successful assimilation among Austrian, German, and Hungarian Jews who, like the Spanish Jews, had been forced to adopt a Christian cultural identity or risk ostracism, violence, and continued discrimination. Among these diverse Jewish populations, passing involved masking one's Jewish origins so as not to be identified (because of dress, language, customs, or physical appearance) as a Jew. In effect, it was a strategy of personal protection intended to obscure differences that, if known, might lead to social rejection or, more gravely, the loss of human rights or perhaps the loss of life.[22] Donna Goldstein presents this view of Jewish assimilation in Hungarian society:

> Historically, Hungarians of Jewish descent have attempted to abide by the strict rules of citizenship governing the ethos of the times: they converted to Christianity or gave up religious practices, adhered to Magyar over German and other minority languages, and became Communists during the era of Soviet influence in Hungary. Such an extreme case of accommodating behaviour can be interpreted as a reflection of the specific demands of assimilation and the requirements of citizenship made on this group during different historical periods, and this can be seen as having flamed the production of what appear to be "closeted Jews."[23]

Similarly, studies of Jewish accommodation in turn-of-the-century Austria and Germany focus on the phenomenon of assimilationism, particularly among European Jews.[24] During this period, Jews living in German-speaking countries understood the importance of adopting the language, dress, and even religious observances of German Christian society, since acculturation was essential to economic and social stability. In this era of Jewish assimilation, antisemitism in Western Europe contributed to the development of self-criticism among upwardly mobile and educated German and Austrian Jews who, in their hopes of passing, eschewed all appearances of ethnicity that their ancestry might reveal. As Sander Gilman points out, such internalized ethnic anxiety led to a split within Austrian and German Jewry, as assimilated Jews stigmatized Eastern European Jewish immigrants whose continued adherence to religious tradition and custom provided a constant reminder of Jewish difference. Gilman explains the effects of this aspect of internalized antisemitism in terms of the value of negative projection for the maintenance of a positive self-concept:

> One of the most successful ways to distance the alienation produced by self-doubt was negative projection. By creating the image of a Jew existing somewhere in the world who embodied all the negative qualities feared within oneself, one could distance the specter of self-hatred, at least for the moment.[25]

A look at Jewish relations during the late-nineteenth and early-twentieth-century immigration to the United States reveals similar divisions between German Jews and those who were emigrating from Eastern Europe and Turkey. In this period of massive Jewish immigration, newly arriving Eastern European Ashkenazic Jews and Turkish Sephardic Jews were both viewed with suspicion by the already assimilated German Jewish populations, who feared that the more ethnically identifiable immigrants would reinscribe images of Jewish difference into public consciousness.[26] In response to the tensions surrounding Jewish stereotypes of coarseness, materialism, and uncleanliness, German Jews expressed their internalized antisemitism through negative Jewish attitudes toward non-German Jewish immigrants, including Eastern European and Sephardic Jews. In addition, as Riv-Ellen Prell points out, internalized antisemitism contained a gender component as well, since Jewish immigrant men's attitudes toward Jewish women reflected their own fears of being labeled as the socially unfit Jew.[27]

In her work on Jewish assimilation, Prell emphasizes the relationship between ethnic anxiety and sexism within Jewish American culture. She persuasively argues that, beginning in the early twentieth century, upwardly mobile Jewish men sought to distance themselves from their ethnic origins by associating negative attributes of Jewish ethnicity with Jewish girls and women:

> Their very ability to become Americans required Jews to make minute distinctions in an antisemitic world. Jews' apparent ability to assimilate to the white Christian world around them only heightened the sense that difference was dangerous. Because, like other Americans, young Jewish women could buy what they wanted with the money they earned, what they purchased was constantly condemned as lacking in taste. . . . From the point of view of the Jews from the Lower East Side, the shop girl was as attuned to style as were the wealthy. To the Jews of the "great middle class," this behavior, by contrast, had to constantly be controlled to protect against embarrassing imitation. Their place in that class remained vulnerable despite their economic standing.[28]

Within a few decades, the stigma of Jewish ethnicity became attached to the notion of the Jewish American Princess who, like the shop girl, came to represent all that was materialistic and negative about Jewish culture. While a target of derision within the Jewish community, the Jewish American Princess served to promote the image of the economically successful Jewish father and husband whose total assimilation was evident in the comfortable middle-class "American" life (with all of its consumer goods) that he could now provide for his family.[29] At the same time, in fostering images of the Jewish wife and mother as the conspicuous ethnic consumer, Jewish men sought to distance themselves from the antisemitic stereotypes that threatened their own social acceptance and mobility within the dominant Christian culture. According to the culture critic Norman Kleeblatt, it was during this period of intensified Jewish acculturation that the ethnic body became the site of Jewish self-deprecation. In particular, the prominence of the so-called Jewish nose began to be looked on as a signifier of Jewish identity.[30] Writing on the popularity of rhinoplasty (plastic surgery for the nose) among Ashkenazi Jews in the United States, Kleeblatt observed:

> Seen as a cure for the prominent "Jewish" nose, the surgery was particularly common in postwar America among Jews seeking to make their physical features conform with widely promoted standards of Anglo-Saxon beauty. The question of why and for whom Jews seek this cosmetic curative to ethnicity is complicated. One plastic surgeon who has analyzed the phenomenon comments: "[Jewish] patients seeking rhinoplasty . . . frequently show a guilt-tinged, second-generation rejection of their ethnic background masked by excuses. . . . Often it is not so much the desire to abandon the ethnic group as it is to be viewed as individuals and to rid themselves of specific physical attributes associated with their particular group."[31]

With this trend toward physiological Anglicization, Jewish women were at the center of the Jewish community's longing for acceptance. A mark of the Jewish American Princess was (and still is) the mandatory "nose job" that rendered the Jewish female more attractive to Jewish men through the transformation of ethnic features.[32] Plastic surgery, along with changes in diet, dress, custom, and family name, thus became the means of achieving the radical assimilation of Jews into contemporary society, an extremism that in part had developed in response to fears generated by the Holocaust.[33]

Like the radically assimilated Ashkenazi Jews of the nineteenth and twentieth centuries, the Spanish crypto-Jews and their descendants engaged in various forms of cultural accommodation, including religious and familial adaptations, that masked their ethnic origins and remnant ancestral beliefs. Although the extent of crypto-Jewish acculturation created a much deeper sense of secrecy and alienation than that experienced by the more traditional Ashkenazi communities, an underlying ethnic anxiety informed the cultural transformation of both populations, since both sought protection from "discovery." Among modern descendants of the crypto-Jews, anxieties about ethnic identification have retained specifically religious overtones, especially because ties to the community are still determined, to a great extent, by the centrality of the Church and Catholicism in the social and economic lives of Latinas/os.[34] Fear of being designated a religious outsider, of being excluded and thus of suffering economic and social consequences, has helped to sustain secrecy in a culture where hidden Jewishness had been a cause for concern for hundreds of years. In the following description of crypto-Jewish family life, a male descendant from New Mexico captures the essence of this centuries-old ethnic anxiety:

> The families are cut off from other spiritual support. There is as a result a deep closing in on one's self and one's own family. There is fear of exposure, disclosure and even an age-old fear of death. There is a turning inward among family members, a deep enmeshment. It is passed on in a secretive way—maybe only one person knows, and she tells no one. If too many people know, you never know when it might be a threat.

## SECRECY AND THE DISCLOSURE OF JEWISH ANCESTRY

What is compelling about the persistence of crypto-Jewish culture is that the turning inward of descendant families did not completely obliterate or erase either the memory or the fear of an ancestral Jewish identity. Rather, it would appear that succeeding generations of crypto-Jews retained knowledge of their origins even as the original act of forced conversion was sustained through long-term strategies of assimilation and accommodation. As this current generation of descendants come to terms with their Jewish ancestry, it is primarily through a veil of secrecy and uncertainty that they come to understand and appreciate the extent to which danger and anxiety remain part of the legacy of crypto-Judaism. Patterns of disclosure within descendant families indicate that less than half the respondents were told of their Jewish ancestry as children and that such disclosures were frequently accompanied by a warning to keep this information inside the family. These accounts reveal that children's questions about family heritage or culture frequently went unanswered, leaving the impression that there were some areas of family history or family life that were not to be discussed. As one woman explained, "We were a very secretive family. . . . 'We don't talk about this,' would be my mother's response when I would ask her questions." Secrecy as a family norm was thus strongly communicated to children, who learned early on that familial privacy was of the utmost importance.

A descendant raised in Mexico recalled the extent to which a norm of silence prevailed within her household:

> The children were not allowed to converse. You are to be seen and not heard so that nothing could be said. It was very strict rules in our home. You were not allowed to bring friends to our house, you are told not to talk to strangers, you don't tell them anything about your family. What happens in your home is never discussed. If there is an outsider in your house and a child would speak, me or my siblings, we knew we had done something wrong. As soon as you began to talk, you would be excused from the table with just a look from our parents.

Another descendant from New Mexico described the culture of silence that was pervasive in her family home:

> When we would ask, we were told, "Only God knows where we came from." That is if we even dare to ask. We were raised not to ask questions. Why were you afraid? That was a foolish question, of course you were afraid, for you knew what it was to be Jew.

In other families where crypto-Jewish heritage was acknowledged, albeit with the caveat to "keep the family secret," storytelling was often used as a means of relating the family's hidden ethnicity. A woman raised outside Mexico City described how her grandmother created narratives of Hebrew ancestry that focused on the image of the wandering and persecuted Jew:

> She would tell me stories, and they would be about the Hebrews who had a lot of problems. They never were accepted anywhere so they had to go everywhere. And she used to tell me the story of the wandering Jew, and she would say, "No, he is not going to rest. For a long time we are not going to have a place of our own. We have to continue to follow the Divine's rules before the world is mended."

In another childhood recollection, a descendant in her sixties related a story that her grandmother told her when she was a young girl living in northern Mexico. The story is of a family who, because of their Jewish faith, refused to eat pork and thus died at the hands of a despotic king:

> My grandmother would never eat pork. She was the only one in the family who wouldn't eat pork. And one of the things she used to tell me was that everybody who ate pork was unclean. And she had a story that she used to tell me. The story went like this: "There once was a king who used to bring all the people together. He wanted everyone to eat pork. And there was a woman that had seven children. And the king told the whole family, 'If you don't eat pork, we're going to kill all the children.' The

> woman shook her head and she held her children by the hand. And she said, 'It doesn't matter if they kill me or my children. The King of the universe gives us death but he also gives us life.' After she said this, they were holding hands and the king cut off the oldest boy's head and he then cut off the next boy's head until he had killed them all but they kept the faith." My grandmother told me that story so that I would know what it means to be Hebrew and to observe the rules that show my faith in God.

The crypto-Jewish themes of apostasy and martyrdom that clearly underlie this family fable are given even greater meaning in light of the Jewish story of Hannah and her sons, a traditional Hannukah story found in Maccabees 2 and from which this crypto-Jewish version appears to be derived. In the original text, a Jewish mother and her seven sons are tortured by King Antiochus for refusing to "partake of swine meat forbidden by the Law." After the first son is put to death, the second son says to the king, "You accursed wretch, you may release us from our present existence, but the King of the universe will raise us up to everlasting life because we have died for His laws."[35] Four more sons are then executed, and as the youngest son goes to his death, his mother tells him, "Do not be afraid of this executioner, but show yourself worthy of your brothers. Accept death, that in God's mercy I may receive you back again along with your brothers."[36] In both the original story and the crypto-Jewish version, the consumption of pork is the symbolic expression of apostasy. This legend would therefore have particular meaning for crypto-Jews who, in abstaining from pork, might, in spite of their baptism, retain their covenant with God. Through the retelling of the parable to children, each generation learns of their secret Jewish ancestry and the means by which they can live as Christians without completely forsaking their Jewish heritage.

Further, this family narrative highlights the significant role that the pig played in the evolution of crypto-Jewish culture. Fabre-Vassas's recent work on European antisemitism illustrates how deceptive practices relating to the pretense of eating pork functioned to protect the crypto-Jews from discovery. She cites the history of the crypto-Jews, or *chuetas* of Majorca, a group who, at least through the seventeenth century, continued to abstain from pork in recognition of their Jewish past.[37] In 1672, the inquisitor Don Juan de Fontamar described the acts of dissimulation in which the *chuetas* engaged as they tried to conceal their observance of Jewish dietary laws:

> For added dissimulation, they buy some pigs, of which they later sell the fat and the leanest meat, make a few grilled meats, adding a great deal

> of cow and lamb meat and so much spice that one can barely tell if there's any pork; moreover, they eat it ostentatiously and manage to be seen by the Catholics, whereas when they eat other foods they hide from them.[38]

According to Fabre-Vassas, other known "deceptions" by the crypto-Jews included the Portuguese preparation of *chorizo de Marrano* (Marrano sausage), a type of blood sausage that resembled a pork sausage but in reality contained no pork or pig fat. Local folklore held that these "fake" sausages would be displayed by crypto-Jewish families as evidence of their Christian loyalty.[39] In what appears to be a continuation of this type of dissimulation, descendants from both Mexico and New Mexico report that pigs were often kept in their families' yards, although pork was rarely eaten in their homes. As children, these respondents were especially aware of certain times and holidays, such as Easter, when their families would make a great display of preparing ham or pork, alongside other meats that were more typical of their family diet.

Dissimulation thus remained a part of remnant crypto-Jewish practices among twentieth-century descendant families who, more often than not, maintained a silence around their Jewish ancestry. Particularly for those descendants who learned of their Jewish ancestry as adults, questions concerning Jewish roots were frequently met with suspicion as if, in seeking out information about Jewish family origins, they had "hit a painful and sensitive nerve," as one respondent stated. In the following account, a male descendant from New Mexico relates the difficulties he continues to encounter when engaging his mother in discussions about their Jewish background:

> Every once in a while, I'll ask her a question about Judaism. I can't ask her too much at once. She gets suspicious. I'm treading on thin ice, but every once in a while she'll give me a little pearl so that I can remember. She'll talk about the semitic bread in the family or covering the mirrors.[40] But then she'll stop suddenly and tell me that I ask too many questions.

Another respondent described the reluctance with which her elderly mother "confessed" that the family did indeed have Jewish ancestry:

> I finally felt comfortable enough to approach my mother. I finally worked up my nerve. It was an afternoon, I remember clearly. She was sitting in her room, rocking. I pulled up the ottoman to her, and I sat in front of her and looked her right in the eye and said, in Spanish, "Are you a Jew?" And she said, "Why do you ask me?" And I said, "You have a lot of Jewish customs." And she said, "*Si,* yes. I had been told when I was a little girl." And she couldn't tell me exactly who had revealed this to her, but the next thing she said to me was,"But it's better if you don't tell anybody."

> . . . And the thing that surprised me was that she blushed when I asked her if she was a Jew, as though . . . it was something that had been hidden for a long time.

As these accounts indicate, adult disclosure is often characterized by secrecy and fear that is reminiscent of earlier historical periods; and, as previously pointed out, such disclosures frequently take place when an elderly family member nears death, as the following narrative illustrates:

> My mother became ill a couple of years ago. By then I was thinking maybe we were Jewish so I had checked out a lot of books on Judaism, and I had them in my arms and went into the hospital room. She looked at the books, and she said, "You need to go to the synagogue over there by the Greek Church on Alameda. You need to go there and they'll teach you everything you need to know." She said that right before she died.

Respondents also gained knowledge of their Jewish origins from unusual deathbed requests. In these cases, a dying family member might specifically refuse the last rites of a priest or request a burial without a Christian religious service or gravestone symbolism. The descendants interpreted these requests as evidence of a Jewish ancestry that, at the time of death, became especially important.[41]

For the most part, explicit disclosure of Jewish lineage by elderly family members came as a welcome affirmation of a suspected Jewish past. Positive responses to such disclosures, however, were not universal. The descendants' narratives clearly indicate that some were more open to the possibility of Jewish ancestry than others. One woman in her sixties expressed a great deal of ambivalence over her terminally ill uncle's reference to a Jewish past:

> I have only told a few other people about this stunning thing that happened before my uncle died. He moved in with my cousin and her family. She is a very religious girl, very Catholic. My uncle got cancer, and she took care of him at home. My cousin and I were having this conversation, and she said, "Well, I remember when Dad died. I was praying the rosary and he said, 'Are you still praying?' and I said, 'Yes, I'm still praying.' He said, 'I guess you think I'm going to die. You're praying to Jesus?' I said, 'Yes', and he said, 'But we are of the House of David.' " My cousin said, "What are you talking about? I think you've gone nuts." "No," he said, "We are of the House of David." . . . Those were his last words, and then he died. When my cousin told me, I just got goose bumps; I got these chills all the way down to my ankle. Why would he say that? To me it doesn't make any sense. Did he know he was a Jew? Did he know his ancestors were Jews? If he did, who told him? I keep asking myself, why would he say that?

Deathbed disclosures such as the one described above may create tensions over whether to accept or reject Jewish ancestry. While the majority of descendants in this study accept and for the most part embrace this aspect of their family history, their narratives reveal a plethora of reactions on the part of other family members, responses that range from good-natured toleration of their "newly Jewish sibling" to disinterest and angry denial. A descendant who was raised in Colorado offered this insight into the conflicting reactions that may exist within one family:

> Let me tell you, when this religious thing first came out, you talk about families. My second brother, he and I used to run from church together, he's not religious and he thinks it's okay. He says, "Well, if mom was a Jew, then we're Jews." And that's as far as he goes. My third brother is not exactly anti-Jewish but very pro-Catholic. We have had some battles, and he doesn't accept it at all, and my father was very upset. He and I had some arguments, and I didn't talk to him for a couple of years. You see, my father is a good man, but he is very uneducated. He thinks all Jews have blue eyes and blond hair. He does. He thinks that. And he'd say, "Your mom didn't look Jewish. You don't look Jewish. You're Mexican." And I would say to him, "Well, Dad, I didn't say I'm not Mexican, I just said I'm a Jew too. If you go to Israel, most of them look like me." We are on good terms now. My dad has mellowed out. He respects me for what I say, but he won't discuss it.

Divisions occur both among siblings and between parents and children. In one account a mother reported that her daughter explicitly refused to discuss the possibility of Jewish ancestry:

> I don't talk to my children about us having any Jewish background. My husband, he talks to them about it. My oldest daughter is very Catholic. She experienced more going to Catholic school, so she has become very Catholic. Her husband is very Catholic, and so she don't want to hear about it. She flat out told my husband, "I don't want to hear about it."

Some respondents explain this tendency toward denial as a response based on fear. A descendant from New Mexico thus spoke of the depth of his mother's anxiety after his grandmother made an elusive reference to their Jewish heritage:

> My mother is still a staunch Roman Catholic. She refuses to budge and think that maybe we are Jewish. They have been covering up for so many years, they cannot think of the shame because to be Jewish was to have your head chopped off. So that way, they preserved themselves. Maybe some day my mother will realize and say, "Oh, my God, we're Jewish. It's real. All of the people that we always feared were ourselves."

Despite the secrecy and tensions that surround awareness and disclosure of Jewish ancestry, a growing number of descendants are seeking to verify the reality of their family's hidden Jewish past. For these individuals, deathbed revelations hold great significance, since such disclosures encourage the reclamation and transmission of a lost cultural heritage.

## COLLECTIVE MEMORY, ANCESTRAL HERITAGE, AND FAMILY SECRETS

Family secrecy, while a form of protection, also helps to create what the French sociologist Maurice Halbwachs called collective memory, a series of recollections that comprise the knowledge and memory of family history as it relates to membership in a particular group at a particular time and place.[42] In his groundbreaking treatise on the sociology of memory, Halbwachs analyzed the relationship between social memory and family recollections:

> Each family has its proper mentality, its memories which it alone commemorates, and its secrets that are revealed only to its members. But these memories, as in the religious traditions of the family of antiquity, consist not only of a series of individual images of the past. They are at the same time models, examples, and elements of teaching. They express the general attitude of the group; they not only reproduce its history but also define its nature and its qualities and weaknesses. . . . Sometimes it is the place or the region from which the family originated or it is the characteristic of this or that family member that becomes the more or less mysterious symbol for the common ground from which the family members acquire their distinctive traits.[43]

The unique and particular context through which knowledge of Jewish ancestry was transmitted to descendants illuminates Halbwach's understanding of the creation of collective memory within families in which secrecy and anxiety remain part of the discourse on religious and ethnic origins. As the knowledge of a Jewish past is remembered through warnings, stories, and family folklore, the older generation re-creates, through the production of social memory, the sense of danger that historically has informed crypto-Jewish identity. Especially in New Mexico, where accounts surrounding a secretive Jewish culture have been most prominent, crypto-Jewish descent is reconstructed through imagery that recalls a more dangerous time of secret prayer and worship. Here descendants frequently draw on the contemporary folklore that has contributed to the romanticization of crypto-Jewish heritage, citing media reports that describe the discovery of hidden religious scrolls and secret prayer rooms.[44] To this construction of a clandestine Jewish past, descendants bring their own family history, as one respondent recalled the memory of a female ancestor who saved a Jewish prayer book:

> I remember that my great-grandmother told me that one time the priest came to their home because he had heard that they were reading strange books. My grandmother's great-grandmother wore a corset, and she immediately left the room, opened her corset and put the book in, and tied it as tight as she could and when the priest came in, he was looking everywhere. And my grandmother's great-grandmother just sat, and she wouldn't get up off the cushion. After the priest left, her husband asked her where it was hidden, and she said, "I have it here," and he said, "Where?" and she showed him. She literally had it against her undergarment so tight that it left a mark for some days. She had saved it. Even through fires, people would rescue the book.

As this narrative reveals, family lore contributes to the creation of a collective memory that not only preserves a history of hidden religious observance but also reinforces the memory of religious persecution by the Church. Through collective memory, one generation instills in another the feelings and knowledge that define the family's history and present cultural experience. Within the history of crypto-Judaism, family narratives have served as an especially important source for creating a collective memory of Jewish heritage. This memory is embedded in a culture of secrecy and danger that continues to inform the ethnic consciousness of those descendants who are now seeking to end the silence and openly acknowledge their families' Jewish ancestry.

CHAPTER 2

# Women and the Persistence of Culture

## *Ritual, Custom, and the Recovery of Sephardic Ancestry*

The persistence of a culture of secrecy poses certain dilemmas for descendants whose religious upbringing bears little resemblance to a Jewish past and whose traces of a Jewish heritage have all but disappeared. In the absence of a surviving cultural community and/or substantial evidence of Jewish religious practice, descendants are faced with the challenge of constructing Jewish origins out of collective memory and remnant ritual behavior. Since memory provides the foundation on which a tie to crypto-Judaism is established, the ritual life of contemporary women offers clues to Jewish ancestry that remain hidden among idiosyncratic beliefs and customs. Through the preservation of both oral history and ritual performance, women have been at the center of the recovery process for modern descendants. Because women's twentieth-century role in the maintenance and transmission of crypto-Jewish culture is reminiscent of the role they played in the medieval period, a review of the historical data on gender and cultural persistence provides a context in which to assess the gendered nature of culture-bearing in contemporary society.

### MEDIEVAL AND PREMODERN WOMEN IN CRYPTO-JEWISH LIFE

Studies of the Inquisition proceedings reveal that women were frequently responsible for retaining Jewish practices and beliefs, both within their families and among community members. While the records suggest that men, on occasion, were accused of teaching Judaism to their children and, in some cases, were suspected of being "secret rabbis,"[1] it was women's privatized ritual and family life that was of particular concern to the Church.[2] Given the importance of women to the perpetuation of crypto-Jewish culture, a great deal of historical work has focused on the significant and central role that women assumed in maintaining and transmitting Judaism under the threat of persecution and danger. In one of the earliest histories of crypto-Judaism, the historian Cecil Roth noted the risks that were taken by crypto-Jewish women to ensure that their children would be schooled in the traditions and practices of Judaism. In 1932 Roth published a text on crypto-Jewish history in which Spanish Jewish women were recognized for their courage and faith:

> At the earliest Inquisitional period in Spain, we are informed how women comprised the vast majority of the few who maintained their Judaism to the end and thus died the deaths of true martyrs. It is significant that women took a prominent part in initiation to Judaism in several known cases, showed an especial familiarity with the prayers, and were in some instances peculiarly meticulous in their observance. It was by the mothers and the wives that the Marrano circle in Mexico, in the first half of the seventeenth century, was presided over and inspired. Ultimately it became customary for a woman to act as the spiritual leader of the Marrano groups.[3]

More contemporary scholars have made an equally strong case for the significance of women to Jewish survival. Writing on the Portuguese Inquisition, I. S. Revah concluded:

> In this continuous or discontinuous transmission of marranism two social groups performed a decisive role: the family milieu and the professional or university milieu. The women have greatly contributed to the perpetuation of marranism, often behind the back of their husbands: they figure also in greater numbers than men in the autos de fe. Marranism was a simplified religion which ignored hierarchy.[4]

The most recent and comprehensive study of women and medieval crypto-Judaism has been conducted by the historian Renee Levine Melammed, whose research focuses specifically on crypto-Jewish women tried for heresy in Spain.[5] Drawing a comparison between these crypto-Jews and the *moriscas* (women of Islamic descent who either voluntarily or through force converted to Catholicism), Levine Melammed maintains that the crypto-Jewish home was a center of resistance where women sought to counter the hegemonic influence of Christian domination.[6] Noting that the Church was well aware of the centrality of the home in sustaining crypto-Jewish life, Levine Melammed illuminates the transition that Judaism underwent during the periods of forced conversion, as Judaism shifted from a public institutionalized religion to a privatized familial faith:

> The demise of Jewish institutional life in 1492 left the male Jew without the framework within which he had functioned. Without the synagogue, the house of study, and the communal organizations, he was destined to be at a loss. . . . By contrast, the women had never been dependent upon a center outside of the home, nor were they overly dependent upon books. . . . Traditionally the women had kindled lights on Friday evening, prepared Sabbath meals, baked matsah, observed the dietary laws, and the like; now these observances were to become the major symbols of crypto-Judaism. The new thrust of crypto-Jewish life was no secret to any of the parties involved, including the Holy Tribunal.[7]

In *Heretics or Daughters of Israel?* Levine Melammed examines the types of customs and traditions that crypto-Jewish women sustained and for which they were arrested, including the observance of the Sabbath, dietary laws, holy days, and fasts.[8] Studies of crypto-Jews in the Americas confirm that similar customs were retained in the colonies and that here, too, women were frequently charged with the heresy of preserving and observing Jewish rituals. Two historians of this era, Seymour Liebman and Arnold Wiznitzer, focus especially on the martyrdom and suffering of crypto-Jewish women in Mexico.[9] Among the most well known of these women were the female members of the famous Carvajal family. Although Luis de Carvajal Jr. is perhaps the best-known martyr of this period of crypto-Jewish persecution, the fate of his mother and sisters illustrates the dominant role that women played in Mexican crypto-Jewish culture and the extent to which women suffered during the Inquisition.[10]

Beginning with the arrest of Luis de Carvajal (senior), the Carvajal family's persecution by the Mexican Inquisition persisted for half a century. Carvajal was a colonial governor of Jewish ancestry whose wife, sister, nieces, and nephew (Luis de Carvajal Jr.) were all practicing secret Jews. Carvajal, however, identified strongly as a Christian. After the death of Carvajal's wife, his niece, Isabel, was reported to have incited Carvajal by requesting that he return to the "law of Moses," as his deceased wife would have wished. Hearing her uncle recite a Christian prayer, Isabel was said to have demanded of her uncle:

> There is no Christ: How can a wise man like you follow the wrong way of the law of Jesus Christ? It means that you will go to hell.[11]

In response to her condemnation, Carvajal reportedly knocked Isabel to the ground and suggested to other family members that she should be "choked."[12] Later, when Carvajal was himself arrested for Judaizing, he testified to his loyalty to the Church, condemning the behavior of his heretical relatives. Eventually, the charges against Carvajal were reduced from heresy to aiding and protecting Jewish apostates. For these crimes, he was sentenced to expulsion from the colonies, and he died in prison before the expulsion order could be carried out.[13]

At the same time that Carvajal was imprisoned, his niece, Isabel, was denounced as a Judaizer by another family relation. Arrested by the Inquisition in 1589, she confessed to her Jewish beliefs and practices, reciting the Hebrew words of the Shema before the tribunal.[14] When asked to name others, she at first implicated only her husband and her aunt, both of whom were deceased. She was then tortured until she named her mother and her brothers, including Luis Jr., as secret Jews.[15] Isabel's mother, Doña Francisca, was then arrested and at age fifty tried on charges of Judaizing. Accounts of her trial and ordeal vividly portray the tortures to which crypto-Jewish women were subjected and the conditions under which they were forced to implicate their own children.

According to the records of her proceedings, Doña Francisca admitted that she was a Jew but refused to recant or name others with whom she practiced Judaism. Tortured for many hours, she eventually asked for mercy, a request that was granted only after she had named her children as accomplices in the observance of secret Judaism. Doña Francisca, her son, Luis, and her daughters, Catalina, Isabel, Mariana, and Leanor, were all reconciled (that is, they confessed and repented) to the Church in 1590.[16] The family's safety was short-lived, however. Six years later, Doña Francisca, Luis, Catalina, and Isabel were found guilty of relapsing into Judaism and were executed at the auto-da-fé of 1596.[17] Then in 1601 Mariana was sentenced to death, and her younger sister, Ana, reconciled. Ana, the last surviving member of the Carvajal family, was executed almost fifty years later during the auto-da-fé of 1649. She was sixty-seven at the time of her sentencing.[18]

The continual arrests and trials of the Carvajal family illustrate the many facets of Inquisition history that led to the persecution of Jewish women and children. Further, the Carvajal legacy illuminates the significant role that women assumed in the observance and teaching of crypto-Judaism in the colonial era. The crimes for which Doña Francisca and her children were tried reveal that women were indeed at the center of crypto-Jewish life in colonial Spain, a finding that is further confirmed by the proceedings from the seventeenth-century trial of Gabriel de Granada, a thirteen-year-old child who was charged with Jewish heresy. The records of de Granada's testimony offer this especially revealing portrait of the Judaizing mother in the Mexican crypto-Jewish household:

> When this confessant was at the age of thirteen years, Doña Maria de Rivera, his mother, called him and when alone with him in the house in which they then lived in the Alcayceria, she told him how the law of our Lord Jesus Christ which he followed was not good, nor true, but that of Moses, that she and her mother Doña Blanca de Rivera and his aunts, Doña Margarita, Doña Catalina, Doña Clara and Doña Isabel de Rivera observed and followed, and because he was her son, and for the love she bore him, she wanted to bring him out of the error and deception in which he was and teach him the said Law of Moses, because it alone is the good, true and necessary law for his salvation . . . and he answered unto his mother that he would observe it if there were whom would teach it to him; and on this occasion and on many others his said mother told him and taught him how in the month of September the fast of the great day must be kept in observance of the said law, bathing on the eve of the day previous and putting on clean clothing and supping on fish and vegetables, and not flesh (meat) and that wax candles must be lighted and put on a clean cloth.[19]

The historical data on the Carvajals and the de Granadas, as well as on other women of sixteenth- and seventeenth-century Mexico, strongly suggest that crypto-Jewish women responded to religious persecution by strengthening their roles as bearers of culture within a religiously repressive political environment.[20] As a result of the forced conversions, the gender boundaries of traditional Sephardic life became blurred as mothers, rather than fathers, fulfilled the commandment to teach their sons the beliefs and laws of Judaism.[21] This shift in women's roles contributed to the development of a female-centered spiritual culture that characterized the crypto-Jewish household. As this culture evolved over time, crypto-Jewish women preserved and transformed the traditions of their ancestors as they struggled to reconcile the contradictory identities of the convert and hidden Jew.

Because it was primarily women who maintained control over the preservation of knowledge and the practice of ritual, an informal system of matrilineal descent emerged in which both ancestry and faith were carried and transmitted through women in the family. Crypto-Judaism thus gave new meaning to the Jewish laws of matrilineal descent that historically traced Jewish lineage through the bloodline of the mother. Within medieval and early-modern crypto-Judaism, it was not only biological maternity that determined Jewish ancestry but also a maternal knowledge of religious ritual and beliefs that, in more traditional settings, would have fallen under male purview. Further, as Robert Ferry's research on Mexican crypto-Jews of the seventeenth century suggests, the female-centered aspects of crypto-Judaism offered the possibility of a shared religious life among women who gathered together in secret to fast, pray, and mourn the loss of their community members.[22] Thus, the survival of crypto-Jewish culture can, in part, be understood through an analysis of gender, since women sought to preserve a religious heritage in which ritual and community provided the continuity and connection from one generation to the next.

Among modern descendants, the persistence of this cultural legacy is found in the secret ritual life of twentieth-century crypto-Jewish women whose hidden customs carry with them an imprint of Jewish ancestry. In comparison to the crypto-Judaism of earlier historical periods, however, twentieth-century remnants of crypto Judaism were preserved primarily as individual or intrafamilial aspects of spirituality. As such, the communal dimensions of crypto-Judaism that were once present in the religious lives of women who shared customs and beliefs with one another ceased to exist. The medieval and premodern forms of crypto-Judaism have been replaced by a fragmentary presence of a Jewish past that is constructed through individualized perceptions and present-day interpretations of familial rites and customs.

## THE SURVIVAL OF REMNANT JEWISH PRACTICES AND THE SIGNIFICANCE OF THE SABBATH

Taken together, the historical texts by Gitlitz, Liebman, Levine Melammed, and Roth attest to the persistence of a crypto-Jewish culture defined by a set of rituals and beliefs that came to characterize the secret observance of Judaism in medieval Spain and premodern Portugal and the colonies of the Americas.[23] Within this form of cultural survival, as elaborated above, women were especially important in the preservation of beliefs and practices. In turning to the narratives and oral histories of modern descendants, it is clear that a number of women-centered rituals have survived through the twentieth century. Although they have been transformed by time, fragmentation, and assimilation, these customs and beliefs retain traces of crypto-Jewish practices that have informed the ritual life of Latina women. Among the most important ritual links that modern descendants maintained with Jewish heritage was the practice of observing the Sabbath. Accordingly, Frances Hernandez writes:

> Of all the suggestions of a Jewish presence in the native population, the persistent observance of the Sabbath is most often mentioned. I have heard many reports of lamps lit at Friday sunset, left burning all night with a long linen wick, and the explanation that the light was an offering for the repose of the souls of dead relatives.[24]

The Sabbath lamp ritual, as described by Hernandez, was also observed by crypto-Jewish women in medieval Spain and is associated with the customs of Belmonte, Portugal.[25] In his work on contemporary Portuguese crypto-Jews, David Canelo offers this explanation of the oil lamp ritual and its origin in the Inquisition period:

> On Friday afternoon, before the sun has set, the family lights a special lamp with pure olive oil and a linen wick made of seven strands. This is the wick of the Lord, as they call it, and reciting at the same time a prayer, they celebrate the beginning of the Sabbath celebration. . . . This lamp must be left to burn to the end. As was the custom of the other Crypto-Jewish communities in older days, the Crypto-Jews of Belmonte also used to put the lamp of the Lord in a clay pot, in order to prevent the light from being seen from the outside.[26]

Descendants who were raised in Mexico reported other concealed Sabbath rituals. One practice involved lighting oil lamps in church on Friday afternoons. One fifty-five-year-old female respondent recalled her mother's weekly lighting of oil lamps in the church:

> Every Friday my mother went to the church and she always had oil to burn. . . . She would pay the church keeper to pour the oil directly into the lamp on the highest altar and she always made sure that they had the oil burning from week to week. It would be two or four in the afternoon. The church was empty, and she would go up to the altar and start praying. And I said, "Who are you praying to? There are so many saints in there," and she would say, "We are praying to ourselves. Don't speak, don't say anything in here. We are praying to the Holiness." And she would never say God, which is *Dio* in Spanish, or Christ or anything. But she always went there and prayed to the Holiness. It was very confusing to me. I knew that Christ was someone special, but that he was not the same as God. It seemed like we were not really true Catholics.

This narrative provides a rare glimpse into what may be the survival of covert practices among modern crypto-Jewish women. Levine Melammed reports that in medieval Spain Jewish women would often supply oil or money to keep lamps burning within community synagogues.[27] Similarly, the descendant in Mexico is described as having taken oil to the church, where she paid attendants to light the lamps on the Jewish Sabbath. Because this ritual was performed at the same time each week, it bears some resemblance to the medieval Jewish custom. Further, the prayers that the descendant's mother spoke in the church invoked an image of God that was more in keeping with the Jewish notion of the divine than with the Catholic conception of the trinity.

As perhaps a crypto-Jewish holdover, this form of ritual observance is illustrative of what James Scott calls hidden transcripts, covert rites, and behaviors that emerge from the experience of oppressive social control.[28] According to Scott's analysis, rituals such as the Sabbath church custom described above function to conceal the performance of hidden transcripts that were associated with a forbidden or dangerous religious practice. Within the context of crypto-Jewish culture, such clandestine behavior appears to have survived into the twentieth century, since the practice of this secretive custom (or hidden transcript) continued to be maintained long after the threat of persecution had become less severe.

The surviving church ritual, however, was unique among the accounts of Sabbath worship provided by the respondents. More commonly, the performance of Jewish-origin Sabbath rites was confined to the private sphere of the home, where unusual ritualized behaviors could go undetected. Sabbath observance was thus maintained in protected areas such as basements, bedrooms, barns, and nearby woods, what Albert Raboteau would describe as "invisible" spaces that conceal the performance of surviving ancestral practices.[29] The persistence of invisible rituals among the descendants of the crypto-Jews was evident in candle-lighting ceremonies that were either hidden from view or masked as Christian-based. A male respondent who was raised in New Mexico offered this recollection of his grandmother's Friday night ritual:

> My grandmother used to light these candles by herself, and when I was about ten years old, I remember asking her, "Why do you light these candles on Friday evening?" I didn't say sunset, I just said Friday evenings. She said very brusquely, "Death of Christ," kind of mumbling under her breath. I said, "Oh. OK." It was like I shouldn't ask. It has always struck me that she never wanted to tell me why she was lighting the candles. . . .
>
> This woman is a very Christian woman, you know, and she was always willing to teach me prayers, and here I am sitting with her and this is not my grandmother that I normally know. She would have given me this big explanation; tears would have come down out of her eyes and she

> would have told me about the death of Christ. And instead, it was very curt. And I said to myself, that was what my grandmother was hiding. She was probably Jewish. I started reading books on Sephardic Jews, and I found her last name among the Spanish Jewish surnames, and that was the beginning of my quest.

The persistence of invisible Sabbath customs, while primarily attributed to women's ritual life, was connected to male covert behavior as well. In three cases, the respondents reported that men within the family conducted secret religious prayers or services on Fridays and Saturdays, gatherings from which women were excluded. Recalling a childhood in New Mexico in the 1940s, a woman in her sixties witnessed prayer meetings in a small church in a New Mexican village on Friday evenings:

> We used to go to this church when we were young. And the thing is, we used to go there with my uncle, and they did their prayer things, and it was late in the evening on Friday nights and so we would go to sleep. My cousin and I would just go to sleep for the night. We would take a little mat with us, 'cause the church did not have any benches at the time; it was just a dirt floor. I know it would be Friday night when we got there, and I remember the men would sing certain songs in the evening and other songs on Saturday morning.

Other descendants remembered their grandfathers or uncles wearing skullcaps and praying in seclusion on Friday night or Saturday morning. In one Texas family, the descendant's great-grandfather reportedly had a special room where he "practiced his own religion." Each week, he would go into this room with a large black book that he used for prayer. With the exception of his grandson, no other family member was allowed to disturb him while he prayed in this separate and enclosed space.

In comparison to these few accounts of male ritualized behavior, the vast majority of Sabbath rituals that were preserved were female centered and took place within the domestic sphere of the home. The lighting of Friday night candles by women, for example, was frequently accompanied by rigorous and mandatory housecleaning. This concern for cleanliness is captured in the memories of a woman who was raised in northern Mexico:

> On Friday evenings my grandmother would change all her beds. The house had to be clean. She would change all her beds, the beds especially had to be clean. She had a small table in her bedroom with two candles, one on each side. Every Friday evening she would light them, and she would not allow anyone in her bedroom except me. . . . And she would say some prayers in words that I did not know.

The association of the Sabbath with cleanliness, a common theme of ritual remembrance, is in keeping with notions of ritual purity that are pervasive in both the historical and contemporary culture of crypto-Jewish life. In addition to the Sabbath observance, ritualized notions of purification are present in the remnants of family purity laws, dietary customs, and the Fast of Esther, suggesting that a preoccupation with ritual purity may account for the types of rituals that remained part of the practice of crypto-Jewish culture.[30]

## RITUAL IMMERSION AND THE SEPHARDIC DIASPORA

Distinctions surrounding the pure and impure within Jewish law can be traced to religious codes that were intended to protect the sacred areas of the original Temple from contact with the profane. According to biblical injunction, people in a state of impurity were prohibited from entering the Temple sanctuary.[31] The laws stipulated that states of impurity included physiological conditions that involved the emission of bodily fluids such as blood and semen. In addition, religious purity laws also governed marital relations, prohibiting sexual intercourse during menstruation and directly after childbirth.[32]

Within this distinction between the pure and the impure, the concept of a *niddah,* "one who is ostracized or excluded," applied to women who were in a state of defilement because of bodily emissions.[33] For those designated as *niddah,* the law stipulated that purification could only be achieved through immersion in a *mikveh,* a natural body of water that had to be drawn from springs, rivers, or other natural sources. As women were defined as a *niddah* in accordance with their menstrual cycle and childbirth, the *mikveh* became a significant and mandatory ritual among Jewish women whose sexual lives were regulated by the commandment to purify one's body of impurities.

During the Inquisition, adherence to family purity laws by medieval Sephardic women became a basis for persecution of the crypto-Jews. Among other crimes against the Church, ritual immersion was prosecuted as an act of heresy.[34] The records of the Inquisition reveal that at the onset of persecution, women continued secretly to visit the community *mikveh* until such visits became too dangerous. They then adapted the *mikveh* to the home, constructing ritual baths that were often shared by female relatives and friends.[35] During the 1486 trial of Maria Garcia of Herrera, Garcia admitted to the Inquisitional authorities "that when I delivered or when my menstrual cycle arrived, I would separate myself from the bed of my husband and would not return to his bed until I had bathed and was clean."[36] In 1500, another of the accused women described two forms of ritual purity in which she engaged, one after menstruating and the other after the birth of a child:

> I observed sometimes when I had menstrual blood or was post-partem and then at its conclusion I washed myself, sometimes I bathed, this as per ceremony, and sometimes after childbirth, at the termination of the seven days, I dressed in clean clothes and had clean sheets put on my bed because I was told that this was a ceremony.[37]

As this testimony reveals, ritual cleanliness in medieval Sephardic culture was associated with three forms of purification: immersing in a ritual bath, putting on clean garments, and preparing clean bedclothes, rituals that could all be observed within the privacy of the home. Further, other women testified that they performed purification rituals that specifically pertained to the custom requiring a woman to pare her nails before entering the *mikveh*. Maria Alfonso of Herrera confessed, "When I was menstruating or had given birth, I separated myself from the bed of my husband and did not approach him until I was clean and had bathed myself and had cut my nails."[38]

The confessions of the medieval crypto-Jewish women attest to the maintenance of family purity laws that took on varied forms in the century after the forced conversions. The persistence of these female rituals appears to have survived beyond the initial persecution period and into the more intensified Christianization of the crypto-Jewish descendants. The findings in this area of ritual behavior indicate that some aspects of immersion customs persisted throughout the Sephardic diaspora and the dispersion of the crypto-Jews into the Americas. During the Mexican Inquisition in the mid–seventeenth century, for example, Rafaela Enriquez was charged with performing ritual cleansing with other women who ceremoniously washed one another. During the same period, Isabel de Ribera testified that she had been told that menstruating women "could not go to their husbands, nor eat what they were to eat, nor touch them with their hands, because it was forbidden by the law."[39]

Recent research among modern-day crypto-Jewish populations indicates that remnant forms of family purity rites also survived into the twentieth century.[40] Gitlitz reports that in Portugal descendants of the Jewish converts have maintained fragments of purification rites associated with childbirth. These customs include reciting the following prayer, which is intended to purify the birth mother:

> Blessed are You, Adonai, God, King of the world, who sanctified us through Your holy and blessed commandments, and permitted us to live to this day, choosing us from the gentile peoples and drawing us away from those who are in error, and giving us these commandments for the purification of our souls. Amen.[41]

Among the female descendants in the Americas, childhood recollections contain references to fragmentary rituals that appear to be derived from Jewish purification customs. These narratives are replete with images of unique rituals in which symbolic cleansing assumed a significant role for women in the family. A woman living in the Southwest of the United States offers this view into the ritual life that came to characterize hidden Jewish ancestry:

> I remember these other rituals my grandmother would do. I realize my grandmother would make us burn our nail clippings or our hair if we cut them. As soon as we cut our hair or our nails we had to put them in the fire, and when she would sweep she would take the contents of the dust pan out and the ashes from the fire as well and take them out of the house—ridding the house of dirt or the unclean. . . . I can clearly remember my grandmother doing this all of the time, as we stepped into a tin tub for our baths, she would always put the water on top of our forehead.

Another descendant who was raised in South America described a similar connection to Judaism through the observance of immersion rituals in her family. The accounts of her childhood reveal the importance of cleansing rituals, especially those focusing on hand washing and cleansing the body. In particular, she spoke of a great-aunt who maintained many of the cleansing customs as well as a rite of immersion:

> One of my great-aunts, she kept all these things. She taught us that we needed to wash ourselves with cold water. We need to do fasting four times a year, and she used a lot of herbs and cleansing for the body. . . . Every Friday afternoon we needed to go out and bathe—and remember, this was in the countryside many years ago, and we didn't have running water. Even if we bathe with hot water, we still needed to rinse ourselves with cold water. . . . When I had my first menstruation, my aunt took me to a river where the water was running, and she bathed me. It was the first of the year, the first of January. And I say to her, "What are you doing?" And she says, "Well, that's the way I want to clean you up." She put me in the water up to my chin and I started feeling different. I saw a teeny drop of blood going in the water. And I will never forget that. Because that was like something that has to do with my feminine inner part. It was very beautiful. I saw that teeny spot of blood flowing through the water, and it was like years of water running through our bodies.

It is significant to note that in this woman's family, a river was chosen as the site for ritual immersion. Other respondents report similar experiences of being taken as teenagers to a nearby river, where they were bathed in running water. This form of ritual immersion may have become common among crypto-Jews, particularly as religious persecution limited access to the synagogue or community *mikveh*. In seeking to maintain the family purity laws, it is conceivable that rivers and streams became customary ritual sites for crypto-Jewish women who sought undetected sources of natural water for immersion ceremonies.

The historical importance of ritual immersion, along with the persistence of Sabbath cleansing rituals, lends support to the view that among women in particular, rites associated with ritual pollution and cleanliness retained a special significance within the crypto-Jewish household. This finding highlights the selectivity of cultural persistence among a people whose concerns for salvation remained tied to a history of forced conversion and Christianization. A survey of remnant crypto-Jewish rituals suggests that the Jewish-origin customs that survived were those rites and traditions that reflected a certain anxiety about purity, sacrilege, and apostasy, anxieties that were evident not only in the preservation of the Sabbath and remnant forms of family purity but also in the maintenance of dietary laws and ritual fasts.

## RITUAL CLEANLINESS AND THE OBSERVANCE OF DIETARY LAWS

In the historical analyses provided by Liebman, Levine Melammed, and Gitlitz, the persistence of Jewish dietary customs assumes a prominent position within the evolution of crypto-Jewish culture.[42] From the medieval period onward, the continued adherence to biblical laws about distinguishing between clean and unclean food, animals, and domestic practices is evident both in the Inquisition proceedings and in the oral histories provided by modern-day descendants. For many individuals of crypto-Jewish heritage, dietary customs relating to the Jewish laws of kashruth are instrumental in reconstructing the evidence for Sephardic ancestry.[43] Such customs include a preoccupation with "unclean" foods and materials, separating milk and meat, examining uncooked eggs for the presence of blood in the yolk, and an aversion to pork, a meat that is a mainstay of traditional Latina cooking.[44]

A woman in her fifties who was raised in Texas spoke of her mother's extreme concern about cleanliness. In describing her mother's fear of the unclean and of blood contamination, the respondent reported that such behavior seemed strange in comparison to the practices of the surrounding community:

> We didn't eat eggs with blood spots in them. They were terrible things. She would just throw a fit, that egg was not to be eaten. And dividing things that were unclean. Things that she considered unclean were never to touch the clean things. She was fanatical about that, about never accepting clothing from anyone that might have had contact with blood or with a dead body. I thought it was odd, and I began to wonder about those things. As a child I questioned them because I thought she was a little crazy doing that. . . .
>
> Oftentimes my mother would ask a lady in the neighborhood to come in and eat with us. She would invite her to eat at our table, because my mother thought she was poor and hungry. But then she would say that this person was unclean. And I would ask her, "Well, how do you know when somebody's unclean?" "Well," she answered, "when people have our customs and our ways they are clean." And after the person left, the dishes would be washed. She had a large double sink. All of the things that she considered unclean would only be washed on this side of the sink, the "nonkosher" side, and then they would be boiled and placed under the sink. I never questioned any of it until I started reading Leviticus in recent years. And then it began to make sense to me.

Further, this same descendant spoke of her mother's disdain for people who ate *"carne de porca"* (meat of the pig), telling her daughter that such people had an unclean smell. As her mother neared death, her fear of contamination grew more intense:

> She was eighty-nine, and she was living with me. I remember bringing her up a chicken breast, with vegetables and what not. She had dinner in her room so I left it and went downstairs and I heard her yelling at me and I ran upstairs to see what was wrong and she said, "*Hija* [daughter], why are you serving me this filth?" And I asked her what she meant by that. And she said, "I don't eat *morano* [pig]," and I said, "But it's not pig, it's chicken." And she wasn't convinced that it wasn't pork so she didn't eat the chicken. It was a few months after that I asked her if we were Jewish and she said yes, but she didn't want me to tell anyone.

It would appear from this account that, as in earlier historical periods, the aversion to pork assumed great significance among a people whose connection to Judaism became linked to abstaining from a food that was so deeply emblematic of Christian acculturation. Additionally, the descendants' narratives reveal that avoiding pork was associated with fears surrounding disease, contamination, and death.[45] A woman raised in South America thus explained:

> My mother always discouraged eating pork, and so did my grandmother. I always asked why, and my mother said that if you eat pork and you get upset, then you could die.

Nowhere is this fear of food contamination more apparent than in the account of a descendant whose mother had suffered a brain seizure:

> Fifteen years before my Mom died she had a seizure, and it turned out to be a trichinosis worm that was inside her system forever. The doctor said that the worm made its way up to her brain, and the first symptoms were paralysis on one side. So I asked my Mom, how did this happen? And she said, "Well, *hijo* [son], in Mexico when all this was going on we ate pork so that people wouldn't think we were *Judeos* or whatever." "You did that?" I said, and she says, "Yeah, don't ever eat it. That's where the trichinosis worm comes from."

In some instances, the association of unclean foods with illness and perhaps death revealed the persistence of ancestral fears surrounding godly retribution, since disease was interpreted as a "curse" for the sins of past as well as present apostasies. These contemporary references to feelings of guilt and shame reflect a deep-seated cultural response to forced conversion that, while having diminished over time, nonetheless remains part of the recovery process for modern descendants. The notion that a family might still be punished by God for refusing to return to Judaism and for the violation of Jewish laws was articulated by a number of descendants. A woman whose sisters had become Christian fundamentalists expressed this fear strongly. She reported that she warned her family that such a religious choice could be dangerous, their mother having already been diagnosed with a serious illness:

> And that was one of things I was telling my sisters, too. I said, "Now, look, you guys are Christians, if you don't convert—if you don't go back to your true religion, you're going to be punished by God." And my mother always used to say, "God's going to punish you." And so I told my sisters, "God's going to punish you. Look what he did to Mom." And we laugh about it. I mean, it's terrible to say, but, I mean, it's true.

In her analysis of purity and danger, Mary Douglas maintains that fears of divine retribution are a result of cultural ideologies in which ritual pollution and contamination are linked to certain behaviors, such as the violation of food taboos, that are perceived to have serious and life-threatening consequences.[46] The lingering tensions surrounding cleanliness and purity among the modern descendants, as manifested in the aversion to pork, represent a legacy of such fears. Further, concerns about ritual purity were also manifested in customs that linked ritual purification to acts of repentance. Fears for salvation were thus evident in the past and present observance of religious fasts that were intended to absolve crypto-Jewish women from the sin of apostasy and forced conversion.

## DESPAIR, REPENTANCE, AND RITUAL FASTING

In reconstructing the effects of forced conversion on the Jews of medieval Spain, the historian Yitzhek Baer describes a culture under siege.[47] Beginning with the pogroms of 1391, fears for the complete destruction of Spanish Jewish culture existed alongside the danger of family dissolution, since apostasy threatened the stability of Jewish life. According to Baer, a deep sense of despair thus became pervasive within the Jewish community, as feelings of anguish and desolation were expressed in Jewish writings and in personal letters that survived this period of persecution. Among the literary scholars of the time, the poet Solomon de Piera was witness to the destruction of his home and to the loss of his sons. Deeply troubled by those who chose conversion rather than martyrdom, he refused to console the newly baptized Christian:

> My friend, why criest thou to icons,
> and why giv'st thou thy praise to idols? . . .
> And how canst thou ask for holy offerings?
> From one who has partaken of untithed crops?[48]

Other surviving documents of this period attest to the conflicts and personal upheavals that resulted from the pogroms and mass conversions. In a letter written to a friend, a Jewish physician laments that among his friend's family, only the mother remained an observant Jew:

> As for your poor, regal mother, I can inform you that she is living in bitterness in her husband's house and continues to abide by the Law [of Moses] and act decorously; and although many are her tormenters and would-be converters, her only reply is that she would die before going over. But now, thanks be to God, nothing hinders her from making her way daily to the *judería,* and she visits the House of God, the women there inquire of one another that she should not have to walk alone, and the good souls among them accompany her to the gate of the quarter.[49]

This letter speaks to the trauma of persecution and conversion that divided families and that caused deep rifts within the Sephardic Jewish community. As the sin of apostasy became part of the discourse of Jewish despair, feelings of guilt and betrayal became especially apparent in the developing crypto-Jewish culture and in the observance of fasts, particularly by women who sought to purify themselves of sin.

Within traditional Judaism, fasting as a form of atonement is derived from a commandment in Leviticus that directs the Jewish people to set aside one day each year for ritual expiation:

> And it shall be a statute for ever unto you: in the seventh month, on the tenth day of the month, ye shall inflict your souls, and shall do no manner of work, the home-born, or the stranger among you. For on this day shall atonement be made for you, to cleanse you; from all your sins shall ye be clean before the Lord.[50]

This commandment is observed as Yom Kippur, or the Day of Atonement, and was known among the crypto-Jews as *el Gran Día de Ayuño* (the great day of fasting) or as *el Día del Perdón* (the day of pardon). Within the seventeenth-century crypto-Jewish community in Mexico, the women of the Enríquez family were especially vigilant in their observance of the Jewish fast day. Catalina Enríquez testified that three months before her mother's death, she and her sisters prepared the home for the *Gran Día,* lighting candles that were to remain lit throughout the day of abstinence. Following a fourth-century Jewish custom of dispensing charity to the observant, Juana Enríquez offered monetary rewards to those who had refrained from eating and drinking during the holy day.[51] Fasting among the crypto-Jews was also evident in their observance of Tishah-b'Ab (the holiday commemorating the destruction of the Temple in Jerusalem). Because of the crypto-Jewish emphasis on fasting, Ana de Leon, the last surviving member of the Carvajal family, became a renowned "performer of fasts," her piousness a model for other crypto-Jewish adherents.[52] Among modern descendant women, ritual fasting appears to have survived in various forms, most notably in the crypto-Jewish celebration of the Fast of Esther.[53]

## FEMALE IMPURITY AND THE FAST OF ESTHER

As a significant penitential custom, the Fast of Esther originates in the biblical story of Esther, who, concealing her Jewish heritage, is chosen as queen of Persia by a powerful and despotic king. As the biblical story unfolds, the king's chief adviser calls for the death of all the Jews in the kingdom soon after Esther has been named queen. This decree presents a moral dilemma for Esther, who chooses to reveal her Jewish origins to the king and to plead for the safety of the Jews. Esther then commands the Jews to fast with her for three days. On the third day, she risks punishment and goes to the king's chambers without permission. The biblical account then records that when the king saw Esther, he was so taken with her beauty that he offered her half his kingdom. Two days later Esther tells him that she is a Jew, and in the following passage from the Book of Esther, she pleads for the survival of the Jewish people:

> And the king said again unto Esther on the second day of the banquet of wine, What is thy petition, queen Esther? and it shall be granted thee: and what is thy request? and it shall be performed, even to the half of the kingdom.
>
> Then Esther the queen answered and said, If I have found favour in thy sight, O king, and if it pleases the king, let my life be given me at my petition, and my people at my request:
>
> For we are sold, I and my people, to be destroyed, to be slain, and to perish.[54]

In the conclusion of the biblical story, the king responds to Esther's plea and saves the Jews.

In traditional Judaism, Esther's courage and bravery are commemorated by the observance of the joyous holiday of Purim, a celebration that was practiced by Iberian Jews before the forced conversions.[55] After the persecutions, however, the commemoration of Esther's triumph became focused on themes of spiritual betrayal as the solemn Fast of Esther replaced the more lighthearted festival of Purim. In sixteenth-century Spain and Portugal, the Fast of Esther was extended from the traditional one-day period to a three- or four-day fast that more closely replicated the repentant acts of Esther in the biblical story.[56] Roth maintains that in Mexico the Fast of Esther was as important as the Day of Atonement and that the length and seriousness of the fast sometimes resulted in a life-threatening situation for observant women.[57]

In remembering the life of Queen Esther, one prayer in particular was reported to have been of special significance to the fasting crypto-Jewish women. This psalm, the Prayer of Esther, was recited during the observance of her fast. As a plea for forgiveness, the Prayer of Esther expressed strong feelings of self-hatred and recrimination. An excerpt from the liturgy, which is found in the Apocrypha,[58] reveals the sense of sorrow and grief that the Fast of Esther engendered among the observant women:

> And Esther, the queen, fled *in prayer* unto the Lord, being seized with an agony of death. And taking off her glorious raiment, she put on garments of anguish and mourning; and instead of the choice ointments, she covered her head with ashes and dung, and she humbled her body *with* much *fasting,* and every place the ornament of her joy she filled with her tangled hair. And she besought the Lord God of Israel and said, "My Lord, our King, Thou art *God* alone; help me who stand alone, and have no helper save Thee: for my danger is in my hand.
>
> "I have heard ever since I was born in the tribe of my family that Thou, Lord, didst take Israel out of all the nations, and our fathers from their progenitors, for an everlasting inheritance, and that Thou didst for them all that Thou didst promise.
>
> "And now we have sinned before Thee, and Thou hast delivered us into the hands of our enemies, because we have given glory to their gods. . . .
>
> "But Save us by Thy hand, and help me who *stand* alone, and have none save thee, O Lord.
>
> "Knowledge has Thou of all things, and Thou knowest that I hate the glory of the wicked, and I detest the bed of the uncircumcised and of any alien. Thou knowest my necessity, that abhor the sign of my proud estate, which is upon my head in the days wherein I show myself openly: I abhor it as a menstruous rag, and I wear it not when in the days of my leisure."[59]

The importance of this prayer lies in the articulation of fears surrounding ritual impurity and acts of sacrilege. In reciting the Prayer of Esther, crypto-Jewish women acknowledged the pain and self-hatred of the apostate. Through Esther's lamentations, they could speak the unspeakable, as they too had sexual relations with an uncircumcised husband and were shamed by a false religion that they were forced to wear like a "menstruous rag." Such allusions to the ritually unclean body, both of the uncircumcised man and the menstruating woman, linked spiritual impurity to physical uncleanliness. Accordingly, intensive fasting in honor of Esther functioned to alleviate the guilt of forced conversion, since the cleansing of the body became a vehicle for the purification of the soul. Like immersion in the *mikveh,* the ritual of fasting focused on the female body as a site of contamination that within crypto-Jewish culture specifically linked the sin of apostasy to the impurity of women whose ritual lives reflected the tensions surrounding Jewish notions of the sacred and the profane.

In accordance with the premodern tradition, the Fast of Esther was still observed in Portugal at the end of the twentieth century. In a modern-day adaptation of this holy day, the crypto-Jews, particularly the women, fasted on Thursday one month before Passover. Between the fast day and the end of Passover they were prohibited from eating pork, thus linking the consumption of pork to ideologies of ritual pollution and bodily purification.[60] Further, the Portuguese liturgy that accompanied the Fast of Esther is thematically similar to the prayer found in the Apocrypha, emphasizing the observant woman's identification with Esther's sin and redemption:

> Like that Queen Esther
> Who covered herself with a sack and ashes
> Give me, Lord, that I do
> That which she would do
> In the Holiest honour,
> In the Holiest praise,
> That I may end the night and the day.
> Amen, Lord, to heaven go, in heaven arrive![61]

In reproducing the guilt and despair that characterized the premodern period, the contemporary European liturgy for the Fast of Esther retains the themes of repentance, purification, and salvation found in the Apocrypha. As illustrated by the surviving ritual practices of the European descendants, the retention of customs surrounding cleanliness, the body, and ritual pollution is particularly significant, even as the original meaning and concern for purification have been obscured over time. While thirteenth-century Spanish Jewish writings on repentance and fasting may have informed the strict conditions under which crypto-Jewish women at first observed the Fast of Esther,[62] the emphasis on female sin and bodily atonement suggests that this ritual of redemption may have also been influenced by Catholicism and especially by the rituals of fasting and self-deprivation that were pervasive among medieval and premodern religious women.[63]

The strong emphasis that the Fast of Esther placed on the female penitent resonates particularly with the Catholic representation of Mary Magdalene, the female sinner of the New Testament. While contemporary Catholic theologians point out that Mary Magdalene was in fact a holy woman who was falsely identified as the sinful woman of the scriptures, the construction of Mary Magdalene as female sinner pervades much of the art and theology of the medieval period.[64] Like Esther's, Mary Magdalene's sins were portrayed as those of the flesh, and like Esther she practiced self-denial through fasting and supplication. Thus, each representation of the female as religious supplicant emphasizes the relationship between sinfulness and bodily purification. As the Jewish symbol of the fasting Esther in sackcloth and ashes converges with similar representations of the sinful Magdalene figure, each of these female personas offers a reminder of a longing for divine forgiveness and salvation. The similarities between these two female images thus reflect a religious syncretism that characterized other aspects of crypto-Jewish observance through the blending of Jewish and Christian beliefs, customs, and symbol systems.

## SYNCRETISM, WOMEN'S RITUALS, AND THE PRESERVATION OF CRYPTO-JEWISH CUSTOMS

As described above, the rites and prayers associated with the Fast of Esther retain religious themes and customs that may be representative of ritual practices in which Jewish and Catholic theologies of sin and purification converge. Such a merging of faith traditions suggests that, as in the case of other colonized and forcibly assimilated religious groups, the crypto-Jews developed syncretic religious forms and beliefs that blended dominant culture ideologies and practices with those of indigenous traditions. While the meaning of *syncretism* has become a contested area of study within cross-cultural research on colonization and forced acculturation, the term is used here to describe the invention of blended rituals and practices that were originally intended to conceal the persistence of forbidden and/or stigmatized traditions.[65] Among the crypto-Jews in New Mexico, for example, Purim was known as the Festival of Saint Esther, a ritual that more closely paralleled traditional Purim celebrations before the Inquisition and that may have been influenced by the presence of Ashkenazic Jewish traders and settlers in the Southwest during the nineteenth century.[66] According to one respondent, this holiday was a family celebration that appeared to bring together elements of the joyous observance of Purim with a feast that honored a Catholic female saint. In one of the oldest ethnographies of crypto-Judaism in the Southwest, a descendant described this unique family custom:

> The Festival of Saint Esther is mainly a women's holiday in our way of doing things. Usually this holiday was dedicated to mothers teaching their daughters the ways of the home and such. Pastries, rolled *empananitas,* made with fried meat and pumpkin, were prepared along with elaborate meals. Everyone dressed up and drinking and singing were indulged in. The women lit candles to Saint Esther and other saints. Wine was drunk, and the oldest person made a blessing over the wine. Although the men did most of the drinking, it was basically a women's holiday. It was held up to about twenty years ago. At that time we had a bishop named Davis

> in New Mexico who started doing away with so-called Jewish holidays and traditions, in this instance by telling people that there was no Saint Esther in the Catholic religion, claiming that Esther, commemorated on Purim, was part of the Jewish faith. [67]

The New Mexican construction of Saint Esther highlights the influence of Catholicism on the evolution of crypto-Judaism, illustrating the influence of syncretic ritual motifs. Within this sphere of ritual practice, the Jewish Queen Esther is transformed by the language and theology of Catholic sainthood. Rather than the penitent Magdalene of European symbology, the representation of Esther in the southwestern United States is more closely aligned with the image of Mother Mary, an especially important icon within the culture of Latin America and Mexico.[68]

This form of syncretism has been identified across cultures as diverse populations have responded to forced conversion and missionization through a blending of indigenous belief systems with the symbol systems and theologies of the colonizing culture. Within Haitian vodou, for example, the symbol of Mary assumes various manifestations within the pantheon of African female deities known as the Ezili. In her work on Haitain religious practice, Karen McCarthy Brown describes the relationship between the Virgin Mary and African spirituality:

> Several female spirits belong to the group called the Ezili. The three most important are Lasyrenn, the mermaid who links ancient African senses of woman power and water power; Ezili Danto, the hardworking, solitary, sometimes raging mother; and Ezili Freda, the sensual and elegant, flirtatious and frustrated one. . . .
>
> Lasyrenn, Ezili Danto, and Ezili Freda are each conflated with particular manifestations of the Virgin Mary: Nuestra Señora de la Caridad del Cobre, Mater Salvatoris, and Maria Dolorosa. But unlike the Mary of mainstream Catholicism, who offers an ideal of perfectly submissive (and virginal) motherhood for emulation, the Ezili are much closer to the human drama.[69]

Similar patterns of syncretism have been found among Native Americans in the United States. William McCloughlin's research on missionary influences among the Cherokees provides this syncretic adaptation of the biblical parable of Noah and the Flood:

> When men were found to be incorrigible, at length a certain dog told his master to make a vessel and take his family and provision and seed to sow because Ye ho waah was about to bring a flood to destroy all their

> wickedness. . . . It was supposed that all kinds of animals went into the vessel. . . . [Afterward] the land becoming dry . . . the man soon commenced preparing the ground for a crop. The family saved thus were red.[70]

The construction of Saint Esther, the belief in Ezili, and the Cherokee story of the flood each contain elements of an ancestral tradition that link the religious imagery and symbolism of Christianity with preconversion beliefs and observances. Within crypto-Jewish culture, such syncretism may also be evident in candle-lighting ceremonies that blend Christmas customs with Chanukah observance and in food rituals that combine the hidden commemoration of Passover with the more overt celebration of Easter. Descendants point out that the Catholic festival of Las Posadas is celebrated from December 16 to 24, a time period that frequently coincides with Chanukah.[71] Because both holidays involve lighting candles on successive nights, some respondents have interpreted this ritual through the lens of religious syncretism. Here a male descendant from New Mexico describes this custom as it was practiced in his home:

> From the sixteenth to the twenty-fourth of December in my grandmother's house, we had to light a bonfire every day. On the sixteenth, one bonfire, on the seventeenth, two bonfires, and the eighteenth, three bonfires, and so on. Every day you had to light one until the ninth day, and then you light the ninth fire and they say that is the novena to the child Jesus. But it really isn't. It's the *shamas*, the ninth candle on the menorah. And my grandmother was very upset if these *luminarias*, the bonfires, were not lit. She said you have to light nine candles, if you don't have enough wood.

For a larger number of descendants, the persistence of Passover has more significance, particularly since two unique dishes, typically prepared during Easter, appear to adhere to Passover dietary restrictions. The two dishes, *capirotada* and *pan de semita,* are believed to be derived from the Passover prohibition on eating leavened bread.[72] In the early twentieth century, the preparation of *capirotada* was sometimes accompanied by other rites such as marking a Jewish home with the blood of a lamb, a Passover ritual that was observed by seventeenth-century crypto-Jews.[73] In one ethnographic account, a descendant associated the preparation of *capirotada* with the appearance of blood on the door of his family home:

> For Passover a bread pudding called *sopa* is made. Among those who have some Marrano connection, you will hear it called *capirotada*. It's made of layers of bread, raisins, cheese and syrup. When my grandparents still lived on the farm they would sprinkle blood on the doors, just a tiny

bit, because otherwise it would be too obvious to the Hispanic Catholic community. The sprinkling of blood is from the Bible.[74]

Another descendant from New Mexico explained the preparation of *capirotada* and *pan de semita* this way:

> My mother makes a *capirotada* with soda crackers. She doesn't make it with leavened bread. In my mother's household this was with crackers, even though in New Mexico traditionally it is made with bread. . . . After my grandmother died—I was seventeen—I started asking my mother, "Did grandma make anything special for Easter, Holy Week?" "Oh," she said, "yes, we used to make this *pan de semita.*" And as a kid I always used to think *semita* was bran. And this bread is heavy, it doesn't rise, and my grandmother baked it in the outdoor oven. . . . My friend and I looked up *semita* in the dictionary, and it means Semitic. I thought it had always meant bran, but it means Semitic. *Pan de semita* is Semitic bread. And this is what we used to eat during the Easter holidays.

The food customs associated with Passover represent a form of ritual persistence wherein food became the symbol system and the ritual codes through which women, knowingly or unknowingly, retained a connection to a Jewish heritage. An interesting parallel may be found in the ritual lives of Middle Eastern women. In a study of elderly Kurdish women in Israel, Susan Sered found that in nonobservant Jewish families, grandmothers would prepare holiday foods that served as a link to Jewish cultural heritage.[75] Sered points out that the Kurdish women self-consciously used holiday cooking as a way to deepen their ties to Judaism in a community where meal preparation became the "ultimate domestic religious act."[76] Modern descendants of the crypto-Jews share Sered's understanding of the role that women's domestic rituals play in maintaining bonds to the religious customs of Jewish ancestors. A female descendant from South America thus explains the maintenance of Jewish-origin rituals as an act of remembrance:

> I ask myself why, why were they doing these things? Why after five hundred years did they keep something? It was twisted and wrong, but theythat identity. They kept that identity only in one gesture, by washing their hands before going to the table, by spending a week out in the country under the stars, by bringing the girl children to the river to be washed, by preparing special foods. They did this to remember the old people. That was enough for them.

For the modern descendant who is grappling with the meaning of these ritual acts, the memory of Jewish-origin practices is imbued with a sense of the sacred as they recall the privatized forms of worship in which their mothers and grandmothers engaged. Through the performance of ritual, these women fostered a spiritual environment that has had a significant impact on the current generation of descendants who are in the process of recovering their Jewish ancestry. The persistence of crypto-Jewish rituals has therefore affected the development of the descendants' spiritual consciousness, informing their religious choices as they find themselves at the intersection of crypto-Judaism and Christianity, each of which has influenced their cultural and religious upbringing.

CHAPTER 3

# The Self-in-Relation and the Transformation of Religious Consciousness

As evidenced by the narratives of the descendants, reclaiming Jewish ancestry involves the disclosure of family secrets and the remembrance of family custom and ritualized behaviors. Together these experiences contribute to the transformation of both the spiritual and ethnic self as each of these aspects of identity are reconstructed through the lens of Sephardic heritage. While the act of ritual remembrance affirms the presence of a Jewish past, the recovery of Sephardic roots opens up the possibility of change for the future. The study of crypto-Jewish descent thus lends itself to an examination of spiritual transformation and the reconstruction of religious identity within a multiethnic and multicultural social context.

From the outset, the discovery and reclamation of Jewish ancestry raises important spiritual questions that center on the meaning and origins of religious beliefs. In responding to the religious and spiritual issues that hidden religious and ethnic ancestry engender, descendants report a variety of responses that range from a recommitment to Catholicism to conversion to Judaism. For almost 20 percent of the respondents, recovering their Sephardic roots ultimately resulted in the retention of an exclusively Christian worldview. These descendants report that although they may have Jewish ancestry, they were raised as Catholics and did not consider a blood tie to Judaism a challenge to their existing belief system. Accordingly, a woman in her midsixties who was raised in New Mexico explains her religious perspective as follows:

> I happen to be an American with Hispanic, Indian, Canary Islander lines, Portuguese, lots of Portuguese lines, Spanish lines, Greek lines, and some from Belgium. All this, along with some Jewish lines maybe adds a new dimension—it's part of the story. I am not a gung-ho religious person, but I am Catholic, and especially when I visit my family in New Mexico, I become very religious. I say the rosary.

For the participants who remained Catholic, the phenomenon of contemporary crypto-Judaism created a number of concerns. Especially troubling were the harsh criticisms of Church doctrine and Catholic clergy that sometimes accompanied discussions of crypto-Jewish history and ancestry. One descendant took particular offense at what she believed to be the vilification of the medieval Spanish monarchs, Queen Isabella and King Ferdinand. Maintaining that the royal family had been misrepresented by a Jewish view of Spanish history, she explained that, although she had found and confirmed hidden "Jewish lines" in her family lineage, Jewish heritage was not an ancestry that she wished to stress or on which she placed a high value.

What distinguished the strongly identified Catholic descendants from the majority of the sample population were a strongly Catholic religious upbringing and the absence of a remnant crypto-Jewish culture in the family of origin. By comparison, the descendants who experienced a shift in spiritual consciousness as a result of their knowledge of their Jewish ancestry were raised in environments where fragments of a crypto-Jewish past could still be discerned. Among these descendants, two patterns of religious change were evident. One pattern revealed a tendency toward faith blending and the desire to bring Christianity and Judaism together in some type of syncretic belief system. The other pattern of responses showed a greater tendency toward conversion to Judaism. Descendants who assumed a more syncretic religious stance, integrating both Jewish and Christian perspectives, tended to be raised in a religiously aware home where multiple spiritual orientations were present. This type of religious acculturation reflected a public/private split that incorporated the public worship of Christianity as well as the privatized observance of remnant Jewish rituals in the home. A male descendant with Indian, Jewish, and Spanish ancestry offered this description of the diverse ritual practices that were evident in his family and that coalesced in the ritual behavior of his grandmother:

My grandmother was a very Christian woman, but she lit candles on Friday night. Heaven only knows what prayers she was saying, because she would always say them sort of under her breath. And she always taught me Catholic prayers, but on Friday nights, I would sit with her and watch her light the candles, and it did not seem Catholic at all. There was a mystery and secrecy around this ritual.

As this respondent explained, the weekly lighting of the Sabbath candles, as well as the practice of other Jewish-origin rituals by his grandmother, had a significant impact on his developing spiritual consciousness. Though he attended church regularly with his family, he began to explore his Jewish ancestry as a young adult, eventually enrolling in classes on Judaism at a local synagogue. Over time, he reformulated his belief in Jesus to accommodate the Jewish notion of the divine. Now, as a man in his forties, he has reenvisioned Christ as a rabbi and great teacher:

Jesus' sensibility was very Jewish. He probably did not have any inkling that he was changing Judaism. He had something new to say, because it was all about love. Because God is love. We should love one another. I don't know if he was the son of God or not, but he was giving Judaism a new perspective, and so he was probably a great rabbi.

While this type of syncretic response was somewhat prevalent among the descendants, the more pervasive reaction to the discovery of Jewish ancestry was a transformation of religious consciousness that led to the adoption of an exclusively Jewish worldview. The prevalence of this response is undoubtedly an artifact of the self-selectivity of the sample population, in that my study tended to attract participants who were leaning toward adopting a Jewish religious identification. These descendants reported that, although their families identified as Christian, they did not attend church regularly and tended to be critical of orthodox forms of Christianity. A thirty-five-year-old descendant who was raised in the predominantly Catholic culture of Albuquerque, New Mexico, describes her parents as self-consciously nonreligious. Nevertheless, when she was a young child her father took her to church so that she and her siblings would have some religious training. The experience resulted in her rejection of Catholicism:

My dad decided that we should have some kind of religion so he decided to take us to the Catholic Church, and my mother refused to go because she had gone on Palm Sunday one time and the priest insulted the congregation and she never went back. We would go to church with my Dad, and about the only thing I remember is the priest started calling the

> congregation sinners and my Dad just got up and took us out to the car and said, "Don't believe anything they said." I don't remember my grandparents ever going to church either. So that was pretty much it.

A comparison of the three spiritual responses to crypto-Jewish heritage (remaining Catholic, developing syncrenistic beliefs, or adopting a Jewish worldview) reveals that the religiosity of the family of origin is an important variable in determining the impact of hidden religious and ethnic ancestry on religious consciousness. A family's preexisting religiosity, belief systems, and cultural practices clearly influence the choices that adult descendants make as they grapple with the knowledge of a hidden Jewish heritage. At the same time, however, familial religiosity is only one important piece of the "spiritual puzzle." Another equally important factor is the absence or presence of a childhood caregiver with whom the descendant shared a privatized ritual life. The importance of caregiving and affective bonding to the development of spiritual consciousness among descendants suggests that self-in-relation theory might be a useful paradigm in the study of changing religious identity within the descendant population.

## SELF-IN-RELATION THEORY AND THE CREATION OF THE SACRED

For the last two decades, self-in-relation theory has become increasingly important in the field of gender studies. As an interactive model of personality formation, this social-psychological theory focuses on gender differences in development and the significance of empathy for the developing self. Originating in the object relations school of psychoanalysis, self-in-relation theory emphasizes the role of female caregivers, especially mothers, in fostering empathic attachment in girls. As perhaps the most widely adopted feminist perspective on personality development, the self-in-relation paradigm has been applied to the study of moral behavior, adolescent social relations, family violence, and early childhood experience.[1]

Given the role that family culture assumes in the recovery of Jewish ancestry, it is useful to consider the self-in-relation paradigm from the perspective of ritual preservation, empathic attachment, and the creation of a Jewish consciousness among modern descendants. Relational theory maintains that psychosocial development emerges from the emotional interaction that takes place between a child and caregiver, what Jean Baker Miller refers to as the "interacting sense of self" that "includes feeling the other's emotions and acting on them as they are in interplay with one's own emotions."[2] In keeping with Miller's understanding of the self-in-relation, the respondents' narratives indicate that their spiritual development, like other aspects of the interactive self, emerged out of the emotional context of familial relationships. More specifically, the accounts suggest that spirituality is influenced by two relational components of early childhood development: the establishment of an empathic bond between the child-descendant and an adult caregiver with crypto-Jewish origins and the subsequent creation of emotional ties to Judaism that originate in the privatized spiritual life of the caregiver.

The narratives reveal that descendants who developed a Jewish spiritual orientation in adulthood reported strong emotional ties to caregivers with crypto-Jewish ancestry. One male descendant, for example, offered this description of his relationship to his grandmother:

> I spent a lot of time with my grandmother. I really lived between her house and my house. My mother always knew that when my father would get angry and chase me, I'd run to my grandmother's house, and my grandmother would stand in front of me and she'd say, "You're not touching this one. All the others you can touch, but not this one." She protected me. When she died, I thought that God was the most horrible person in the whole world—to take my grandmother away from me.

Following this pattern of childhood attachment, the formation of a Jewish spiritual consciousness evolves out a process of religious socialization in which the crypto-Jewish caregiver creates a spiritual environment that fosters the development of feelings and emotions associated with the hidden observance of Jewish rituals and customs.

In his work on religious ritual, the anthropologist Clifford Geertz describes religion as "a system of symbols which acts to establish powerful, pervasive and long-lasting moods and motivations," a psychological response that engenders feelings of awe and respect.[3] Within crypto-Jewish culture such feelings of awe and respect became associated with the practice of rituals and the disclosure of secretive belief systems through which Jewish religious symbols and ideas are transmitted. A descendant raised outside Mexico City described how her grandmother secretly taught her about the family's "special" faith:

> On Saturdays my grandmother would read to us in the back of the shop that our family owned. I remember when I was about five years old, she read real quietly, passages about Abraham, Ruth, and Moses. And when people came by the shop, she would be quiet and say, "Don't discuss this with anybody." She called it the Holy Testament, and when we

> asked her about it, she said it was very special. . . . She used to put it very, very colorfully. She used to say, "All you have to remember is that Jesus was a Jew and that Jesus was a really good man, and he was a prophet. And he was a very highly intelligent Jew, just like any other, like Moses. And that very, very religious Hebrew people always ask their fathers for help. So you have to accept that for yourself, because we are Hebrews."

Through the transmission of hidden beliefs, this descendant's grandmother created an atmosphere of clandestine emotional bonding, laying the foundation for the descendant's affective attachment to Judaism, an emotional connection that she described as a feeling of "coming home."

As the spiritual climate of remnant crypto-Jewish culture was expressed through the moods and emotions of the family member who preserved Jewish beliefs or performed remnant Jewish rituals, the development of a nascent Jewish consciousness emerged from the exchange of emotion that took place between the adult caregiver and child descendant. Particularly in those cases in which the descendant had observed some form of private worship as a child, a sense of mystery and awe informed the memory of these unique family interactions. A woman in her sixties remembers with great emotion the special relationship that she had with her father, a New Mexican Latino whose religious life became centered in his home after he lost his sight. As a child this descendant would pray with her father each week in a ritual of private devotion. It was during these privatized religious interactions that she first became aware of her father's unique customs:

> This is when I noticed that my father always wore his hat all day, right up to the moment when he lay his head on his pillow at night. In the morning it was his hat he would put on first. Another thing for sure, he never forgot his prayers, morning, noon, and night. I used to go over there on weekends, and I would walk six miles to see my father. And he used to have me read from this book that he had. It was always the same, the same things that he had me read, and the verse at the end of the prayer was always the same. And it stayed with me for years. And whatever book it was, it was not the Bible or a songbook but something else. For years I looked for that prayer—it was really a hymn—that he had me read, and then I went to this banquet and a man sang this same hymn and I was just enthralled. And he explained that this was possibly a song that was sung at Yom Kippur, because this is the only hymn that does not make reference to Jesus Christ. This was the hymn and phrase that my father would read every time.

In the father-daughter relationship recounted here, the emotional context of the sacred is bound up in the special attachment that this descendant developed to her father, a parent whom she did not actually meet until she was nine. In the course of their developing relationship, her father's nurturing became linked to his creation of the sacred in the shared moments of prayer and ritual that brought them together. As an adult, these emotional memories have served as the basis of her emerging Jewish spirituality that she expressed through a burgeoning belief in the Jewish notion of God:

> I will pray to the God of Moses who through him God gave us the commandments. Release your children as you did in Egypt when you released them from bondage. . . . When Moses led them out and wandered in the desert those were our ancestors.[4]

From a psychoanalytic point of view, the descendant's emotional attachment to Judaism might be understood as a response to the "uncanny," a term that Freud used to describe the primal feelings associated with early childhood perceptions of magic and the supernatural.[5] Freud's explanation of the uncanny, as an emotional response to that which is concealed, would seem to be particularly applicable to those crypto-Jewish descendants who associated their remnant family rituals with the occult practices of the "magical schools" of kabbalistic Judaism.[6]

## RITUAL HEALING, EMOTIONAL ATTACHMENT, AND THE UNCANNY

Although the origins of Jewish mysticism date to the first century, it was in thirteenth-century Spain when Jewish mystical tradition first began to flourish.[7] The growth of Spanish Jewish mysticism was facilitated by the dissemination of the *Bahir* and *Zohar,* two texts that formed the basis of the secret teachings of the Kabbalah. Over time the *Zohar* became the most widely studied of these texts and the main focus of mystical Judaism among the exiled Spanish Jews and their descendants. As a Jewish mystical tradition, the Kabbalah conceptualized the existence of a godhead, Ein Sof, an unlimited, unqualified, and unchangeable divine principle. According to the mystical beliefs, this godhead created the world out of its own infinite being through a process of divine emanations *(sefiroth).* The task of the mystic was to contemplate the various emanations of the godhead and thus to transcend ordinary consciousness by contemplating the mysteries of creation.[8]

In addition to the contemplative aspects of kabbalistic Judaism, a more contested arena of kabbalistic practices also exists, which includes the "magical school" of Jewish mystisicm known as magical or practical Kabbalah. Characterized by the use of incantations and amulets, this school was denounced by rabbinic scholars such as Maimonides who deemed these practices as "fit only for the ignorant and unlearned."[9] Despite these condemnations, the magic or occult school of the Kabbalah appears to have influenced rabbinic healing practices in medieval Spain.[10] After the expulsion of the Jews, the school of magical Kabbalah became especially prevalent in the exiled Sephardic communities where incantations and herbal formulas were used for protection, childbirth, love, and prosperity. Fragments of these formulas were recorded in the writings of the sixteenth-century kabbalists and have survived into the nineteenth and twentieth centuries in Greece and Jerusalem.[11] Victor Perera thus recounts a Sephardic family history in which his grandfather and great-grandfather were renowned holy men and spiritual healers:

> In the Salonika of Yitzhak Moshe's father, according to historian Michael Molho, the art of preparing amulets against the evil eye was a highly prized gift from God, possessed only by tzaddikim [holy men]. The rabbi or *escriba*—scribe—prepared parchments by hand, transcribing passages from the *Zohar* and invoking the names of protective angels: Uriel, Rafael, Gabriel, Michael. . . . Around the neck of a sickly child, or of one considered pretty enough to arouse the envy of neighbors, Yitzhak Moshe Perera might have hung a thread from the tallith of his father, or a small bag of garlic, salt or cinnamon stick. . . .
>
> My great-grandfather's studies in the Kabbala and his gift of healing went hand in glove. The primary, overarching purpose behind the medicinal amulets, the prayer-making and Kabbalistic formulas was to invoke God's protection to keep at bay the malefic influence of the *ayin hara* [evil eye] and its author, Shatan, the devil.[12]

The legacy of spiritual healing that Perera identifies in his ancestral family can also be found in the family narratives of crypto-Jewish descendants who maintain that kabbalistic healing characterized certain aspects of crypto-Jewish life in the Americas where women often carried on the healing traditions of their Sephardic ancestors.[13] These descendants believe that their family's healing traditions were informed both by *curanderismo,* the folk medicine practices of indigenous culture, as well as by Spanish Jewish sources.[14] A descendant in his forties recounted his childhood experience as the son of a *curandera* (spiritual healer) in Colorado:

> We never saw physicians growing up. My mother treated us with medicinal herbs. I would ask her about it, and she would say, "Well, your grandmother

> taught me." And then she would do things like if a baby had a stomachache, the neighbors would call her, and she would do this egg ritual, and the stomachache would go away. I don't know how it worked. I don't know if anybody does. I say to her, "Where does this come from?" She says, "It's from the Kabbalah, the ancient sages. The rabbis would treat patients this way. See it's Spanish, but it was Hebrew before that."

Similarly, another descendant discussed his relationship with his grandmother, a healer who cared for him as a child and whose vision of the sacred became part of his healing vocation as an adult. Here he describes his spiritual calling as a result of the confluence of Native American and Jewish ancestry that informed his grandmother's mystical heritage:

> She and I were always together. People called my grandmother a *bruja,* a witch. When I'm born she tells my mother I have the power of three Marys. I have no idea what that means, but like her, I have medicine. My grandmother was really an herbologist. Everyone came to her for healing. She was a very powerful woman. But people in the village think that she was a *bruja,* because she could do great things. She knew exactly when people were going to die and when they were pregnant. I use a lot of herbs that my grandmother used, including Native American and Jewish ones that she knew from her Jewish ancestry.

As these descendants re-create the memory of spiritual healing within their family of origin, they recall the powerful feelings that they experienced in the presence of nurturing women healers. In adulthood these emotional memories, imbued with a sense of the uncanny, become the foundation on which notions of a Jewish soul are given meaning in the descendant's changing worldview. Ritual remembrance therefore becomes part of the construction of a Jewish spiritual perspective, particularly as this memory is infused with deep feelings of connection to those family members who have preserved the memory of crypto-Jewish practices and beliefs.

It is significant that this relational phenomenon is not unique to Spanish crypto-Jewish culture but is also evident in other spheres of Latina/o religious life. The research on popular religiosity among Latina women, for example, analyzes the significant role that primary attachments play in the development of spirituality in the Catholic Latina/o household. As an alternative to hierarchal Christianity, popular religiosity among Catholic Latinas is a privatized form of worship that exists outside the institution of the Church, offering members of disenfranchised groups a personal access to God and salvation.[15] In their research on Catholic Latinas, Milagros Peña and Lisa M. Frehill argue that popular religiosity, as a home-centered spiritual tradition, is a form of resistance that creates "one cultural space in which Latinas have been influential" and where they have been actively engaged in the production of religious culture.[16]

Like the descendants of the crypto-Jews, Catholic Latinas practice various forms of religious rituals within the domestic sphere, personalizing the relationship to God through the creation of sacred spaces within the home. Such spaces are established through the maintenance of altars and the placement of ritual objects that become the focus of privatized worship among family members. Thus, as in the crypto-Jewish household, a sense of the sacred is communicated to children who observe and participate in the emotional rituals that characterize the spiritual life of the family. This phenomenon is evident in the personal narrative of a Mexican American woman who participated in the Hispanic Women's Liberation Theological Project. As she describes the origins of her spirituality, she offers this glimpse into the religious environment that she experienced in the extended family of her childhood:

> In the house my mother had an altar, my grandmother had an altar . . . and when this uncle would wake up, the first thing he would do was to pray. And I was very curious and was always asking questions, and I would ask him, "Uncle, what are you doing?" And he would explain to me how to start off his day, first of all he was talking to God. When it came time for breakfast, which was nothing elegant because we were very poor, I would notice that, even if all he had to eat was a tortilla or a piece of bread with his cup of coffee, he would not put anything in his mouth before asking for God's blessing. . . . The example my grandmother, my mother, this uncle gave me was of having faith in God.[17]

As this account illustrates, the individual's attachment to God emerges from her connection to significant childhood caregivers. In this narrative, a close family member affectively mediates between the world of the sacred and the world of the profane, providing an emotional link to God that lays the foundation for spiritual feeling in the psyche of the young child. This relational interpretation of spiritual development suggests that attachment to God develops within the dynamic that takes place between the child and a more powerful nurturing figure, since the child experiences the feeling states of those to whom he or she feels deeply connected. Among the crypto-Jewish descendants, such exchange of feelings creates the emotional context through which an affective tie to Judaism and to the Jewish notion of the divine is established. Such ties become especially significant following the death of the family member whose crypto-Jewish practices had helped to instill a sense of the sacred in the child descendant.

### MEMORY, SPIRITUALITY, AND THE SIGNIFICANCE OF ATTACHMENT AND LOSS

The self-in-relation model, as elaborated above, provides a framework for understanding the construction of spirituality in childhood. In addition, the relational paradigm also helps to explain the emergence of a Jewish worldview in adulthood following the death of a parent or other significant caregiver with crypto-Jewish origins. For more than a third of the descendants, their adoption of a Jewish belief system, whether in whole or in part, was informed by the experience of loss and mourning. Research on death and bereavement among adult children suggests that identification with a parent is a common response to loss.[18] While such identification may be expressed through the adoption of physical characteristics or behavioral changes, the narratives of the crypto-Jewish descendants strongly point to the significance of spiritual identification in the period of bereavement. For the descendants, adopting a Jewish worldview thus became a means to sustaining an attachment to the deceased. Here a male descendant offers this observation on the relationship among memory, loss, and spirituality:

> It took a long time for me to get over my grandmother's death. When I went to seminary I learned about memory. To remember is to keep my grandmother close. It all makes sense to me that she hasn't gone, that she is still here because of my memory. And people ask me why I do things a certain way, pray a certain way that is different because of our Jewish ancestry. And I say, These are the old ways. These are the ways that they were done. I don't know how far back they go, but I venture to say that they are probably very, very old. And I am not going to change them. . . . They are part of our tradition. Whether they are right or wrong is immaterial to me. I will practice them the way I was taught by my grandmother.

In modern crypto-Jewish culture, the secret religious heritage of the primary caregiver becomes a spiritual signifier that helps the descendant to sustain an emotional bond with the deceased. Such a bond is strengthened through the descendant's acknowledgment of Jewish ancestry and his or her developing belief in the Jewish faith. This spiritual response to death is evident in the account of a descendant who felt ostracized by his family after making the decision to remove his dying mother from life support:

> I think that now, seven years later, I understand all the emotion. But my dad blamed me, my brothers, my sisters. So I was pretty much ostracized forever. And I started going into a very deep depression, very deep. You've got to understand, I was the oldest. I was mother's favorite, and I was just lost. She was very tender with me. And I didn't know what to do. I even contemplated suicide. I was really in a depression. And I started remembering things she would say about how bad things were for the family and it was always Judaism that kept them going, and I kept remembering this. And I'd just keep hearing "Judaism, Judaism, Judaism" in my mind and you know, I didn't really know what Judaism was. . . . And so I called a colleague of mine and we had lunch. I said, "You know, I'm a Jew." He said, "What?" I said, "I'm a Jew." He said, "How could you be a Jew?" I said, "My mother told me, I'm a Jew. We're Jews." After that, I decided to take classes at the temple.

Another male descendant converted to Judaism soon after witnessing the deathbed conversion of his mother:

> Mom had a deathbed conversion almost a week to the day before dying. . . . And I remember Mom [had] a gasp of realization that the end was near. So I remember her gasping and then us going through the ceremony, all of us in tears, including the rabbi going through that conversion. . . . There were prayers, and you know, I was just so moved emotionally. I was just on a different plane. I was just psychically embedding that whole scene into memory. It was beautiful and sad at the same time. But you know, I am glad she did it. She died the way she wanted to. She died in September, and I began the conversion process a month or two before. The rabbi had planned on converting Mom in December, so I converted in December. It was kind of a symbolic identification with Mom, me being alive and converting. There was that kind of connection that I made.

As these accounts suggest, spiritual development begins with an empathic connection between child and caregiver to which the adult descendant returns as death represents a final separation from the deceased. Because death and loss frequently result in a rekindling of childhood emotional states, the adult mourner experiences a longing to reclaim the hidden Jewish belief system that formed at least part of his or her spiritual consciousness as a child. Thus, with the death of the caregiver, the descendant's connection to Judaism becomes especially important.

For some descendants, this connection is reinforced through dreams, a medium of remembrance in which the worlds of the living and of the dead converge. A number of descendants reported that the deceased came to them in dreams and, as if directed by God, reminded them that they were indeed spiritual Jews. Dreams such as these, while indicative of an unconscious longing to return to a nurturing parent figure, engendered feelings of attachment both to the deceased and to Judaism. This emotional dynamic is illustrated by the experience of a woman from South America whose family kept a lambskin in their home as a reminder of their Jewish ancestors. Just before her father died, she reported having had the following dream:

> In this dream I was here in Texas in the house where I work. It was about 7:00 in the morning, I suppose. I saw my father in a huge, huge home. And there were all my cousins and everybody eating outside in the front room. I went into the next room, and there was my father in a big bed with lots of pillows. He was dying, and he called, "*Mi hija* [my daughter], come here." And I sat down by his bed. Then he called to his wife to take some paper from a big room. She brings the papers and my father passes them to me. Then he told my daughter to come into the room and to come close to him. He took a *kipah* [skullcap] and put it on her head. And he looked at me and said, "Remember, the name of Abravanel [a renowned Portuguese Jewish family]. These are members of your family." Then we walked out of the room, and I am holding my daughter's hand. And there is a little bit of snow on the ground, and I say to my daughter, "Where we come from, there is no snow." In the same hour I was having my dream, my father was dying in South America.

In the months after her father's death, this descendant came to believe that her father had visited her in her dreams so that neither she nor her children would forget their Jewish ancestry. This dream, coupled with her memory of the crypto-Jewish ritual life of her aunts, reinforced her emotional commitment to Judaism.

## GENDER, SPIRITUAL DEVELOPMENT, AND THE SELF-IN-RELATION

As the above narratives reveal, the presence of empathic bonds between family members of different generations crosses gender lines, since attachments are formed between daughters and fathers, sons and mothers, daughters and grandfathers, and sons and grandmothers. Within this cross-gendered phenomenon, the emotional bonds between women and boys appear to be especially strong within the crypto-Jewish family. This finding is particularly significant in light of the emphasis that relational theory places on the development of male autonomy as an outcome of maternal separation. As discussed earlier, the relational paradigm stresses the importance of empathic attachment between mother and daughter. Male development, by comparison, is explained as a process of separation from the mother as primary caregiver. Nancy Chodorow's analysis of European American families thus concludes:

> Internally, the boy tries to reject his mother and deny his attachment to her and the strong dependence upon her that he still feels. He also tries to deny the deep personal identification with her that has developed during his early years. He does this by repressing whatever he takes to be feminine inside himself, and, importantly, by denigrating and devaluing whatever he considers to be feminine in the outside world.[19]

In applying Chodorow's model of development to Latina/o culture, Denise Segura and Jennifer Pierce suggest that, unlike in European American families, personality development in Chicana/o culture is informed by the extended family structure characteristic of Latina/o communities.[20] Thus, the construction of the gendered self may be influenced by multiple female caregivers, including mothers, aunts, and grandmothers, all of whom participate in the upbringing and socialization of both male and female children. For the male child, one consequence of this pattern of nonexclusive mothering is that issues of separation and differentiation become centered on multiple female caregivers rather than on a single maternal figure. According to Segura and Pierce, this structural arrangement may result in one of two paths toward masculine identity formation:

> Nonexclusive mothering may make Chicanos more responsive to women—or conversely it may make them more disdainful. The presence of several female caretakers may actually ameliorate male contempt for women because the Chicano child is not completely dependent on any one woman. The opposing view is that nonexclusive mothering makes it much harder for the young Chicano boy than for his European-American counterpart to achieve a masculine identification because the energy involved in repressing feminine identification is greater—a difficulty exacerbated by the disadvantaged structural position of Chicanos.[21]

The research on spiritual development within Latina/o crypto-Jewish culture supports the supposition that the presence of multiple female caregivers may lead to a more rather than less female-centered developmental process for Latino males, at least as far as the construction of the spiritual self-in-relation is concerned. This finding may in part be explained by the role that women play in cultural persistence in historically threatened religious and ethnic communities. The role that women assume as bearers of culture may strengthen the empathic bonds between female caregivers and male children, lessening the impact of emotional repression and female rejection on the psychological development of the male child. In this regard, Chodorow's assumption about a mother's tendency "to identify less with her son, and to push him toward differentiation" may be more characteristic of nonethnic American European families than of those families that are ethnically and racially diverse.[22]

In the crypto-Jewish families described here, empathic connections between male children and female caregivers are in part centered on a privatized spiritual life that originates with the secrecy of crypto-Jewish culture. Instead of "pushing" the male child toward differentiation, women in crypto-Jewish households create and sustain a close identification with their sons and grandsons. Within this developmental paradigm, a shared ethnic and religious heritage becomes at least as important as gender difference in the personality formation of boys. This finding would suggest that the process of gender development in the descendant crypto-Jewish household, as well as in other ethnic families, is influenced by multiple factors, including family structure and the historical and contemporary presence of diverse forms of cultural oppression and forced assimilation.

As this research suggests, the religious realm may have become one sphere of social life where cross-gender ties became especially important. It is therefore not surprising that both male and female descendants found that, as they integrated the memory of ritual practice and their emotional attachment to the practitioner, their understanding of themselves as ancestral Jews took on new spiritual meaning. Further, cross-gender identification may also help to explain the gender shift in culture bearing that has been found among modern descendants, since men are now taking a more active role in transmitting Jewish heritage to the next generation. This gender shift will be elaborated more fully in the conclusion. In a number of families, cross-gender development has influenced patterns of religious change, as illustrated by the deathbed conversion described above. Another example of this trend is found in the narrative of a male descendant who rejected Catholicism soon after his grandmother began to identify as a Jew:

> My grandmother used to believe in Jesus. She believes in God now, but she believes in Judaism. She's not Catholic anymore. She goes to temple once in a while, but she says, "I pray in my house. I pray in my garden. God is with me all the time. You have to pray. God is the biggest thing." She

> calls him Nuestro Señor, Our God. She wears the Star of David. She used to have a cross, but she bought a Star of David in Israel. She's been there three or four times. She's been to Egypt to see the pyramids. She said, "I saw where we built the pyramids." It wasn't like, "where the Jews built them," it was, "where we built them."

In the case of this descendant, his grandmother's religious transformation placed his awareness of Jewish heritage in a more spiritual context, a shift in perspective that ultimately led to his informal conversion to Judaism. For other respondents who were more steeped in the religious life of Christianity, crypto-Jewish descent created a less dramatic change as they sought to bring together Judaism and Christianity in a more unified approach to religious beliefs. In the chapters that follow, both syncretism and conversion will be more fully explored, as each of these dimensions of spiritual transformation reflects vastly different approaches to the recovery of Jewish ancestry.

CHAPTER 4

# Syncretism and Faith Blending in Modern Crypto-Judaism

The previous chapter established a theoretical model for understanding how religious belief systems are constructed in a culture where multiple ethnic identities inform the development and adoption of a spiritual worldview. As described in the self-in-relation analysis, one response to the discovery of crypto-Jewish heritage is the formation of a syncretic religiosity that integrates the diverse belief systems to which the descendant feels connected as a result of childhood attachments and religious acculturation. In a further exploration into the construction of spirituality, this chapter will explore the syncretic response to crypto-Judaism in greater depth, since the experience of the descendants illuminates the complex nature of syncretism in contemporary religious culture.

As a significant area of research, syncretism has been the subject of postcolonial interrogations into the effects of forced acculturation on colonized populations. Within the discourse on responses to colonization, the notion of "blending theologies" has been understood as a form both of accommodation and of resistance within ethnic and racial communities that have been subject to forced conversion and missionization. Charles Steward and Rosalind Shaw discuss the diverse ways in which syncretism has been explained in the literature on religious cultural adaptation:

> Syncretism refers to the synthesis of different religious forms. It is a contentious and contested term which has undergone many historical

> transformations in meaning. Some see it as a disparaging, ethnocentric label for religious traditions . . . which are deemed "impure" or "inauthentic" because they are permeated by local ideas and practices. Yet in other contexts religious synthesis may have positive connotations as a form of resistance to cultural dominance, as a link with a lost history, or as a means of establishing a national identity in a multicultural state.[1]

In an earlier chapter on crypto-Jewish history and cultural persistence, syncretism was presented as a form of resistance to domination, an act of religious persistence that led to the survival of Jewish spiritual identity in successive generations of crypto-Jewish descendants. Building on this historical analysis, this chapter will examine religious syncretism as a postmodern response to the recovery of Jewish roots. Within the context of theological transformation, syncretism among contemporary crypto-Jewish descendants can be understood as a process of partial conversion whereby individuals select aspects of their newfound Jewish faith and combine these with their preexisting Christian beliefs to create a syncretic belief system that incorporates both dimensions of their cultural and religious heritage. Through this process of integration, the descendants become what Brigit Meyers has described as active agents in their own religious biographies.[2] As a postcolonial phenomenon, syncretism thus becomes the means by which descendants reconcile the existence of two divergent religious worldviews that when brought together create the possibility of a new, more inclusive ethnic and cultural identity.

Within the history of crypto-Judaism, syncretism as a response to conversion developed in the fifteenth and sixteenth centuries in Iberian cultures, where converts had access to Jewish resources and Jewish communities that retained Sephardic beliefs and practices. The Jewish-Christian traditions that emerged in this era of Christianization were thus grounded in a knowledge and awareness of Hebrew texts and ritual life.[3] In contemporary society, the syncretism of crypto-Jewish descendants arises out of a very different cultural milieu, in that modern descendants, for the most part, are far more conversant with Catholic culture than they are with Jewish tradition and ritual, to which they have had very little exposure. As a result, the process of "faith blending" among modern descendants starts from a Christian theological position that over time is modified and restructured to include a Jewish perspective. The respondents frequently described this religious restructuring as the acquisition of "lost" religious knowledge. Thus, the reclamation experience of the descendants can be compared to that of other ethnic groups, such as Native Americans, who also have a history of forced conversion.

Among indigenous peoples, recovering ancestral religion, belief, and custom is frequently accomplished through studies with elders in the community who have retained the pre-Christian traditions of their tribal cultures. This form of cultural recovery is illustrated by the experience of Mary Crow Dog, a Lakota Sioux, whose efforts to return to tribal religious practice strongly conflicted with the desires of her devoutly Catholic mother:

> To be an Indian I had to go to the full bloods . . . I felt drawn to my stubborn old full-blood relatives, men like my Uncle Fool Bull who always spoke of a sacred herb, a holy medicine which was the Creator's special gift to the Indian people. . . . I listened to these stories and one day I told my mother, "I'm gonna grow up to be an Indian!" . . . She did not like it. She was upset because she was a Catholic and was having me brought up in her faith. She even had me confirmed. I sometimes try to imagine how I must have looked in my white outfit, with veil and candle, and it always makes me smile. I was then white outside and red inside, just the opposite of an apple.[4]

As Mary Crow Dog's experience suggests, the recovery of ancestral religion among Native Americans takes place within the tribal and family culture of Indian society. With the absence of an equivalent surviving religious culture in the historical evolution of crypto-Jewish communities, crypto-Jewish descendants, by comparison, turn to the institutional structures of mainstream Judaism (and in a few cases to other crypto-Jewish adherents) to acquire religious knowledge. In the majority of cases, a local synagogue provided the venue for the descendant's introduction to Jewish theology and ritual. Here a female descendant living in Denver described her initial experience with the study of Torah.[5]

> Before I could start classes at the synagogue, I met with a woman who was sponsoring me for the class. I explained everything to her. She told me that I had to buy this big huge collection of books and the Torah. I just finished reading the Torah about three weeks ago, from beginning to end. I am thinking about it, looking at it as a guide and as rules that we have to abide by as part of the chosen people.

As the attainment of Jewish knowledge broadens their view of religious beliefs and theological concepts, descendants tend to choose one of two paths toward religious change: They either adopt Jewish beliefs completely or modify an existing Christian worldview to incorporate Jewish perspectives. For a small number of respondents, this spiritual reorientation involved reinterpreting Christianity within the framework of Jewish cultural origins. In a reversal of the medieval phenomenon in which crypto-Jewish converts transformed Judaism to accommodate and/or resist the imposition of Christian doctrine, modern descendants engage in a Judaization of Catholicism. Through a theological recasting of Jesus and Mary as historical Jewish figures, the descendants create a link between Christianity and Judaism that parallels their own ancestral histories of Jews who became Christians. Within this sphere of cultural and religious identification, three syncretic motifs emerge from the theological adaptations of the respondents. These motifs are Jesus as Jewish Messiah, Mary as Divine Jewish Mother, and Jesus as Suffering Jewish Martyr.

## JESUS AS JEWISH MESSIAH

Within the sociology of religion, the study of messianic Judaism has primarily focused on the modern aspects of this movement among young North American Jews who, in search of a meaningful spiritual path, have become part of a Jewish messianic religious group that accepts Jesus as the Messiah.[6] While a number of descendants have been drawn to such movements in an effort to resolve the conflicting spiritual identities of their crypto-Jewish heritage, the respondents in this study generally have rejected such religious groups, choosing instead to create or sustain their own form of messianic Judaism that is more closely tied to the religious culture of their crypto-Jewish ancestors.

The messianic motifs that emerge in the spiritual narratives of the descendants appear to have their origins in the religious discourse that characterized the development of both Christianity and Judaism in the century immediately following the forced conversions of Jews in Spain. The polemical debates in the postconversion period focused on the question of whether Jesus was actually the Messiah. For both the Church and the Jewish community, this theological debate was at the heart of the conversion dilemma. During this period of forced conversion, Jewish and Christian writings proliferated as rabbinic scholars sought to refute the efficacy of the Christian position, while Christian theologians, most notably those with Jewish backgrounds, defended the principles of Christianity. The theological discourse specifically on the Messiah reached a critical juncture with the public debate that took place in Tortosa in 1412.[7]

The disputation of Tortosa, which for the Spanish Jews was among the most important and painful religious debates of the medieval period, was initiated by the physician Geronimo de Santa Fe, a well-known convert who before his conversion was known as Joshua Lorki. Knowledgeable in both Hebrew and Jewish law, Geronimo de Santa Fe appealed to the crypto-Jews in their own language and with an understanding of their culture. His arguments were based on an earlier disputation between the thirteenth-century convert Paulus Christiani and the Jewish scholar Moses Maimonides. In a public debate held in 1263, Paulus Christiani stressed the belief that the Messiah had come in the person of Jesus and that he was a divine being. Following Paulus Christiani's argument, Geronimo de Santa Fe claimed that the authors of the Talmud believed that the Messiah had already come. Because of Geronimo de Santa Fe's position and authority, the Church hoped that the crypto-Jews would accept Jesus as the Messiah and become true Catholics.[8]

More than a hundred years after the Tortosa disputation, a significant anti-Jewish treatise emerged in Portugal after the expulsion of the Jews from that country and the ensuing forced conversions. Like the earlier disputations, this treatise, authored by Franciso Machado, was aimed at the newly baptized converts who continued to practice secret forms of Judaism. Drawing on rabbinic sources, Machado's work, which was entitled *Espelho de Christâos Novos (The Mirror of the New Christians),* claimed that Jesus embodied twenty characteristics of the Messiah. Further, Machado's writings argued that the destruction of the Temple in Jerusalem was punishment for idolatry and the death of Christ.[9] Within the framework of religious doctrine espoused by the Church, both Geronimo de Santa Fe and Machado intended to establish Jesus as the true Messiah within a culture of crypto-Jewish adherents.

Fears that the Christian interpretation would appeal to the crypto-Jews led to Jewish refutations of the Christian treatises. The most elaborate of these was produced by the exiled Spanish Jewish thinker Don Isaac Abravanel, who, at the turn of the sixteenth century, produced three works: *The Wells of Salvation, The Announcer of Salvation,* and *The Salvation of His Messiah.* With these tracts, Abravenel hoped to encourage belief in a Messiah who was still to come and faith in the teachings of the Torah. In seeking to mitigate the despair and hopelessness of a people who had suffered exile and forced conversion, Abravanel predicted a future of redemption and the coming of the Messiah.[10] During the same period, Rabbi Abraham ben Eliezer Halevi, an exile who had settled in Jerusalem, played a central role in a messianic movement that had grown in importance in the early part of the sixteenth century. His work, like Abravanel's, included messianic calculations and an apocalyptic view of redemption that emphasized the importance of the fall of Constantinople.[11]

As the historical data reveals, the culture of crypto-Judaism first in Spain and then in Portugal was influenced by two competing messianic motifs, a Christian account of death and redemption and a Jewish theology steeped in despair and hope for true salvation. In Spain, the crypto-Jews were especially influenced by spiritual movements that foretold the coming of a Messiah who would put an end to the suffering by the Inquisition. Many of those who prophesied the coming of the Messiah were young girls of twelve or thirteen whose visions of redemption created large followings among poor and working-class converts. The most well known of these "prophets" was Ines of Herrera (also called the "maiden of Herrera"), a child who was reported to have ascended to heaven, where she witnessed the salvation of the persecuted Jewish souls.[12]

Among the crypto-Jews who settled in the colonies, such messianic themes took expression in a seventeenth-century belief system that was deeply influenced by the experience of exile and Jewish suffering. This phenomenon was exemplified in the arrest and testimony of Manuel Diaz, who was tried by the Inquisition in Mexico in 1596. During his trial, Diaz predicted that the Messiah would come by the year 1600, a prediction that was based on a dream that he had while imprisoned for Judaizing. Diaz's dream foretold of the coming of the Messiah and the freeing of Jewish prisoners by the God of the House of David. Similarly, the trial of Blanca Enríquez revealed that she, too, had predicted the arrival of the Messiah, who would liberate the Jews from persecution.[13]

Other messianic themes present among crypto-Jews in sixteenth- and seventeenth-century Mexico represent a blending of Christian and Jewish features. In particular, divine birth narratives among crypto-Jews predicted that the "savior" would be born to a crypto-Jewish mother. In one such narrative, crypto-Jews reported that they believed that Blanca Enríquez's daughter, Juana, would give birth to the Messiah. During her pregnancy she was believed to have made nine visits to a painting of "St. Moses."[14] Another narrative focused on Blanca Juarez, a twenty-two-year-old woman who was considered a *santa* (holy woman) because of her pious and religious ways. It was hoped that after her marriage she would give birth to the Messiah. The records of Blanca Juarez's trial indicate that the crypto-Jewish community held prayer vigils in which Blanca Juarez was seated in the center of a circle, surrounded by visitors who prayed for the Messiah's birth.[15] Accounts such as these clearly illustrate the extent to which crypto-Jewish culture was influenced by Christian theological constructs of the birth of Jesus. In these syncretic motifs, the notion that the Messiah was still to come was retained, while at the same time redemption was conceived as the as-yet-unrealized birth of a male child from within the crypto-Jewish community.

In turning to the syncretic beliefs of modern-day descendants, messianic themes of salvation are found in diverse religious orientations that have developed out of the descendants' recovery of their Sephardic roots. The family history of one Mexican descendant in particular illuminates the relationship between crypto-Jewish descent and the adoption of a spiritual worldview that incorporates messianic themes from both the Hebrew Bible and the New Testament. According to this descendant's oral history, her religious transformation began in pre–World War II Mexico, when, as a young woman, she discovered her Jewish ancestry and soon thereafter became a member of a church near Juarez that was led by a minister with crypto-Jewish origins. Before joining this church, the descendant had been a self-taught Catholic:

> When I met Brother Q I was a very devout Catholic at the time. I taught this Catholic doctrine to myself, because neither my mother nor my grandmother was very Catholic, and I was looking for something. My grandmother lit the candles on Friday night, and she never ate pork. She told me stories about people who ate pork and who were unclean. I suspected we were Jewish, and then the Brother told me that my family was Jewish and that there was a way to know by checking the coat of arms of my family. Soon after, I became involved in this religious community led by the Brother. He spoke Hebrew and taught me the Shema[16] and was close to the Mexican Jews who were also living in this village. They wanted him to go to their synagogue. They thought that they would make him a rabbi. They wanted him to become a rabbi, but he would need to be circumcised, and he didn't want to do that. He would teach about the Messiah, but it was not the Christ that most people believe in.

This descendant explained that, after leaving Mexico a number of years ago, she and her extended family, including her brothers, children, and grandchildren, established a church in Arizona that carries on the Jewish-Christian tradition of the now-deceased minister from Juarez. Accordingly, they observe the Sabbath from sundown on Friday to sundown on Saturday, and they hold services each Saturday afternoon. The religious beliefs at the core of their spirituality focus primarily on the notion that Jesus was the Jewish Messiah:

> The Christ of most people is an idol. We do not believe in idols, because we follow the Ten Commandments. There is only one God, the God of Israel. The Christ that is taught to us is the Son of God, and he is the Messiah but is not the same Christ that everyone believes in. It is not the same Christ that is celebrated in December or on Easter. Our Christ is the Christ which is found in the Book of Isaiah. The other Christ is false, is an idol. We find the Messiah in the Old Testament, when he is going to be born and all the circumstances. It is chapter 53 in Isaiah and then it is in the New Testament in Matthew, 2, 7, and 9; there is a star to announce his birth. . . . When you understand everything, it's beautiful. You feel the glory of God—Israel.

This view of messianic Judaism is consistent with the perspectives of other messianic movements that cite Isaiah as proof that Jesus fulfilled the prophecies of the Hebrew Bible.[17] The Juarez congregation described by the descendant appears to be an offshoot of the Church of God (the Seventh-Day Adventists), which emphasizes a return to Hebrew tradition through the observance of the Sabbath.[18] At the turn of the century, the Church of God had a strong missionary presence in Mexico.[19] Because of its emphasis on Hebrew biblical interpretation, the Church was believed to have attracted many converts of crypto-Jewish descent.

While the Mexican descendant in this study acknowledged the similarities between her family's "Church of God" and other Adventist movements, she and the other members of her family maintain that their theological orientation is more authentic and that it represents a distinct Jewish-Christian framework unique to Brother Q's own Jewish sensibilities. As evidence of their Jewish orientation, they describe a ritual life that, in addition to the observance of the Sabbath, involves the recitation of morning prayers and the celebration of Chanukah and Passover. Although they do not circumcise their sons, they adhere to the notion of a spiritual covenant with God that they describe as "circumcision of the heart."[20]

In observance of the Jewish prohibition on idolatry, the Mexican descendants do not permit any representation of God in their small church or in their homes. The only religious symbol permitted is the Star of David, which is worn as an adornment and which, in the form of a small neon light, is lit every Friday night in the descendant's home and remains lit until Saturday at sundown. The Star of David is viewed as a symbol of the Messiah Jesus who, descended from the tribe of Judah, will return after God's commandments have been fulfilled on earth. Further, the descendants do not celebrate Christmas or Easter, maintaining that these holidays promote idolatry and misrepresent the divinely inspired birth and resurrection narratives of the Hebrew Bible.

Within this religious framework, Passover, which they also call the Lord's Supper, is a particularly important holiday in which they equate the sacrifice of the lamb with the sacrifice of the Messiah, as one family member explained:

> In Israel the priests sacrificed the lamb for the remission of Israel's sins as a symbol of the Messiah—to make it a reality. He [Jesus] celebrated the Passover when he was on earth. And he also came and fulfilled the prophecy, and he instituted the emblems of the sacrifice to liberate the Jews and also everybody else. The emblems of the sacrifice are the matzoth that we eat and the Mogen David kosher wine that we drink—all the things we have at our seder. And we also sing the song of Israel, the Hatikva, when we celebrate our seder.

In contrast to this Protestant-inspired form of syncretism, a very different messianic approach has been adopted by one New Mexico descendant. This respondent, now in his midsixties, became a Russian Orthodox priest as a culmination of a long spiritual journey in which he attended Catholic seminary and studied Judaism before finally choosing to become Russian Orthodox.[21] At home now in the monastic world of the Russian Orthodox Church, this descendant believes that he has found a spiritual avocation in which his belief in Jesus as the Messiah can be sustained within a theological framework that also incorporates a Jewish notion of God:

> I am what they call a messiahist, you understand? For me there is Jesus, the flesh, the son who you can see, whose image is of a man. But there is also God the father, like in Judaism, who is unseeable. When they ask me how I see God, I say for me God is a ball of fire. God is a blaze of light. Jesus is flesh that is derived from the center of the fire, from the flames of God.

In this theological construction of the divine, the descendant combines the Hebrew symbol of the burning bush with the Christian representation of Jesus as the divine son. His religious worldview is centered on the saintly images of Jesus and Mary that characterize both the Mexican American Catholicism of his upbringing and the Russian Orthodoxy of his current faith. Thus, unlike the messianic Jewish-Christians who forbid representations of God, he surrounds himself with religious icons that have both Jewish and Christian origins, creating a unique religious environment where representations of saints coexist with Judaic ritual artifacts.

In the small monastery where this Russian Orthodox descendant resides, a statue of the Virgin Mary holding the infant Jesus provides a focal point for a religious space that is adorned with portraits of the last czar and czarina of Russia. Not far from the statue of Mary and Jesus stands a wooden and glass bookcase housing a porcelain Messiah doll that has been in the descendant's family for many generations and thus may be a legacy of the Messiah culture of earlier crypto-Jewish periods. According to the descendant, the doll, while not God, symbolized the longing for a Messiah who has yet to come:

> The Christ doll tradition in our family is meant to represent the Messiah as a child [who] we always expect will come some time. It is like a woman who is carrying a child nine months is always expecting. When a Christ doll was presented, passed down from one generation to the next, from one family to another, it was not meant as the Christian God but as the promise of a Messiah represented as a child waiting to be born.[22]

Along with these Christian symbols, the monastery also contains Jewish iconography. A doorpost in the house bears the symbol of the mezuzah, a parchment containing scriptures from the Torah, while the entry to the monastery is adorned with a ceramic plaque on which the Hebrew letters for God, יהוה, are inscribed.[23] The mixed religious symbolism that characterizes the monastic home of this descendant expresses the confluence of traditions informing his understanding of himself as a Jewish Christian. As the religious statuary suggests, however, the most significant of these symbols are Mary and Jesus, holy mother and divine child. Because Russian Orthodoxy celebrates the human maternity of Mary, it is she, as Christian religious symbol and Jewish mother, who offers the possibility of spiritual reconciliation between the two traditions.

## MARY AS DIVINE JEWISH MOTHER

In the syncretic belief systems created by a number of the descendants, Mary provides a bridge between Jewish spiritual ancestry and modern Catholic upbringing. In the case of the Russian Orthodox convert, the descendant places special emphasis on the Jewishness of Mary within a theological framework that stresses her humanity. Thus, his conversion to the Russian Orthodox Church provides an institutional setting for his personal syncretic vision. The Russian Church emphasizes the corporeal nature of Mary who, although human, was able to attain spiritual perfection by following God's will completely. Within the Russian Orthodox worldview, Mary is venerated as a loving and forgiving mother whose benevolent maternity can be experienced by all humankind. According to this tradition, Mary is associated with the principle of Divine Wisdom (the "Mother Church"), a feminine presence of God that encompasses Jesus and allows for the redemption of humanity.[24]

It is this concept of Mary to which the Russian Orthodox descendant subscribes, creating a syncretism that incorporates the idealization of Mary as the benevolent and powerful Jewish mother. In veneration of the young Jewish Mary, the descendant has painted a portrait of the saintly mother on the outer wall of the small Russian Orthodox Church that is connected to his monastery. Inside the building, a "miracle" picture of Mary hangs on a prominent church wall. This painting of Mary is believed to weep real tears for the death of Jesus and thus has become a source of healing for those who attend this church. Maintaining that his role as healer is derived from the kabbalistic practices of his crypto-Jewish grandfather, the descendant performs rituals in which he attends to the emotional and physical ills of his mostly Mexican American parishioners, many of whom bring *milagros* (healing amulets) to hang on the walls surrounding the weeping image of Mary. At the request of his parishioners, the descendant will perform a healing ceremony in which he uses Mary's tears as a source of spiritual power. As a healer, priest, and confidante, this descendant believes that his followers are attracted to his church particularly because of his distinctly crypto-Jewish spirituality:

> That is why the others come to see me. What I do is familiar to them. When we come in here [the church], they call on me to bless their children and their land and to baptize them. I understand who they are. I can also help them to heal.

The appeal of Mariology both to this descendant and to other Mexican American crypto-Jewish respondents is undoubtedly tied to the significant role that Mary, in her representation as the Virgin of Guadalupe, plays in the religious life of Mexican Americans.[25] The story of the Virgin of Guadalupe, as a narrative of divine intervention, signifies the intersection of native and Catholic religious cultures, since the sixteenth-century apparition of the Virgin is believed to have appeared to Juan Diego, a converted Indian who saw a vision of Mary near the mountains of Tepeyac. Jeanette Rodriguez thus describes Mary as an inclusive "symbol of both cultural and religious identity" whose image is that of kindness and compassion.[26]

For Mexican American descendants, the image of the Virgin is pervasive. She appears in the religious iconography of the Church and of the home and in popular cultural venues such as T-shirts, street murals, and car ornamentation.[27] Within both popular and traditional religiosity, Mary assumes a powerful function as divine healer and loving mother. It is these two dimensions of spiritual and human maternity that are incorporated into a modern crypto-Jewish syncretic worldview in which Mary is idealized as the Jewish mother who gave birth to the Jewish Messiah. A mixed-race descendant with Native American, Jewish, and Spanish ancestry thus conceptualizes Mary within a Westernized Christian understanding of Mary as Wisdom:

> I now have a very old Jewish notion of the divine. For me God is a divine presence; that is how I see God. I used to say, "Praise ye Lord Jesus," and all these things. I rarely ever talk about Jesus now. Instead, I always talk about Christ, the Messiah. . . . Jesus, as prophet or Messiah is the spirit of the people, and Mary is another aspect of God, she is the attendant to God's learning. She is *Hokhmah*. She is wisdom.

In referring to Mary as Hokhmah, this descendant uses the Hebrew term for Sophia, the Greek word for the feminine principle of Divine Wisdom.[28] His conceptualization of Mary as Wisdom derives from his extensive study of religion through which he has constructed an image of Mary that embodies ancient notions of the female as creator. Within this imagery, Mary as Wisdom is a maternal figure who is perceived as having divine power.

For those descendants who have incorporated the notion of a female divinity into their Jewish-Christian worldview, Mary assumes the qualities of nurturance, understanding, and wisdom. These are maternal attributes that, according to the theorist Ana Maria Rizzuto, have their origins in early childhood attachments to nurturing maternal figures who were experienced as all-powerful. In keeping with the relational understanding of spirituality as discussed in the previous chapter, Rizzuto's analysis maintains that a person's image of God is informed by the parenting that he or she received. An individual's conception of God, as either nurturing or punishing, will therefore be a manifestation of his or her relationship to a parent who was either nurturing or hurtful.[29] Within the cultural framework of crypto-Jewish experience, in which female nurturers played a significant role in the emotional and spiritual life of the descendants, it is therefore not surprising that a number of descendants have sustained their belief in Mary and in her powers to heal, love, and forgive.

## JESUS AS SUFFERING JEWISH MESSIAH: SYNCRETISM AND THE PENITENTES

As empathic attachment and love form the social-psychological foundations on which the connection to Mary is sustained among descendants, connections to Jesus as her suffering and tormented son provide yet another view into the relationship between syncretism and spirituality. Within this emotion-centered worldview, the symbol of the crucifixion is interpreted as a specifically Jewish aspect of persecution with which the descendants strongly identify, as the following narrative suggests:

> I hate the symbol of the cross. To me it represents death. I hate that image of Jesus hanging on a piece of wood above the altar. To me, Jesus is like a family member, part of the Tribe of Judah, like a cousin. That's how I look at it, that I am related to the rabbi of Nazareth, that he is Jewish, and so am I.

The conceptualization of Christ as a Jewish martyr figure, as articulated by this male descendant, has particular significance for those descendants who link the survival of crypto-Judaism to the proliferation of the Penitente Brotherhoods in northern New Mexico and southern Colorado. According to some respondents, this unique religious culture provided an emotional venue for a secretive religious culture in which the suffering of the persecuted Christ figure became the focus for clandestine rituals and practices.

Beginning with colonization, secret religious societies known as *Los Hermanos Penitentes* (the penitent brothers) gained a strong following among Latino men living in remote regions of New Mexico.[30] The Penitente Brotherhood that characterized the spiritual lives of many New Mexican Catholics in the eighteenth and nineteenth centuries developed within communities where the chapter house, or *morada* (Penitente chapel), provided a place of worship and a source of communal activities. The observances of the secretive, all-male brotherhood were focused on Holy Week rituals, Corpus Christi processions, and feast days.

Although there is little scholarly evidence to support the link between the Penitente Brotherhoods and the colonial crypto-Jews, at least ten descendants believe that, in some remote areas of New Mexico, the chapter house became the place where crypto-Jewish traditions were actively preserved by men within the secret and isolated Catholicism of Penitente culture. In the following account, a male respondent offers his view of the relationship between the Penitentes and the survival of crypto-Judaism:

> I think that in some Penitente chapters there were people who were all coming from the same background. What happened was that the converted Jews that arrived here had to keep up their traditions somehow, so they create these rituals, and it just evolves within the Penitente movement. They have their own hymnbooks, but the Catholic Church doesn't. They have their own prayer services, which the Catholic Church doesn't have. And that way they maintained some semblance of their heritage, with the women being very separate.

While this descendant's view of the Penitentes in New Mexico remains purely speculative, he believes that the Penitente Brotherhood was in fact a sacred institution that brought together his family's Catholic history and Jewish ancestry. The chapter house to which he still belongs has served as a spiritual home not only for him but also for his brothers and uncles. Since his childhood, the brotherhood has been at the center of his family's religious life. Among those who were deeply involved with the Penitentes was his elderly grandmother, with whom he shared a strong emotional bond. As a member of the women's auxiliary, his grandmother was extremely active in this female "arm" of the brotherhood, assuming responsibility for the sick and for meal preparation.[31]

Soon after his grandmother's death, this descendant began to delve into his family genealogy and to rethink the unusual rituals that his grandmother performed on Friday nights and around Passover and Chanukah. Convinced that there was a link between his family's involvement with the Penitentes and his crypto-Jewish ancestry, he began to take classes in Judaism, developing a knowledge base from which he has constructed a new syncretic faith that remains centered in the Penitente Brotherhood. Accordingly, this descendant has reinterpreted many of the Penitente rites from the perspective of crypto-Jewish practices. Among the customs that he views as having crypto-Jewish origins is the rite of scarification. This ritualized aspect of initiation involves carving a symbol of brotherhood into the back of the initiate, signifying his membership in the secret society. Because this ritual involves cutting the initiate's flesh, the descendant believes this rite was once a substitute for circumcision:[32]

> Initiation into the brotherhood would normally occur some time during adolescence. All of them have the rite of scarification. This rite of initiation is the same for every chapter house. The main form of initiation is scarification. I think that in some chapter houses where there were crypto-Jews, the scarification replaced circumcision. Because they cannot circumcise because they will be suspect, they scarify.

In addition to scarification, the descendant reflected on other aspects of the brotherhood, such as the exclusion of women from the most sacred areas of the chapter house and the covering of one's head inside the chapel, as rituals that resonate with traditional Jewish practice. Because of these and other customs, the descendant strongly believes that this form of nontraditional Catholicism developed out of a theological perspective that was grounded in Judaic notions of the sacred. Thus, he describes the inner sanctuary of the *morada* as the place where the presence of God is acknowledged through rituals of purification and respect that are similar to those found in Sephardic Judaism:

> You should be there on Friday night. So here we are in the chapter house, and when you enter there's ritual bathing and you always wear a black scarf for prayer. We never wear shoes in the sanctuary, and the eldest man of our chapter house always has to say, "The reason that we have to take off our shoes is because the place is holy." It is just like Moses going up to Mount Sinai. And the Lord God says, "Take your shoes off, for this place is holy." This looks like Roman Catholic. The prayers are Roman Catholic, but this is not Roman Catholic!

As this descendant reimagines the brotherhood as historically linked to crypto-Judaism, he refers to the inner sanctuary of the *morada* as sacred ground, comparable to that of the ancient Temple in Jerusalem where the "Holiest of Holies" resides. In drawing parallels between the chapter house and Jewish observance, he referred to the differences between the inner and outer sanctuary of the *morada:*

> One thing that has always struck me in our chapter house is that when we are praying in the public prayer room we always kneel. But inside the chapel—the *oratorio*—where only the members can go, if anyone wants to pray, they stand. We had some brothers from another chapter house come to visit us. And they were very upset with us because we didn't kneel. They said to us, "Even in here you should be kneeling. To pray you kneel." And we said, "We've never observed this in this chapter house.

> Never have we prayed in this room kneeling. We pray standing." Then the eldest member gets up and he says, "We pray standing because when we are in this room, we are in the kingdom of heaven. In this room we are actually in the presence of God."

For this respondent, the distinction drawn between kneeling and standing in prayer, between being within or outside God's presence, further affirms his conviction that his family's chapter house is a remnant culture of crypto-Jewish belief and practice. Seeking to integrate this historical perception with a contemporary religious orientation, he conceptualizes Jesus as separate from God, envisioning Christ as a Messiah who suffered for his role as Jewish prophet:

> I always talk about Christ, the Messiah, you know. Not as Jesus, but that Jesus was one of many. We always had Messiahs. Jesus was a great man, and fortunately I went to Roman Catholic seminary and they taught me about the Christian writings, what the Christians had attributed to the words of Jesus. The words of Jesus were very Jewish. His sensibility was very Jewish. . . . And so I go back to Jesus, and I think, "Oh, he only wanted to clean up Judaism—giving it a new midrash, a different perspective, and so he was probably a great rabbi."[33]

Although this descendant conceives of Jesus as a rabbi and a prophet, it is Christ's humanity that is most significant for him as he attempts to reconcile his Catholic upbringing with his crypto-Jewish origins. Because the brotherhood emphasizes Jesus' suffering, the Penitentes offer a religious culture that resonates with the notion of Christ as persecuted Messiah. Within the penitential orientation of the brotherhood, the chapter house itself provides a reminder of Christ's painful death. Large wooden crosses typically mark the entrance to the small adobe building, while, in some Penitente landscapes, a struggling Christ figure is situated near the isolated and almost windowless *morada.*

The life-size wooden crosses found at Penitente sites are used annually in Holy Week observances, when the Penitentes reenact the passion of Christ through rituals focusing on Jesus' spiritual agony and the physical torment that Jesus experienced at each station of the cross. The commemoration of both the physical and spiritual pain that Christ endured is expressed through passion plays and through the recitation of hymns that recount the multitude of harsh punishments to which Jesus was subjected. Accordingly, it is Jesus' pained and wounded body with which the crypto-Jewish descendant identifies and with which he creates an emotional and spiritual bond. As Jesus' pain and sacrifice are brought to life each year, the Penitente Brotherhood offers a spiritual home where the descendant's individualized version of faith blending can be realized and expressed.

The creative adaptations formulated by the Penitente descendant, as well as the syncretic worldviews adopted by other respondents, comprise a unique dimension of crypto-Jewish experience, wherein the recovery of Sephardic roots has contributed to the development of innovative and varied belief systems. In the diverse narratives of contemporary syncretism elaborated here, the descendants have created and sustained religious perspectives in which a Jewish-Christian belief system is given new meaning through the redefinition of church and ritual. In a departure from the medieval and premodern syncretic solution to religious persecution, wherein Jewish beliefs and practices became Christianized, the modern-day phenomenon is characterized by the Judaization of Christianity as Christian institutions become the site for the absorption of Jewish ritual and theological approaches.

For the descendant family from Mexico, the syncretic response has resulted in the establishment of a new immigrant Church of God that reflects the influences of early-twentieth-century crypto-Jewish clerical concerns. For the descendant who has chosen the Penitente Brotherhood, it is the existing institution of the secret religious society that provides a structure in which to integrate a messianic worldview with Catholicism. Finally, for the Russian Orthodox priest, the Russian Orthodox Church offers an institutional framework for the merging of crypto-Jewish heritage with a Christian-based theology. As these cases clearly demonstrate, the appeal of syncretism remains strong for a current generation of crypto-Jewish descendants who seek to reconcile the competing faith traditions of their multicultural heritage.

CHAPTER 5

# Conversion and the Rekindling of the Jewish Soul

For a little more than half the descendants who participated in this study, the discovery and exploration of their Jewish ancestry resulted in conversion and the adoption of a Jewish religious worldview. These descendants identify both spiritually and culturally with modern Judaism and with the religious heritage of their Sephardic ancestors. While attachment to crypto-Jewish family members is an important part of nurturing an emotional connection to Judaism (see chapter 4), the decision to convert is informed by a diverse set of circumstances that the descendant brings to the conversion experience. For some descendants, converting to Judaism marks the end of a long search for a meaningful spiritual tradition, while for others, Judaism is appealing because it resonates with the descendant's prior religious orientation. Thus, one descendant chose Judaism after experimenting with Buddhism and Hinduism and another because the study of Torah was similar to her study of scripture in the Assemblies of God Church. In the latter case, the descendant recalled:

> In my growing up as a Protestant, we read what I now know to be the Torah. And with such love for Israel, you know, it sounded like there's this love for the community and God's special relationship to Israel. . . . The fundamentalist element in Mexico and Latin America is what I've now come to understand as the survival of the essence of the Torah.

Because the descendants come to Judaism from widely different backgrounds and spiritual paths, their varied encounters both with the religion and with the conversion process illuminate the multifaceted nature of Jewish conversion in contemporary society. The narratives therefore reveal the intersecting and dynamic relationship among law, history, and theology in the modern construction of Jewish religious identity. Accordingly, a discussion of the legal issues affecting conversion provides a good starting point from which to consider the religious response to ancestral Judaism among modern crypto-Jewish descendants.

## MODES OF CONVERSION AND THE POLITICS OF JEWISHNESS

Within the contemporary discourse on Jewish conversion, the questions surrounding birthright and Jewish legal status are especially salient for crypto-Jewish descendants, since ancestral attachments have different meanings within the spectrum of religious orientations that comprise Jewish thought and practice. According to Jewish law, the most important signifier of Jewishness is being born of a Jewish mother.[1] Thus, in Orthodox and Conservative traditions, conversion is required of all those who cannot trace matrilineal descent, even if the father is Jewish by birth.[2] The legal definition of Jewishness stipulates that any child born of a Jewish mother is by law Jewish, regardless of what future religious paths the mother, father, or child may take.[3]

The emphasis on maternal religious inheritance can be explained from a social and political perspective that locates concerns about Jewish lineage within a biblical and historical framework. The religious rationale for matrilineal descent is derived from a passage in Deuteronomy that prohibits a Jewish father from arranging a marriage between his child and a gentile. The directive from God is contained within a series of commands that God gives to the Jews as they are about to enter the land of Israel after exile in Egypt. In these Torah passages, God directs the Jews to cast out all other nations and expressly prohibits intermarriage between Jews and non-Jews:

> 2. and when the Lord thy God shall deliver them [the Hittites, Girgashites, and Cannanites] up before thee, and thou shall smite them: then thou shalt utterly destroy them; thou shalt make no covenant with them, nor show mercy unto them; 3. neither shalt thou make marriages with them: thy daughter thou shalt not give unto his son, nor his daughter shalt thou take unto thy son. 4. For he will turn away thy son from following Me.[4]

The prohibition on intermarriage reflects anxiety about Jewish constancy, since it is feared that the child born of a Jewish mother and a non-Jewish father will reject the Jewish faith and, more significantly, the God of Israel. Talmudic interpretation of this passage concluded that a child born of a union between a gentile father and Jewish mother is, by law, a Jew, because the child in the Deuteronomy passage is considered the child of the mother's father, the Jewish patriarch to whom this commandment is directed.[5] Through this reasoning, it is the maternal grandfather through whom Jewish lineage is actually inherited. Modern Jewish commentary on the Talmud's view of the Deuteronomy passage thus explains matrilineal descent in the following manner:

> Since the Torah, on this interpretation, calls the child of an Israelite mother and gentile father the "son" of an Israelite grandfather, it was deduced therefrom that the child is to be regarded as being of the same race and faith *as the mother*. Consequently, the child of a Jewish father and non-Jewish mother follows in Jewish Law the religious status of the mother.[6]

While the religious rationale for matrilineal descent offered by Talmudic scholars reinforced the primacy of the Jewish patriarch and his legal authority over his daughter's child,[7] other explanations maintain that matrilineal descent developed in response to concerns over paternity.[8] Within this interpretive framework, the importance of the mother's Jewishness in religious law can be explained in terms of the effects of rape and foreign acculturation on Jewish survival. According to this perspective, historically the survival of Jewish culture was at risk because of both intermarriage and sexual violation among a people who were constantly at war and under foreign domination. Religious inheritance through the mother therefore sustained the Jewishness of the child, regardless of the religion or nationality of the father.

Whether the religious laws were intended to establish the primacy of the Jewish patriarch or to deflect fears surrounding unknown or non-Jewish paternity, the result of matriarchal descent has been the development and maintenance of legal codes that today perpetuate a biological definition of Jewishness linking blood to religiosity and race to beliefs. As a legal construct, the transmission of Jewishness through the mother has grown in importance in recent decades, placing crypto-Jewish descendants in a contested arena of Jewish identity where traditional laws governing conversion limit access to membership in the religious community. Thus, Marc Angel, a leading Sephardic rabbi in the United States, while expressing kinship with Spanish crypto-Jewish descendants, nonetheless maintains that unless matrilineal descent can be established, conversion is required before they can be recognized as Jews:

> When Jewish spokesmen tell the people in New Mexico that they are accepted as Jews because they have gone through a lot, because they love Judaism, because they have ancestors who were Jews several hundred years ago—they are misleading these individuals . . . a compassionate and wise guide would tell them that he is glad of their interest in embracing Judaism, and that to be accepted as Jews they should follow the necessary procedure: halakhic conversion.[9] In this way these individuals can achieve a genuine and universal acceptance among the Jewish people.[10]

Within the boundaries set by Angel and other Orthodox religious authorities, only one descendant in this study was recognized as Jewish through blood ties to the mother. In this case, the descendant's mother suffered from Creutzfeldt-Jacob disease, a degenerative disease of the central nervous system that has been linked specifically to Sephardic ancestry.[11] When the descendant approached a rabbi in Colorado, she was told that because of her mother's illness, she would not have to go through a formal conversion before beginning the practice of Judaism:

> The rabbi said, "You're Jewish. It doesn't make any difference if you are an atheist, you are Jewish. You don't have to convert. You can just start practicing the laws if that's what you want to do."

In recalling this aspect of her search for Jewish roots, she spoke of both the relief and sadness that accompanied her mother's diagnosis and the rabbi's affirmation of her Jewish lineage:

> It was great to find out positively that I was Jewish. I had already been researching it, so I was pretty sure that we were Jewish. So I was relieved that I didn't have to research my mother's side anymore. We knew my mother was ill. We knew she had a condition that wasn't getting any better. You know, it was hard knowing that my mother was ill in the first place. That was pretty tough. So the emotions were kind of mixed, because I was relieved that we were Jewish, but, you know, it's heartbreaking to see your mother go through that.

For the vast majority of descendants whose "birthright" remains a more complicated and disputed area of religious identity, decisions to convert invited a wide array of responses. For some descendants, external recognition of Sephardic ancestry lies at the heart of their conversion dilemma. A woman of Mexican descent recounted a trip to Israel in which she brought along her genealogical documents with the hope that the rabbinic authority would recognize her blood ties to Judaism:

> I went to the chief rabbi, and I brought him a write-up of my whole story. I demanded to be heard, to be accepted, and I never even saw him. They would not even allow me to present my case to him. The deep pain, the deep rejection, that I felt when I left there. But then I recovered. I remembered that *Hashem* [God] knows all that counts. I did not need this rabbi to make me a Jew.

Other descendants voiced similar feelings of disappointment and anger when their Jewishness was called into question:

> When I was twelve or thirteen, my dad took me to see a rabbi, and he was a Conservative rabbi, and he starts asking me about my mother and her family. I wanted a bar mitzvah. I wanted to read Hebrew, but that's not what happened. To me, I made the commitment when I was thirteen. I've lived it as much as I can every day. I've done everything to educate myself in my own way. When rabbis would talk to me I would listen. . . . When I lived in Venezuela, I went to a synagogue. I went to the rabbi's office and told them that I would be there for a year and that I wanted to join the synagogue. So I went to see the rabbi, and the first thing he says is, "You don't have a Jewish name." He wanted me to get a letter from my rabbi here and send it to him verifying who and what I was. The entire year I was down there, I never once went to that temple. I didn't bother. . . . I walked by there every day. It really upset me. It was a beautiful temple. I was miserable.

In response to his rejection by mainstream Judaism, this descendant started attending a Lubavitcher synagogue in the United States, where he is permitted to read from the Torah and where his Jewish authenticity has not been challenged.[12] Other descendants have found similar affirmation in synagogues in Europe. A descendant who was raised in South America took her family genealogy to a rabbi in Portugal who without question accepted her as a Jew:

> I went to the rabbi and I explained to him about my history. I took all the papers and pictures of my family, and they believed me! The synagogue and the people over there—it was like being in your own land, and you come to them and tell them you are here, and they accept you.

As exemplified by these diverse accounts, the indeterminate status of crypto-Jewish descendants has raised difficult and troubling issues within Jewish legal circles, since rabbis from different sectors of the Jewish community have taken various approaches to the question of conversion. Within the liberal sector of Reform Judaism, a small number of rabbis in the United States have created special ceremonies welcoming the descendants into Judaism. One such ceremony at a Reform synagogue in the Southwest brought a number of descendants together in a rite of return. In this special service, participants held the Torah as they recited prayers, publicly declaring their commitment to Judaism. Although a portion of the descendants have embraced rites of return such as these, the majority of participants who identify as Jewish have chosen to undergo a more traditional conversion. As one male descendant explained:

> The fact that I was Jewish once upon a time, I mean by ancestry and blood, is not enough, because I never practiced Judaism. I never studied Judaism. So how could I say that I was a Jew? . . . My personal opinion, in my case, was that, yes, my ancestors were Jews, but I was not. And maybe I wasn't a Christian, either, so I was nothing. But in order to become a Jew, I thought the first thing I had to do was to study Judaism and then I have to be circumcised, which is what I did.

Once an individual decides to convert, she or he must then decide which denomination of Judaism to pursue. Depending on whether a descendant seeks membership in an Orthodox, Conservative, or Reform synagogue and whether the congregation is Sephardic or Ashkenazic, the conversion experience will vary greatly. Although all forms of Jewish conversion require the convert to make a commitment to follow the commandments of the Torah, the extent to which the commandments are studied and observed will differ according to the orthodoxy of the congregation and the prerogatives of the supervising rabbi. Differences also exist in conversion policies over the requirements of circumcision and ritual immersion.

Among the Orthodox, conversion requires intensified instruction in Torah, circumcision for males, and ritual immersion, all of which are overseen by a *bet din,* a rabbinic court made up of three Orthodox rabbis.[13] The Conservative Movement, which takes a more moderate yet traditional approach, also requires instruction in Torah, circumcision, and ritual immersion. Here, however, the rabbinic court need not be composed of Orthodox rabbis. The Reform Movement, the most liberal of the three approaches, involves some religious training and education but does not usually require ritual immersion.[14] These variations within Judaism are further complicated by the dilemma posed by the Orthodox authorities, who will only accept a Jewish convert whose *bet din* is comprised of Orthodox rabbis. Finally, because Sephardic Judaism has no Reform or Conservative dimension, a descendant who wishes to become part of the Spanish Jewish tradition will have no choice but to become Orthodox.

Against this backdrop of diversity and disagreement, the descendants have chosen different modes of conversion. Some have selected orthodoxy because of its emphasis on tradition and the fear that they or their children might be denied Israeli citizenship if their conversion were contested. Others have chosen Reform and Conservative approaches, finding an openness and flexibility that provides a needed bridge between their non-Jewish past and their desire for a Jewish future. Still others specifically seek out Sephardic congregations, where the culture of Spanish Judaism prevails. Finally, in choosing a congregation, how their motivation to convert is interpreted may also influence the descendant's decision.

Beginning with the earliest history of Jewish conversion, rabbinic authorities expressed concern about the sincerity of converts. In the twelfth century, the rabbi and scholar Maimonides established criteria for judging the convert who might be motivated by money or love rather than by belief in God:

> When a man or woman comes to be converted, one makes enquiries lest it be for the sake of money they will come to possess, power they will gain or out of fear, that they have come to seek entry into the religion. If it is a man one makes enquiries lest he has set his eye upon a Jewish woman. If it is a woman one makes enquiries lest she has set her eye upon a young man of the young men of Israel. If no such cause is found, one informs them of the weight of the yoke of the Torah and the difficulty involved in observing it for those who come from other nations, in order that they may depart. If they accept and do not depart and one can observe that they are returning out of love, then one accepts them.[15]

Maimonides' cautious stance on conversion remains part of Jewish rabbinic attitudes today, and it is not uncommon for some test of faith to be given someone requesting conversion. One woman from Mexico described her struggle to find a rabbi who would agree to convert her after she had emigrated to the United States:

> When I came to this country, there were so many things I experienced. I mean, I went to one rabbi, and he threw me out of his office, literally. I went to another rabbi, and this rabbi would not hear of it. He heard my story and then he said, "I'm sorry, I don't even want to talk to you about it." And then I went to another place, I called another synagogue and I asked if I could convert, and the rabbi said he would talk to me. He gave me about two weeks before I could talk to him. And then he said, "What do you want to talk to me about?" Of course he had written down

> that I wanted to convert and that I would be seeking somebody to convert me. He said, "We don't do that. Just forget it, we have enough problems, you have enough problems without being Jewish." But I said, "I already go to temple." And he said, "You have to be certain. You have to be willing to learn all these rituals and laws." I said I was willing and that I knew some of it already. Finally, he agreed. I find out at the end that they are supposed to do that, discourage you, to see if you come back.

The case cited above was among the more extreme instances of faith testing. While other respondents also reported that they had been treated with skepticism in their initial enquiries, many explained that, within time, the rabbi with whom they first spoke became increasingly open to the possibility of conversion.

Still other descendants reported that they were encouraged to pursue their interest in Judaism from the outset. In Texas, for example, two small and relatively new congregations, one Orthodox and the other Reform, offered descendants two very different but receptive environments in which to undergo conversion. A more in-depth look at each of these congregations will help to characterize the varied conversion venues that the descendants encountered as they sought a Jewish religious identity.

## RELIGIOUS CONVERSION AND THE SYNAGOGUE EXPERIENCE

On the outskirts of Dallas sits a comparatively new Reform synagogue with a recently established congregation that embraces a wide range of converts from varied ethnic and cultural backgrounds. The rabbi, who welcomes converts into his growing and diverse congregation, is especially open to those with crypto-Jewish heritage and to others who may have ancestral connections to Judaism. Lodged in a recently renovated warehouse, the synagogue has a unique and eclectic quality. Among the newly converted congregants are crypto-Jewish descendants and Europeans whose families have ties to the Holocaust.

During one Friday-night service, two European congregants described keeping their own Judaism hidden in response to growing up in Europe in the aftermath of World War II. In the years following the Holocaust, fears associated with antisemitism had kept them from identifying as Jews, although in both cases, the congregant's mother had been Jewish. In the last few years, as "their roots began to pull" at them, both of these European congregants chose to convert, having been drawn to this Reform synagogue where individuals like them were engaged in a return to Judaism. Along with the crypto-Jewish descendants, the European converts have created a spiritual home in this small yet inclusive congregation. The prayers and rituals are mostly in English, and there is a focus on the study of Torah as a guiding text for both the secular and religious realms of life. One crypto-Jewish descendant who attended this congregation described the importance of Torah and prayer within the context of the religious community:

> Even before I converted, I always felt that there was one God and I would pray to him and talk to him. And I always felt that but this experience of conversion has opened up other things, becoming part of this intellectual Jewish community. Through the study of Torah, it's like experiencing life in a different way. I have become more meditative. I understand why we act the way we act. And we're really blessed with this rabbi. He is very intellectual, a man of learning. He interacts with the congregation and he is very helpful. Learning from him and being part of this congregation, you understand that Judaism is a way of life and that you have to keep studying.

As described above, community, prayer, and Torah are also at the center of religious life in another small congregation that, like the Reform synagogue, exists on the margins of Dallas's mainstream Jewish community. The members of this congregation, however, are Orthodox, having recently immigrated to the United States from countries such as Iraq, Yemen, Tunisia, and Morroco. This largely Middle Eastern community holds services in a house that has been transformed into a Sephardic synagogue. The living room serves as a sanctuary and is divided by a *mechitzah* (a latticed wooden partition) so that men and women can worship separately. Although the ark holding the Torah is on the men's side, the women are able to view the scrolls at designated times during the service when the Torahs are lifted above the partition by the male congregants.[16]

A female descendant who was raised in Mexico attends this synagogue every Saturday. It is here that she feels most at home in her Judaism, the Sephardic melodies and customs having greater resonance for her than the liturgies and rituals of the Ashkenazic service:

> I remember the first day I walked into this little congregation. I wept as the Torah was being read. Oh, the Torahs are so gorgeous. They have this gold, this beautiful crown; the velvet is red, and the cover has royal blue velvet and gold. And the men were such an inspiration, reading the Torah, and I thought, how come I have not found a place like this in all these

years? The men and the women really come to pray. I mean they close their eyes when they pray, and I love it because that's what I do. For the first time, I truly felt at home. I have been to Israel and I went to Israeli congregations, and I thought this place is just like a neighborhood Sephardic synagogue in the middle of Jerusalem. But it's right in the middle of Dallas! It's a very special place.

This narrative speaks to the affinity for Sephardic Judaism that the respondents frequently express, and yet this descendant was among the very few who were attracted to the Orthodox Movement. The vast majority of respondents joined Ashkenazic Conservative and Reform congregations, which along with being more liberal in their approach also exist in far greater numbers in the United States. In becoming members of these synagogues, however, some of the descendants reported that, unlike in the Dallas Ashkenazic congregation described above, they did not always feel welcomed by the religious community. In recalling the difficulties one descendant encountered in attending services, he provided this account of his experience in a Reform synagogue in the Southwest:

When I came out as a Jew, I began to go to synagogue. I put on the tefillin and the *talit* [prayer shawl] and would pray and chant in Spanish. So we would come in and there would be three or four rows vacant where the Marranos would always sit. We were segregated within the synagogue, and the more we held to tradition, the more we were rejected. Finally, when we would begin to pray, they would turn their faces away from us. I stopped going. It was a very painful experience. We were not accepted by these Ashekanzic Jews. We had been in hiding hundreds of years, and when we finally came out, we were not accepted.

The rejection that this descendant experienced in part reflects the marginalization of Spanish Jewish culture within Judaism more generally, since the relationship between Sephardic and Ashkenazic Jews has historically been fraught with tensions. Up until the eighteenth century, Sephardic Jews outnumbered those of Ashkenazi origin, and the first Jewish immigrants to the Americas were Spanish Portuguese Sephardim whose religious and social culture predominated in the seventeenth and eighteenth centuries in North America. By the early nineteenth century, however, mass emigration of German Jews created a demographic shift, giving prominence to the German Jewish community in North America. During this time, the descendants of the colonial Spanish Portuguese populations retained a certain status and respect because of their historical link to the Spanish Golden Age, when Jewish culture flourished on the Iberian peninsula. Ashkenazic attitudes toward the Sephardic immigrants who emigrated from Turkey in the early 1900s, however, were quite different.[17] As discussed in chapter 1, early-twentieth-century concerns about Jewish assimilation among Ashkenazic populations in the United States led to the rejection and devaluation of the Turkish Sephardic refugees, whose dress, custom, language, and general appearance presented a less European image of the Jewish immigrant.[18]

As a minority population among European Jews, the Sephardim were marginalized by the predominant Ashkenazic communities, which were larger and had greater visibility. By the mid–twentieth century, Sephardic Judaism in the United States had effectively been silenced and rendered invisible within the larger German Jewish population. Debra Regina, a writer of both Sephardic and Ashkenazic ancestry, describes the gradual suppression of her Spanish Jewish heritage:

> I grew up with the best of both Jewish worlds: half Sephardic/half Ashkenazic, yet most of what I felt as a Jew was influenced by Sephardic culture, food, tradition, memory. Growing up, my family exclusively attended Sephardic services during the High Holy Days. . . . Trying to meld that knowledge of Sephardic culture within an Ashkenazic-based Jewish community was often confusing, painful and alienating. . . . There were big gaps; I truly felt like a minority within a minority.[19]

Despite or perhaps because of the tensions that have surfaced over the treatment of the Sephardim generally and descendants of crypto-Jews more specifically, the descendants in this study speak of a desire to return to an imagined Jewish community where ethnic and racial boundaries dissolve in the re-creation of a universal Jewish religious identity.[20] Accordingly, they seek out welcoming congregations where participating in Jewish ritual and prayer provides the spiritual context for the realization of the idealized Jewish community. A descendant thus explained:

> Going to synagogue is such a treat. I mean, you are hearing the chants. They echo the prayers to each other. It feels so ancient. I don't read Hebrew or speak Hebrew, but in that congregation, it's always right. My soul hears the Hebrew, feels the Hebrew, and then my brain and my mouth utter the prayers in Spanish. The prayers in English don't mean the same thing. This place is really special.

For creating a spiritual resonance with Jewish ritual and prayer, the Hebrew language is especially significant in fostering a universal sense of Jewishness that is experienced through the sounds and chants of Hebraic songs and prayers. The cadence and rhythm of the religious language establishes a milieu in which the convert experiences a connection to Jewish spiritual traditions, as another descendant stated:

> When I go to services, I feel a very spiritual connection to the whole process. I don't understand a thing that is being said. I hear the Hebrew chanting and the prayers, and then I read it in English and I get a very emotional connection. So although I'm not reading the prayers in Hebrew, I still have this really deep connection with what's going on. I see the eternal light there and the Star of David behind the rabbi, and I feel like I've come home and it is really spiritual.

In seeking to reclaim a Jewish spiritual self, the descendants voice a longing to return to God and to Torah, since both these aspects of Judaism are understood through a deep and lasting bond to the descendants' Spanish Jewish ancestors. As such, conversion, whether in Sephardic or Ashkenazic communities, incorporates a theology of return that has become part of the contemporary discourse on Jewish religious experience.

## ANCESTRAL TIES AND THE MEANING OF *TESHUVAH*

Jewish thought conceptualizes conversion as both answering the call of God and returning to God though a fundamental change in inner beliefs and spiritual understanding. As such, the Jew who has fallen away from God and who returns to Judaism is the *baal teshuvah,* an individual who responds to the calling and who has "truly returned."[21] Within the theology of exile that has characterized Jewish thought since the Diaspora, the concept of *teshuvah* ("return") has had varied interpretations. A modern-day perspective on this concept is articulated in the writings of Adin Steinsaltz, a rabbi and scholar, who explains the meaning of *teshuvah* this way:

> *Teshuvah* occupies a central place in Judaism and has many facets. As individuals differ from one another, so too do their modes of *teshuvah,* in both motive and form of expression. Broadly defined, *teshuvah* is more than just repentance from sin: it is a spiritual reawakening, a desire to strengthen the connection between oneself and the sacred. . . . For at the root of the notion of *teshuvah* lies the concept of return *(shivah)*—return, not only to the past (one's own, or one's ancestors), but to the Divine source of all being: "You shall return *(shavta)* to the Lord your God."[22]

Steinsaltz's perspective illuminates the varied layers of meaning that the notion of return may have for ancestral Jews who feel that they have been separated both from their Jewish roots and from God. This understanding of *teshuvah* therefore provides a useful context for exploring the spiritual meaning of conversion and return for crypto-Jewish descendants, who describe their initial experience of Jewish spirituality as an emotional return to the religion of their Jewish ancestors. This return is frequently signified by a public rendering of the Shema, the prayer that gives testimony to the belief in a unitary notion of the divine.[23] Here a male descendant conveys the feelings he experienced when, as a newly converted Jew, he recited the Shema for the first time:

> When I uttered the Shema in front of the Torah and witnesses—"Hear, O Israel, the Lord our God, the Lord is One"—that was enough. I mean, it's a powerful experience. The Shema means something to me. It's my vow, my return.

Within the history of crypto-Judaism, the acknowledgment of a unitary God posed certain dangers for the forced converts. During the Inquisition, the belief in a unitary God was often used as evidence of blasphemy for those accused of Judaizing, especially among converts who referred to God in the Spanish singular, *El Dio,* rather that the Christianized term, *Dios,* since the latter nomenclature carried with it the implication of a tripartite divinity.[24] The survival of the concept of *El Dio* has been found among contemporary descendants; a number of respondents reported that their mothers and grandmothers refer to God only as *El Dio,* in contrast to what they had been taught in church.

Within present-day crypto-Judaism, the importance of a unitary concept of God underlies the emotional attachment to Judaism that becomes evident in the conversion process, especially in the symbolic recitation of the Shema. One descendant explained her acceptance of the Jewish concept of a unitary God as a "lifting of the veil" from her eyes:

> I believe God is the hope. And it is like there is one God, and he did these things. . . . I find that as I take the veil off of my eyes and look at the symbolism here, I find there are so many opportunities out there. And that to me is the exciting part. . . . And I remember the first time even thinking that I was Jewish, I guess deep down knowing that I came from a crypto-Jewish family. I had always been proud of my Hispanic tradition, but when I realized what a Sabbath meant on a Friday night, it was like, how many thousands of years have my people done this? . . . It's about returning, it's a return to everything. It's a return to Judaism, to my roots and to who I am.

In keeping with Steinsaltz's view on *teshuvah,* the concept of return as expressed by this descendant embraces a notion of one God that is given meaning through her connection to her Jewish ancestors. The reclamation of a Jewish spiritual perspective is deeply rooted in ancestral attachments that frame the emotional context through which contemporary conversion takes place. The significance of ancestral ties for descendants represents a deepening of the spiritual self-in-relation, since the descendants' affective ties to Judaism extend beyond the boundaries of childhood familial attachments to the historical community of Jews in ancient Israel and in medieval Spain. This affective link to Jewish ancestry thus represents a tie to the Jewish people and to God, through which the spirit of Judaism becomes manifest in the rituals of return that signify the descendant's reentry into an ancestral faith. This phenomenon is evident in rituals such as the bar and bat mitzvah that serve as adult rites of passage among crypto-Jewish converts. In one case, a male descendant shared his bar mitzvah with his wife and thirteen other adults, some of whom had also recently converted to Reform Judaism. In describing his feelings as he read from the Torah for the first time, he emphasized the suffering of his ancestors in Spain:

> When I had my bar mitzvah, I felt like I was a bridge between the old generations and the new ones. I really feel that way. My part in the service was the Shema, and I told the rabbi when I read it out loud that these words were the last words of Jews that were killed and burned by the Inquisition. And so, I said that I felt that some of my ancestors or relatives had been subject to that and then here I have an opportunity to proclaim my faith openly, and I was hoping that I was going to be a bridge between my ancestors and the new generations. I hope I live to one hundred, but if I die tomorrow, I'll be happy. I'll be in peace.

As a descendant who returned to Judaism, this respondent identified with the interconnection between family lineage and cultural survival. His bar mitzvah therefore symbolized a ritualized reentry into Judaism that was done both for him and on behalf of his Sephardic ancestors. This relational aspect of *teshuvah* was especially apparent among women who chose ritual immersion as their rite of return. In entering the *mikveh* for the first time, female descendants reported that they performed this ritual both for themselves and for their Spanish Jewish foremothers who secretly retained the traditions of Judaism in the face of danger and religious persecution.

## *MIKVEH* AS A WOMEN'S RITE OF RETURN

In modern Jewish society, the *mikveh* remains a somewhat controversial immersion ritual required of Orthodox women who are designated as *niddah* (ostracized or excluded) because of menstruation or childbirth[25] and of the convert (male or female) who undergoes an Orthodox or Conservative conversion.[26] In this regard, Orthodox Jewish law stipulates that the convert finalize her or his conversion to Judaism with a ceremony involving immersion.[27] A number of women in this study thus chose this ritual of purification as their reentry into Judaism, explaining that for them the *mikveh* provided passage into the world of their female ancestors. In one case, a Latin American woman living in Texas explained that she wished to perform this ritual for past generations of crypto-Jewish women:

> The rabbi asked me, "Why do you want to do this?" And I say, "I want to do this for the old people, for the ones who had to hide, for the last person who could be cleansed and say *Shema Yisrael* in public. After that, they had to go underground. Let me do this wonderful thing for them." I don't think I even knew what I was doing exactly. But I wanted to do it, to make it official in some way, for the old people. And then I went to the *mikveh,* and they gave me a lady to be with me and when I was getting undressed, I told the lady, "I have waited five hundred years, I cannot wait one more minute. Let's do it." . . . The feeling was indescribable. It was like putting a puzzle of five hundred years together, like pieces of all the souls came together. I was looking up at *Hashem* [God] and I said, "This is not for me. I am doing this for that day that you came to the desert and talked with Moses. You were the burning tree. I am Jewish, and I want to be part of that story. For me and for all of the Marranos, I want to come back." And that is what I did.

In this poignant narrative of ritual immersion, the descendant speaks of her longing to be part of the Jewish people. The imagery she invokes is that of her soul coming together with other Jewish souls to end their spiritual separation and exile. As a ritual of return, the *mikveh* provides the connection between past and present lives, between the fate of the persecuted Spanish Jews of medieval Europe and the survival of the hidden Jews of modern Western culture. As such, the *mikveh* offers a ritualized context for the "birth" of the Jewish self.

The notion that ritual immersion signifies the convert's rebirth has Talmudic origins. Ancient Jewish law maintained that through immersion "one who has become a proselyte is like a child newly born."[28] In adapting this Talmudic interpretation to a modern-day view of conversion, Steinsaltz maintains that ritual immersion thus provides entry into a new faith through a rite of purification that

> represents a symbolic return to the primal state—of the individual, of life, and of the world as a whole. One who immerses himself sinks back into

> the primordial reality and emerges as a new creature. His previous life is then of no consequence. It is both renewal and rebirth.[29]

The themes of renewal and rebirth are especially evident in the narrative of a Mexican descendant who offered this perspective on her *mikveh* experience during her conversion to Judaism in the United States:

> What I found was that conversion was a very, very deep experience for me. It was that I was finding my identity totally. I did all the reading and I knew, to be Jewish and to convert, you have to do it all the way or not go through it at all. So when I had the *mikveh,* they cut my hair very, very short. And having a *mikveh* really strengthens you; it strengthens your self. It's water from the rain. They explain to you that it is natural water that they store and fill up with this huge pan, and thank God I knew how to swim. . . . You have to immerse yourself and say these prayers under the water, you know. Open your toes, your eyes, your hands, and everything. They gave me dental floss, toothbrush, a clean towel, and this lady was there. She was an Orthodox Polish lady, and she didn't speak English. After all the cleaning, then I was ready. The rabbis were there, Orthodox rabbis with beards all the way to their knees. They stood behind these sheets so they couldn't see me. They said prayers and chanted. I memorized the prayers, and it was very spiritual at the end. . . . For my identity, for my own spiritual being, I wanted to do it.

As a rite of spiritual reclamation, the *mikveh* ceremony creates feeling states in which connection to both the past (forced conversion) and to the group (Jewish community) become possible.

Among some female descendants, the *mikveh* is particularly significant because it is a custom specifically identified with women's ritual lives in traditional and medieval Sephardic culture. The modern descendants, however, give the act of ritual immersion new meaning. In entering the *mikveh* for the first time, the women experience a sense of inclusion in both the present-day Jewish community and the lost Jewish world of their female ancestors. For these women, ritual immersion signifies an end to the legacy of forced conversion and the prohibition on their Jewish religious roots. In this interpretative framework, traditional concepts of *niddah* and female bodily impurity remain somewhat obscured.

Within the discourse on ritual purification and conversion, it is interesting to note that in comparison to the modern crypto-Jewish perspective on ritual immersion, Ethiopian Jews who have recently immigrated to Israel take a more political view of cleansing rituals. Until 1975, Ethiopian Jews entering Israel were required to undergo ritual conversion, despite the fact that they had been part of a practicing Jewish community in Ethiopia. As the number of immigrants increased in the 1960s and 1970s, the Sephardic rabbinate ruled that Ethiopian Jews were by law Jewish and thus were not required to undergo conversion in order to participate in Jewish life and custom. Although the Ashkenazic authorities agreed with the Sephardic position, in 1988 the chief rabbi of the ruling Ashkenazi rabbinate initiated a policy that required all Ethiopian Jews to undergo a symbolic conversion if they wished to be considered religious rather than secular Jewish citizens in Israel. The Ashkenazic authorities maintained that although the Ethiopians were conversant with the Torah, they had no contact with Talmudic texts. This ruling, which primarily affected marriage laws, led to charges of discrimination and demonstrations by the Ethiopian community.[30]

Amid this controversy, the *mikveh* became a site of resistance as ritual immersion grew to be symbolic of the Ethiopian Jews' religious and political denigration. Since no other immigrant Jewish community is required to engage in a symbolic conversion, recent Ethiopian immigrant women have refused to observe family purity laws in Israel, though they had done so in Ethiopia, in protest over the ruling. Additionally, studies of Ethiopian ethnicity found that some women rejected the *mikveh* on other political grounds, refusing to adhere to the immersion ritual as it is practiced in Israel because it is reminiscent of baptismal rites that Ethiopian Jews were forced to undergo in Ethiopia in prior historical periods.[31] Among the crypto-Jewish women, one descendant held similar views, refusing to undergo ritual immersion as a part of her conversion because of the rite's association with Christian forms of baptism.

For the most part, however, crypto-Jewish women who visited the *mikveh* embraced ritual immersion as a rite of return that signified cultural continuity and their inclusion in a transnational and transhistorical Jewish community. This perspective on immersion, which contrasts sharply with the Ethiopian women's position, is more likely to develop under historical conditions in which ethnic groups have been denied knowledge and access to ancestral tradition. Unlike the Ethiopian women, crypto-Jewish descendants do not have ties to a living Jewish community. Accordingly, the *mikveh* is experienced as a sacred custom through which attachment to female ancestors and cultural tradition becomes possible and through which traditional patriarchal interpretations of pollution and female impurity are replaced by values of connection and relatedness.[32]

Amitiyah Elayne Hyman, a scholar whose work focuses on the African diaspora, explains this approach to traditional religious practice as the power of ritual to reclaim a lost heritage:

> Ritual is a bridge by which those of us who have almost forgotten and those of us who know can cross over into remembering who we were, who we are, and who we are intended to become. Ritual can assist us by naming and validating the essential worth of our experience. In our collective search for meaning, relatedness, worth, and assurance, we are anchored by ritual. . . . We choose those rituals that come out of the past and our common life together in another place and time.[33]

The practice of traditional ritual, as described by Hyman, is especially significant to those individuals, such as the descendants of the crypto-Jews, for whom almost all traces of ancestral culture have disappeared.

An important element of the women's ritual reentry into Judaism is the role that the body plays as the medium through which Jewishness is felt, apprehended, and remembered. As the narratives of the descendants reveal, it is the female body that holds the memory of familial bonds and ancestral ties through which the individual feels the deep and lasting connections to Jewish culture and to God. As the site of ritual return, the *mikveh* therefore creates a sacred space where spirituality becomes embodied, as the feelings and sensations of religious emotion are experienced in the intermingling of body and spirit in the liminal world of Jewish custom.

The importance of the body, the physiological domain through which religious emotions are apprehended, was first articulated by William James in *The Varieties of Religious Experience*.[34] As an innovative approach to the study of religion in the nineteenth century, James's work challenged the traditional notions of the mind/body split, suggesting that religious experience cannot and should not be understood solely through the articulation of theology and philosophy. Rather, James maintained that the study of emotions and feelings, as they relate to the body, is essential to a complete understanding of spiritual awareness. Drawing on James's theory of embodied spirituality, recent research has focused on the importance of the body in contemporary healing movements in the United States. Wade Clark Roof and Sarah McFarland Taylor thus observe:

> We see a reorientation of spirituality toward the primacy of the body. We see that, for these groups [healing movements], religion is not so much about creed and philosophy as it is about emotion and performance, an immediacy between bodily experience and religious emotion. We see,

> therefore, that the movement toward centering religion in the space of the body becomes linked to a movement toward "spirituality" or rather a movement toward James's redefinition of "religion." Religion, in the body-centered context, draws the focus away from ecclesiastic institutions and theology and toward a more autonomous, more personal, more immediate "spirituality."[35]

James's redefinition of religion, as elaborated by Roof and Taylor, provides a conceptual framework for the emotional conversion experiences described by the crypto-Jewish descendants. For many of the respondents, the relationship between body and spirit is of particular significance, since descendants believe that their bodies hold the memory of their Jewish heritage.[36] This sensory connection to Judaism was frequently articulated by David Kazzaz, an Iraqi-born Jewish psychiatrist and founder of the Hispano Crypto-Jewish Resource Center in Denver. Speaking to the notion that Jewishness is a feeling that runs deep in the physical as well as spiritual being of the descendant, Kazzaz maintains that knowledge of Jewish ancestry is in the "bones" and thus cannot be denied. As feeling states become an affirmation of Jewish heritage, the body becomes the medium through which spiritual awareness and connection to Judaism converge. Within this sensory understanding of Jewish spirituality, the *mikveh* provides a religious milieu where cultural memory is engendered and emotional ties to Jewish ancestors are given meaning and expression.

## EMBODIED SPIRITUALITY AND THE CONVERT'S "RETURN" AT THE WESTERN WALL

In a further illustration of this sensory-oriented spiritual phenomenon, the Western Wall in Jerusalem has become another site of ritual return where the relationship between body and spirit figures prominently in the cultural memory of the crypto-Jewish descendants. The Western Wall of the Second Temple stands at the southeastern corner of the old city of Jerusalem. It is part of the sacred shrines of the Temple Mount, the ancient hill site of the biblical Mount Moriah, where it is believed that Abraham brought his son Isaac to be sacrificed to God. The first Temple was built by King Solomon during the tenth century B.C.E and was destroyed by the Babylonians. The Second Temple, which was constructed by King Herod on the same site (first century B.C.E.), was demolished by the occupying Roman forces in 70 C.E. As the original site of the First and Second Temples, the Temple Mount is a sacred area for Jews where the past is revered in the remnants of the Second Temple that remain standing.[37] These remnants are composed of three portions of the original retaining walls built by King Herod. Of these, the Western Wall of Kotel is considered the most holy of the temple walls, because it is believed that the ancient ark was situated closest to this outer temple structure.

Since 1967, the Wall has been within Israeli territory. As a religious archeological monument, the Wall, although not a synagogue per se, is under the supervision of Orthodox rabbinic authorities and is subject to Orthodox rules of prayer and behavior. Because the Western Wall falls under the jurisdiction of the Orthodox rabbinate, this site, like the *mikveh,* has become an arena for dissension and conflict. Governed by the Ministry of Religious Affairs, the Wall is a sex-segregated area where, until very recently, women were prohibited from praying in groups, from praying audibly, and from carrying the Torah. For the last decade, protests at the Wall have been met with violent responses by the ultra-Orthodox community in Israel.[38]

According to Jewish beliefs, the spiritual power of the Wall is found in the ancient stones that retain the presence of God and that embody the spiritual essence of Judaism. Today these stones have become the medium through which visitors to the Wall communicate with God, often by placing written messages in between the nooks and crannies of those parts of the stone edifice that remain accessible to the public. Amid the thousands of tourists and pious who visit the Wall each year, the descendants of the crypto-Jews have found special meaning in the Temple ruins, a monument to Jewish survival that provides a visible connection to a heritage that is both felt and desired. While Israel may be the homeland to which the descendants return in their search for Sephardic roots, the Western Wall is the sacred shrine where Jewish history, the Jewish people, and God can be experienced through a sense of touch that connects the body to the materiality of the sacred. A woman whose family originated in Mexico described this dynamic between spirit and body when she visited the Wall of the ancient Temple for the first time:

> Most people ask me, "What did you really feel when you got to the Wailing Wall?"[39] I said there was no doubt in my mind that the power still exists in there, that Abraham and my ancestors did not imagine anything. As I got closer to the wall and I put my hands out, there was this feeling like gravity or electricity, energy pure energy. In Spanish there is a word for

> what I felt, like a person crying in pain when you are so deep in sadness because you have lost someone and you are very emotional. I felt that definitely. I could not say anything; not one word came from my mouth. There were no words, but tears, all tears. I just wept for what I felt now and for what had been lost. I asked a rabbi who was standing close by why I felt so overwhelmed, and he said it was because this is where the spirit of God has spread itself so we can feel it.

As a sacred site of return, the Western Wall engenders feelings both of overwhelming sadness and of awe among descendants for whom a return to Judaism simultaneously creates feeling states associated with loss and godliness. The emotional pilgrimage to the Temple site captures many threads of *teshuvah* as the descendants mourn a lost tradition, while, at the same time, they celebrate the power of God to bring them back to the spiritual home of their religious ancestors. In this regard, the Western Wall is an especially powerful symbol of return and cultural survival, a sacred place that engaged the descendant in an act of spiritual reunification, as the following account suggests:

> I went to the Wall, and the first time I was there, I just stood there. I mean, you can't describe it. For me it was like I found it, I made my full journey, because it was for ancient Jewry—my family who thousands of years ago were in Israel. And that was very spiritual and mystical. And no matter how many times I went and for how long—I think one time I just stood there for three hours—it was just this cleansing weeping. That's a special place.

Like the hidden rituals in the descendant's life, the Western Wall holds the spiritual memory of Jewish lineage. A respondent of Cuban Jewish ancestry spoke of the Western Wall as a holy monument where he could actually touch God and where the pride of his Jewish heritage resides:

> The Wall is a connection to Judaism. Growing up you learned to say the Hail Mary and Our Father and all that. Now, it has just become words. I learned those prayers for protection. It was my family's plan for these hundreds of years to have papers saying you are Christian or Catholic, untouchable by the Inquisition or any other faction like the Nazis. But going to Israel is like breaking away and actually going somewhere, to touch the stone of the Wailing Wall is like touching God. It is a connection to who you are, what we fought for, and where we are going. . . . The Temple is the only thing left of our grandeur, of who we were as a people.

Like the *mikveh,* the Western Wall provides a sacred venue for the descendant's emotional reconnection to Jewish ancestry and to the Jewish religion. The accounts of the descendants, in fact, suggest that these two forms of emotional attachment are inseparable from each other in that the descendant understands him- or herself as a Jew who has returned both to a faith tradition and to an ancestral history. As such, the experience of *teshuvah* among crypto-Jewish descendants is characterized by an embodied spirituality. As the mystical and the familial merge, the historical frame through which the converting Jew approaches her or his newfound religion is elaborated through a theology of suffering that comes to define the Jewish worldview of the descendants.

## ANCESTRAL ATTACHMENT, REMEMBRANCE, AND A JEWISH THEOLOGY OF SUFFERING

In her thoughtful and provocative book on Chinese and Jewish cultural memory, Vera Schwarcz discusses the relationship between Jewish attachment to history and theological practice.[40] In this work, she elaborates the biblical injunctions that command the Jews to remember their past transgressions against God and to recall God's acts of redemption for the faithful. According to Schwarcz, the religious laws surrounding the observance of holy days such as Rosh Hashanah (Jewish New Year) and Passover represent the fusion of ritual and remembrance:

> Another side of the attachment to history is embodied in the commandment to remember on Passover. This is a celebration of freedom that every Jew is enjoined to reenact personally. "I left Egypt," the phrase that is the center of the Seder ritual and of the Haggadah, the story we tell, is oriented toward the present. Then, as we raise the matzah, we recite, "*Ha lachma anya*. This is the bread of affliction that our ancestors ate in the land of Egypt." Both the words and the gesture are meant to awaken memory. . . . This bond of memory is also at the heart of the Rosh Hashanah liturgy—a holy day known in Hebrew as *Yom Hazikaron* (Day of Remembrance). On this occasion, which marks the beginning of the Jewish New Year and recalls the birth of the world at the same time, we sound the shofar in order to inspire the full range of emotions associated with memory.[41]

Schwarcz concludes that Judaism is a religion founded on memory, since Jewish prayers connect the worshiper to the past through the practice of emotion-filled rituals that recall the lives and deeds of the matriarchs and patriarchs of Jewish culture.

The narratives of the crypto-Jewish descendants suggest that Schwarcz is indeed right, that Judaism is in part a religion of remembrance encoded in the ritual life of the descendants who become bar and bat mitzvahed, who immerse themselves in the ritual waters of the *mik-*

*vah,* and who pray before the Western Wall in Jerusalem. Yet it is not remembrance alone that distinguishes Jewish theology. Underlying the act of remembrance is a belief system that embraces a history of suffering and loss. Through the recollections of slavery in Egypt, exile from Jerusalem, the persecutions of the Inquisition, and the horrors of the Holocaust, Jewish scripture and ritual provide constant reminders of the persecution and suffering of the Jewish people. On Passover, for example, it is not only the eating of matzo that links contemporary Jewish life to the oppression of one's ancestors. Suffering is also emphasized in the readings of the Haggadah (the book containing the Passover service) that recount the history of Jewish slavery and the seder rituals that commemorate the oppression of the enslaved Jews.

Among the ritual practices of Passover is dipping green vegetables such as celery or parsley into salt water, the greens representing the fruit of the earth and the salt water representing the tears of the Jewish slaves in Egypt. During the seder (the Passover service), the participants also eat *charoseth,* a mixture of apple, wine, and nuts that symbolizes the mortar the slaves used in brick making. To invoke the pain of slavery, bitter herbs, typically in the form of horseradish, are to be consumed. As the herbs are eaten, the traditional Haggadah explains:

> These bitter herbs which we eat, what is their meaning? They are eaten to recall that the Egyptians embittered the lives of our forefathers in Egypt; as it is written: "And they embittered their lives with hard labor: with mortar and bricks, with every kind of work in the fields; all the work which they made them do was rigorous."
>
> In every generation one must look upon himself as if he personally had come out from Egypt, as the Bible says: "And thou shalt tell thy son on that day, saying, it is because of that which the Eternal did to me when I went from Egypt."[42]

In this ritual of consumption, the body is once again the medium through which a connection to Judaism is maintained. During the Passover seder, the boundaries between the modern Jew and the enslaved ancestor become merged, since the liturgy requires the seder participant to identify with the slaves who God brought out of Egypt. This ritualized ceremony reinforces the notion that the twentieth-century Jew must never forget the suffering of the biblical Jew or God's role in the salvation of the Jewish people. Such sentiments give rise to a spiritual sufferance that underlies the celebration of the Passover liberation story. In some modern and less traditional Haggadic texts, this theme of suffering is given a wider emphasis as references to the Inquisition are included in the narrative of remembrance that accompanies the storytelling of the liberation of the Jews from Egypt. In a revised version of the Haggadah created by Aviva Cantor, the Inquisition is recalled with a poem by the Yiddish poet Avrom Reisen:

> Tell me, Marrano, my brother, where have you prepared your seder?
> —In a room in a deep cellar, there my seder is ready.
> Tell me, Marrano, my [sister], where will you get white *matzot?*
> —In the cellar, under God's protection, [I] kneaded the dough.
> Tell me, Marrano, how will you manage to get a hagada?
> —In the cellar, in a deep crevice, I hid a hagada long ago.
> Tell me, Marrano, if your voice is heard, what will you do then?
> —When the enemy captures me, I will die singing.[43]

While Cantor's Passover service contains one of the few references to the Inquisition found in modern Jewish observance, the Holocaust is more frequently remembered through a variety of liturgy and practice. Since World War II, the memorial service for the Jewish Day of Atonement, traditionally recited in memory of deceased family members, has been expanded to include a communal prayer for the six million Jews who died in the concentration camps. Typical of the Holocaust prayers is the memorial liturgy (mourner's kaddish) of the Conservative Movement:

> Extolled, compassionate God, grant perfect peace in Your sheltering Presence, among the holy and pure, to the souls of all our brethren, men women and children of the House of Israel who were slaughtered and burned. May their memory endure, inspiring truth and loyalty to our lives. May their souls thus be bound up in the bond of life. May they rest in peace. And let us say: Amen.[44]

With the inclusion of the mourner's kaddish for the victims of the Holocaust, contemporary Jewish practice has continued the tradition of linking religious ritual with Jewish history and Jewish cultural identity. Because the death and suffering of the historical Jew are remembered alongside the death of a parent, sibling, or child, cultural suffering and personal loss become merged within the theology of atonement and forgiveness that pervades the prayers and supplications of the Yom Kippur service.

Since the historical suffering of the Jews defines important aspects of the religious culture, Jewish ritual has been a site of commemoration first for the enslaved Jews of ancient Israel and more recently for the victims and survivors of the Holocaust. To this dynamic of history, remembrance, and ritualization, the descendants of the crypto-Jews bring their own culture of exile, loss, and mourning, a culture in which the ritual life of the contemporary convert is informed by the suffering of the medieval Spanish Jews. The memory of the Inquisition, like that of the Holocaust, becomes part of a theology of remembrance that underlies the descendant's return to Judaism, as attachment to the suffering of persecuted ancestors is reflected in the Jewish spirituality that emerges from the descendant's ritual experience.

The theological themes characterizing the conversion experience of the returning descendants—ancestral attachment, embodied spirituality, remembrance, and suffering—all contribute to the development of an emotional connection to Judaism that is expressed through the language of relationship. To be Jewish is to know and acknowledge the lives and suffering of one's ancestors, to feel that connection in one's body and one's soul, and to experience God through the history of oppression that is inseparable from the history of the Spanish crypto-Jews. In choosing to adopt a Jewish worldview that includes a spiritual orientation toward ancestors, memory, and religious persecution, descendants choose to become a part of a Jewish cultural community that is defined both by collective religious worship and by a shared history of suffering.

CHAPTER 6

# Jewish Ancestry and the Social Construction of Ethnic Identity

Through the recovery of Sephardic ancestry, crypto-Jewish descendants embrace not only an ancestral spiritual tradition but also a cultural past steeped in the unique and complex history of the Jewish people. The integration of Jewish ethnicity thus involves an identification with shared history, values, and spirituality that together form the emerging Jewish self. Among the descendants, the adoption of a Jewish ethnic identity is tied to a longing for community that has developed in response to social alienation and the growing importance of ethnic identity in the contemporary culture of the United States. Beginning with a discussion of ethnic revivalism, this chapter will examine the social construction of ethnicity from the perspective of stigmatized identities and the creation of ethnic alliances among modern descendants for whom Jewish ethnic identity has both social and moral implications.

## ETHNIC REVIVALISM, THE "STRANGER," AND THE DESIRE FOR JEWISH ETHNICITY

Recent cultural trends reflect a heightened awareness of ethnic origins among diverse ethnic groups in the United States. Richard Alba thus describes the ethnic revivalism that has come to characterize social relations in the postmodern era of ethnic consciousness:

> It is almost hard to remember the time—only a few decades ago, in the aftermath of World War II—when the expectation was widespread that

> ethnic Americans would assimilate, largely along the lines of an Anglo-American prototype, and hence the consciousness of ethnicity would gradually disappear. This was a time when the melting pot was the prevailing image of American society, and it is difficult to identify the forces that overturned this image. . . .
>
> Whatever the cause, the celebration of ethnicity and the perception of the stubbornness of ethnic difference have come to occupy a place of honor. Ethnic festivals and parades are familiar in most communities; ethnic cooking has achieved a lofty niche in American cuisine, far removed from its humble immigrant origins; and evidence of ethnicity in the form of names, accents, and behavioral styles is pervasive in the media. Accompanying these surface changes is a belief, among scholars and the lay public, that ethnic differences form a possibly permanent substructure, if not the ultimate bedrock of American society.[1]

The current ethnic revivalism described by Alba has been attributed to a number of different social trends that reveal important racial and generational differences in the celebration of ethnic identity. Within communities of color, the focus on ethnic and racial pride has been explained as a response to the persistence of racial discrimination in American culture. Scholars argue that emphasizing the value of diverse ethnic backgrounds helps to balance the denigrating treatment of racial minorities in the United States. The emergence of ethnic consciousness among white ethnic groups, by comparison, has been explained as the result of generational shifts in attitudes toward ancestral heritage. This view holds that highly assimilated third-generation European ethnic Americans, unlike their parents and grandparents, take pride in claiming an ethnic identity that fifty years earlier would have been seen as an obstacle to social and economic advancement.[2] Further, contemporary research on ethnicity has shown that current attitudes on cultural and racial origins have been influenced by the effects of assimilation on more recent immigrant communities who are at risk for losing important cultural values in the pressure to become "Americanized."

Within this shifting cultural paradigm, the ethnic revivalism of the late twentieth century has had a significant impact on crypto-Jewish descendants, many of whom long for membership in an ethnic community in which the bonds of a shared history, culture, and religion might be realized. The longing for an alternative ethnic identity and the desire for connection to the Jewish community are rooted in the experiences of social alienation that have informed the sociocultural development of the descendant population. Research on social estrangement thus has particular relevance for the study of Jewish cultural identity among modern descendants. More specifically, the theoretical perspectives of Georg Simmel, the nineteenth-century sociologist, provide insight into the relationship between crypto-Jewish ancestry and isolation in contemporary society.

In chapter 1, Simmel's theory of secrecy in society helped to illuminate the role that secrecy played in the development and maintenance of crypto-Jewish culture. In another of Simmel's important essays of the same period, he elaborated the role of the outsider in society, introducing the study of the "stranger" to European sociology. For Simmel, the stranger was symbolized by the Jew in nineteenth-century European culture who, regardless of assimilation, would always be viewed as the "*potential* wanderer," the ethnic outsider whose origins deprived him or her of full membership in the European community.[3] Tomas Atencio insightfully applies Simmel's theory of estrangement to the medieval and premodern crypto-Jews, whose ambiguous religious status placed them on the border between Catholic and Jewish cultures, where they were variously construed as either apostate Jews practicing Catholicism or as heretical Christians observing Judaism.[4] Atencio observes that the legacy of the crypto-Jewish stranger can be seen in contemporary cultural traits that originate in cultures of secrecy and seclusion. Both Simmel's and Atencio's insights on the status and marginality of the "Jewish stranger" provide a perspective from which to consider the social and emotional dimensions of ethnic identification among modern descendants, whose search for Sephardic roots is steeped in a consciousness of difference and separateness.

As described in the earlier chapters, for the respondents, the choice to become a spiritual Jew grew out of a deep emotional attachment both to primary family members as well as to Jewish ancestors whose imagined religious lives provided the spiritual connection to Judaic beliefs and practices. In seeking to find a spiritual home within modern-day Judaism, many descendants expressed a sense of spiritual alienation that formed the core of their experience as religious outsiders in the predominantly Catholic Latina/o culture of Latin America and the southwestern United States. As nonreligious or nominal Christians within the church-centered culture of Latina/o society, the descendants grew up in an environment where difference often meant exclusion or separateness, occupying a somewhat marginalized position that created a sense of social as well as spiritual alienation. Although the descendants ethnically identified as Hispanic or Latina/o, their Jewish ancestry, whether hidden or acknowledged, created a culture of difference within their families that contributed to a self-perception of otherness that affected their social integration.

The concept of other, as derived from the work of Simone de Beauvoir, therefore provides a useful framework for examining the descendants' desire for Jewish ethnic identity. In *The Second Sex,* de Beauvoir proposes a theory of difference in which Simmel's view of the stranger is elaborated through the analytic categories of One and the Other.[5] De Beauvoir writes:

> Otherness is a fundamental category of human thought.
>
> Thus it is that no group ever sets itself up as the One without at once setting up the Other over against itself. If three travelers chance to occupy the same compartment, that is enough to make vaguely hostile "others" out of the rest of the passengers on the train. In small-town eyes all persons not belonging to the village are "strangers" and suspect; to the native of a country all who inhabit other countries are "foreigners"; Jews are "different" for the anti-Semite, Negroes are "inferior" for American racists, aborigines are "natives" for colonists, proletarians are the "lower class" for the privileged.[6]

Within the nature of social relations conceptualized by de Beauvoir, medieval crypto-Jews (as well as other converts) and their descendants came to occupy the role of Other in cultures in which political and social boundaries were drawn between those with "pure-blood" Christian ancestry and those whose backgrounds included Jewish heritage. Centuries later, the persistence of a consciousness of difference and separateness can be found among the descendants whose families never quite fit into the tightly connected communities of Catholic Latina/o culture. In a small number of cases, the boundaries that were drawn between the descendants' families and the Christian culture in which they were raised were maintained through clerical antisemitism. A male descendant in his sixties describes how he first became aware of his crypto-Jewish background as a child:

> I remember when I was young and I was taken to my first communion and I went to church, and the sister would not let me in. "What is your name?" she asked, and I told her. And she said, are ___ and ___ your brother and sister? And I said, "Yes." She said,"You can't come in here. You are Jews." And I was only ten years old, and I said,"I am Catholic. I just had my first communion," and she said, "Even so, you are Jews and you cannot come into the sanctuary." . . . It was a time when we were still

> taught that the Jews killed Christ, and now I was being told that I was a Jew. I was crying. It was very hard. From that moment on I became two people. I learned to live in two worlds—as a Christian and a hated Jew.

Through this childhood experience, the descendant came to see himself as an outsider within his own culture, internalizing the image of himself as the detested Jew. His narrative illuminates the vulnerability of the child who through the trauma of prejudice begins to feel the stirrings of self-hatred that arise out of stigmatized identities. Frantz Fanon provides an exceptionally powerful insight into the psychodynamics of this form of internalized racism. In his revolutionary autobiography, *Black Skin, White Masks: The Experiences of a Black Man in a White World,* he recounts a moment when, while traveling as a soldier in France, he became the racialized other in the eyes of a young French boy who pointed and jeered at him:

> "Look, a Negro!" It was an external stimulus that flicked over me as I passed by. I made a tight smile.
>
> "Look, a Negro!" It was true. It amused me.
>
> "Look, a Negro!" The circle was drawing a bit tighter. I made no secret of my amusement.
>
> "Mama, see the Negro. I'm frightened!" Frightened! Frightened! Now they were beginning to be afraid of me. I made up my mind to laugh myself to tears, but laughter had become impossible.
>
> I could no longer laugh, because I already knew that there were legends, stories, history and above all *historicity*. . . . I was responsible at the same time for my body, for my race, for my ancestors. I subjected myself to an objective examination, I discovered my blackness, my ethnic characteristics; and I was battered down by tom-toms, cannibalism, intellectual deficiency, fetishism, racial defects, slave-ships.[7]

With this encounter on the train, Fanon's image of himself is forever changed by the fear and racism that pervaded the young boy's response. From that moment on, Fanon recalled that he ceased to be the "man among men" and instead became the composite of racial stereotypes that were linked to his African heritage. Thereafter, Fanon saw himself through the eyes of white culture, his character discredited by what Erving Goffman has identified as the "stigma of race."[8]

Similarly, for the crypto-Jewish descendant who learned of his or her Jewishness in a culture in which Jews were still considered the perpetrators of deicide, internalized images of the hateful and stigmatized Jew informed their understanding of themselves as the differentiated and devalued other. Such experiences of overt antisemitism, however, were comparatively rare. More commonly, the descendants reported that their sense of otherness was reinforced through a distinctive family culture that differentiated their family from those around them. Among the most significant differences described by the descendants was the absence of a strong Catholic familial orientation in a community where the church was at the center of both religious and social life. Here descendants reported that they felt different from other Latina/o families who went to church regularly, who had icons and religious statues in their homes, and who feared and respected the Catholic clergy. A woman from Texas vividly recalled her mother's response to the Church and to the local priest:

> My mother was not really a Catholic. She never went to church, and she was not a religious person in that way. She acknowledged God in her own way but never in an open display. She was suspicious of people that did that. . . . We used to have a priest that would walk our neighborhood on Saturday mornings. And I remember I would be outside playing with the other kids. And they'd run up to him. They'd stop what they were doing and kiss his hand. And I remember standing back; it was so vivid. I would stand back and wonder, am I supposed to do that same thing? And I ran home to tell my mother and ask, "Am I supposed to kiss his hand?" And I remember my mother getting very upset about that and telling me I was not to kiss his hand, because he was just a man.

The indifference to and, in some cases, outright rejection of Catholicism, while rarely explicitly tied to crypto-Jewish origins, nevertheless created a social distance between the descendants' families and the surrounding religious culture. Thus, the majority of participants in the study attributed their sense of difference to the family's religious idiosyncrasy. As one descendant from Mexico explained:

> We did everything that the other kids did except on the Sabbath. Then we did what the Jews did, especially on Saturday. We ate a special bread that my grandmother baked, and we said prayers before and after each meal. I knew that something was different in our house, that we were just different, even though I never confronted my mother or grandmother or asked why on Saturday we couldn't do a lot of things that everyone else did.

Although differences in religious observance and attitudes were for the most part the basis on which the child descendant first began to understand him- or herself as an outsider, the descendants recalled other aspects of a distinctive family culture as well. In particular, a number of descendants who were raised in the Southwest of the United States framed their sense of difference within the context of social and racial distinctions that separated their families from the mixed race or mestiza/o (Indian and Spanish) culture. In these narratives, European or colonial origins were construed as the demarcation between the descendant's family and its neighbors, as the following account reveals:

> I lived in a segregated neighborhood. We grew up in a Mexican neighborhood, but my Mom never said we were Mexican. She said we were Spanish. We're not Mexican, because we didn't come from Mexico. Our ancestors came from Spain, and the affinity for Spain was always there. Mom always impressed upon us to know your language, to know your culture, to know your roots. And she always used to tell us, you know, we're different from the other people who live in the neighborhood.

In a similar narrative, a female respondent offered this view of the stratified racial culture that distinguished her family from those with Mexican (mixed-race) ancestry:

> When I was growing up we lived in a border town. I always felt different from everyone else. I didn't think that my family was like the other Chicano families around us. I would ask if we were Mexican, and my parents always said no. I would never identify with the other families.

The "separatist" perspective, as articulated by this respondent, has racial overtones that are indicative of the social and racial hierarchies of the southwestern United States, where "pure" Spanish lineage has historically accorded individuals a more privileged position and social standing that, for some descendants, was a source of both status and social alienation.[9]

Taken together, the findings on social boundaries and outsider status indicate that social estrangement emerged from a complex set of social interactions that were not the same for all respondents. Clearly some individuals felt ostracized by their Jewish ancestry and thus internalized a stigmatized self-image that was tied to antisemitism. Others associated difference with their European origins. Finally, most descendants' experience of social alienation stemmed from their families' religious and cultural difference. What links all the descendants together, however, is a sense of alienation and exclusion that reinforced feelings of separateness and difference. A respondent who was raised as a Protestant in Mexico succinctly and poignantly expressed the loneliness of the "outsider":

> In Mexico as Protestants we always considered ourselves somewhat different because we were not like everybody else. We knew we were different. Then we came to this country, and I thought maybe we'll find people that

> are like us, but we felt even more different here. It was like going to Mars; I had nothing in common with most of the Hispanics who were Catholic, and I had nothing in common with the other Protestants. And then in junior high and high school it was so lonely, because I had nothing in common with anyone, and so it was very hard. And then when I went off to college I thought, well, maybe in college where there are a lot of people from so many different cultures and so many walks of life [it will be better]. I looked at every ethnic group you can imagine, and nothing made any sense until I started reading about the Jews.

In much the same way that this descendant turned to her family's Jewish heritage as a means to end her social isolation, so too did other respondents adopt a Jewish ethnic identity to resolve the dilemma of the "stranger."

## CREATING ETHNIC ALLIANCES: PERSECUTION, SUFFERING, AND JEWISH ETHNICITY

As an ethnic category in modern Western culture, Jewish identity occupies a somewhat unique position in what Alba characterizes as the "ethnic hierarchy" in the United States. Jews are identified by religion, ancestry, and a set of ethnic stereotypes that both value and stigmatize them as the perennial outsiders, a people defined both by a history of suffering and by a persistent and unshakable image of materialism. Aware of the historical legacies of European antisemitism, descendants of the crypto-Jews express a certain ambivalence about the discovery and recognition of Jewish ancestry. A woman raised in Texas articulated the "dilemma of Jewishness" that the descendants confront as they integrate the knowledge of a Jewish family background into the reality of antisemitic violence:

> When I read about Hispanics rediscovering their Jewish roots, I knew there was something to it, that they were talking about me. And I remember feeling something very heavy inside. I started to cry, because it was a very deep, overwhelming feeling, and for those few minutes I felt very complete—almost as if I had come home. It wasn't mental; it was more of a spiritual thing. It was a very, very heavy feeling. But then when my mind took control, I realized that the Jewish people had been persecuted for two thousand years, and there was no reason in the world why I wanted to be a Jew. . . . I still struggle with this. What do I do with this part of my history—do I accept it? I ask myself why am I doing this, and then I see my relatives like my aging aunt, and I'm more determined to find my Jewishness, because these people are so unique.

The notion of "coming home," coupled with the anxiety of being Jewish, captures the deep emotional response of the adult descendant whose Jewish ancestry creates the possibility of choice: Descendants either can choose to assume membership in an ethnic group that has faced horrific persecution, or they can reject that part of their historical selves that has been obscured by family secrecy and cultural assimilation. For the vast majority of descendants in this study, the desire to "belong" and to honor a history of suffering and religious perseverance led to their decision to choose Jewish ethnicity. The search for Sephardic roots thus resulted in the creation of ethnic alliances through which the descendant reinterpreted his or her social biography within the framework of Jewish history and an association with Jewish cultural values and characteristics. This dynamic of ethnic identity formation is discussed by Simon Herman in his work on the social psychology of ethnicity:

> The alignment with an ethnic group implies a relationship to the group beyond a given moment in time—to its past and future as well as its present. It points to the individual's link with "the unique values, fostered by an unique history, of his [or her] people." The identity of the group itself reflects the impact of the traditions and experiences of the past and also of the hopes and aspirations for the future. [10]

Because the establishment of ethnic alliances relies on the construction of past as well as present connections to the group, family genealogy took on particular importance for the descendants. Through an arduous and time-consuming study of ancestral roots, descendants established links to Jewish heritage and to a history of family persecution that legitimized their claims to Jewish ancestry and provided an emotional tie to the image of suffering that characterizes Jewish ethnicity in modern times. More than two decades ago, Herbert Gans put forward a theory of Jewish ethnicity that stressed the importance of the Holocaust as a symbol of Jewish identity. In his essay on symbolic ethnicity, Gans discussed the increasing significance of the Holocaust in post–World War II Jewish consciousness:

> The interest of American Jews in the Holocaust has increased considerably since the end of World War II; when I studied the Jews of Park Forest in 1949–1950, it was almost never mentioned, and its memory played no part whatsoever in the creation of a Jewish community there. The lack of attention to the Holocaust at that time may, as Nathan Glazer suggests, reflect the fact that American Jews were busy with creating new Jewish communities in the suburbs. It is also possible that people ignored the

> Holocaust then because the literature detailing its horrors had not yet been written, although since many second-generation American Jews had relatives who died in the Nazi camps, it seems more likely that people repressed thinking about it until it had become a more historical and therefore a less immediately traumatic event. As a result, the Holocaust may now be serving as a new symbol for the threat of group destruction.[11]

Gans's analysis foreshadowed the growing and significant importance of the Holocaust as a cultural signifier of Jewish identity. Since his essay was first published in 1979, the Holocaust has become memorialized as the defining Jewish experience of suffering and persecution with no parallel in history or culture. For the past two decades, there has been a proliferation of memorials, popular films, memoirs, and academic scholarship that has kept alive the memory of genocide and the ever-present knowledge of Jewish vulnerability. As a transnational and transhistorical symbol of Jewish identification, the Holocaust reinforces the link between group membership and violence against the Jews. The effect on the descendants of the crypto-Jews has been significant. As a first step toward the creation of Jewish identity, many of the descendants have carved an ethnic alliance out of a history of ancestral suffering and pain. Within this historical framework, the descendants view the Inquisition as an antecedent to the Holocaust, since each of these periods of persecution represent different but related aspects of Jewish victimization.

As modern descendants come to know the history of Spanish Jewry, they become painfully aware of the links between the Inquisition and the Holocaust. As discussed in previous chapters, the writings of the medieval clergy espoused the virtues of genocide, while the blood-purity laws institutionalized racial discrimination. Similar to the German authorities, the medieval and premodern Church officials maintained meticulous records on the disposition of the Jews. Comparisons with the Holocaust therefore became inevitable. Like many Holocaust survivors and their families, the descendants of the crypto-Jews sought to obtain detailed documentation of their ancestors' persecution. Through research at the Inquisition archives in Mexico City and Madrid, they discovered evidence of their families' Jewish background that brought a present-day reality to the suffering of the medieval Spanish Jews. During one interview, a male descendant in his late fifties brought out a large black loose-leaf notebook containing copies of original Inquisition records that had been carefully preserved in the medieval Spanish script. The descendant offered this notebook both as proof of his Jewish heritage and as a material witness to the persecution of his forebears:

> I have located twenty-nine cases of Sephardic Jews who went to trial, and some are clearly related to me. It's all here in Spanish. And it tells you exactly what was done with each one. All of them were physically examined by surgeons, and the majority of them had crude circumcisions. It's fantastic. The names are right here. When I read about this, I feel like my ancestors were denied from practicing their religion. This is sad. . . . There is only one way I can go with all this information that I have. Within myself, I know I have found myself. Even if I don't go to a synagogue, I feel very strongly that my ancestors were deprived, persecuted. This is why I made these copies. On these copies from the Mexican Inquisition it gives you some of the customs, their habits. How they would fold their clothing on the end of the bed for their big day. Their big day was apparently Friday and Saturday. And they fasted from Friday in the evening until Saturday in the evening, twenty-four hours. And how they bathed, and so forth. When I read them I feel as if I know my ancestors—what they were like. I spent six months reading those records, and some are very hard to read because they are in the actual handwriting of the officials of the Inquisition. In the documents they are referred to as the Holy Office.

Another descendant had also obtained documents from the Inquisition archives. Pointing to a name on a four-hundred-year-old ledger, he explained:

> One of my ancestors, Oscar, his name was Oscar de Los Reyes, was a pharmacist, and his family were doctors and medical people. The sad part about Oscar was that he was killed. He was in the auto-da-fé of the 1500s and was burned at the stake in Mexico City. I have documentation for this. Here, look at the record. It says the name of the accused, the date, his occupation as pharmacist, the charge of blasphemy, and then his death by the auto-da-fé. They took place at the central plaza. This is where the Jews who were accused were murdered and burned at the stake. I mean, there were thousands of us.

The use of the word *us* in this narrative clearly establishes the sense of connection that modern descendants share with the crypto-Jews of the past. In establishing an ancestral link to the crypto-Jews of medieval Spain, the respondents identify with the martyrdom of the adherents who chose death rather than renouncing their faith. The image of the burned and tortured Jewish body thus becomes a reference point for the construction of an ethnic identity that is tied to Jewish suffering and destruction. Nowhere is this more apparent than in the narrative of a female descendant from South America who first learned of her Jewish ancestry through a neighbor's reference to the Inquisition:

> When I was very young, maybe nine years old, I had a very bad experience, because I fell on the fire and I was all burned. I couldn't walk for weeks.

> I was very hurt. Then after a couple of weeks, I went to visit a family from Cataluña who lived across the street from our house. They were Catholics who lived in our town. And the gentleman says, "Here comes the burned one. The burned one." And I say, "Oh, thank you. I am very well." And he says, "No, no. You are the burned one from before." When I arrived home, I asked my papa, "What does he mean, 'the burned one from before'?" He asked me, "Do you remember the story of the French lady, Joan of Arc, who was burned because she didn't believe like everyone else?" I said, "Yes." "Well," my papa said to me, "when we did not believe like they believe, they would burn us like her." This was the first time that I had consciousness that I was a Jew.

In this narrative, the descendant's connection to her Jewish ancestors is established within the historical context of martyrdom and religious persecution. Having learned of her Jewish heritage in association with the Inquisition, she came to believe that the accident in which she had been burned as a child was a sign of her ancestors' past suffering:

> The first time I thought of myself as a Jewish person was after the incident with the neighbor. It was a physical connection at first, and then later I had this spiritual experience. I was only about nine when I was badly burned. I was dancing around the room, and back then the houses were heated by big cast-iron stoves with coals, and my mother said, "Be careful," and when she said to be careful, I went backwards and I fell into the hot coals. They were boiling milk with sugar to make a typical dessert, and when I fell into the stove, the coals went all over me. I felt like I was on fire. I was burning, mostly on the feet and neck. One of the charcoals went into my arm. I think I had a memory then of being burned before, and then the neighbor said I was the burned one, and my father told me about our ancestors, and it felt like this accident was a way of bringing this part of my history to consciousness. It is the mystery of things, how things can happen many generations later, and they are like a sign of who you really are.

This narrative strongly illustrates the ways in which cultural and individual identity coalesce for the descendant who is unable to distinguish her suffering from that of her ancestors. For this descendant, who has internalized the painful past of the Jewish people, victimization becomes the defining social and psychological reference for her developing consciousness as a Jew. As the memory of the Inquisition is reconstructed through images of physical suffering, associations with violent persecution characterize the descendant's understanding of her family's place in Spanish Jewish history.

Within this framework of violence against the Jews, the portrait of well-known historical figures who suffered under the Inquisition provide visual reminders of the persecution of the Spanish Jews. Among the most famous families known to the descendants are the Carvajals, whose Inquisition history and persecution were briefly described in chapter 2. A powerful painting of one of the young Carvajal women, Mariana, commemorates the deaths of Mexican crypto-Jews during the late sixteenth and early seventeenth centuries. In this artistic rendering, Mariana is shown at the autos-da-fé as she awaits strangulation, while all around her, other Judaizers are already burning at the stake. This portrayal of the crypto-Jewish victim has been reproduced in texts such as Seymour Liebman's *The Jews in New Spain: Faith, Flame, and the Inquisition.*[12] It is therefore well known among the descendants, some of whom wept openly as they spoke of the emotions that such images engender. Despite the centuries that have passed, paintings such as these personalize the suffering of the historical crypto-Jew, connecting the descendants to the harsh reality of their ancestors' lives. In this way, the artistic rendering of Jewish persecution provides a medium of remembrance and connection that contributes to the development of a shared ethnic consciousness.

The emotion with which the participants respond to the sorrow and travails of Spanish Jewry suggests that, in creating a Jewish identity, a descendant's identification with the victim/martyr deepens the emotional ties between her or him and the Jewish community in which she or he seeks membership. The classical sociologist Emile Durkheim described this aspect of group identity formation as a merging of consciousness between the individual and the social group.[13] In Durkheim's study of religion, this form of merged identity developed out of the ritual life of the community that bonded the individual to the culture. In the experience of the descendants, it was often the family environment, rather than religious ritual, that provided a social milieu for the development of a shared consciousness of suffering. Most notably, the descendants reported that their families were particularly drawn to the memory of the Holocaust. A descendant thus described her mother's intense interest in the Holocaust in post–World War II Texas:

> I can remember my mother used to watch World War II movies, and she would make me sit and watch them with her or she would take me to the movies. She'd take me to these movies where they'd show the concentration camps, and she would sit there and weep. And she did not like the German people, which now I understand.

In remembering this aspect of her childhood, the descendant linked her mother's emotional connection to the Holocaust to a deep-seated fear of antisemitism within remnant crypto-Jewish culture. Similarly, another female respondent recalled how her parents made her aware of the dangers of religious persecution:

> When we were growing up, we seldom talked about religion. But we talked a lot about the Spanish Inquisition, we talked a lot about the crusaders, and we talked a lot about the Holocaust. My parents made an absolute point of making it very clear to us what had been done. They felt very passionate, very sorry about all those things that had been done to the Jewish people. And they always sided with them. You know, they were always very compassionate. We would sit down and discuss it. We would discuss all the different things that happened during the Inquisition. They would talk about all the explorers, about the fact that Jewish people had scattered again, were thrown out of Spain. They talked about all the tortures, burnings at the stake, those kinds of things, and the same thing with the Holocaust. It was the same sort of thing. Any time there was a special on the Holocaust, we'd watch it. They'd make a point of making sure we'd watch it.

In constructing links to Jewish ethnicity, descendants drew on these kinds of childhood memories, which provide a glimpse into how identification with Jewish persecution informed families with crypto-Jewish descent. In relation to this identification, descendants speak of "feeling Jewish" in a very deep and personal way that is tied to the experience and the horrors of the Holocaust. A thirty-six-year-old man whose family originated in Cuba described how, as a teenager, he discovered his family's Jewish lineage and soon thereafter began to see himself in the image of the victimized Jew:

> By the time I was thirteen, I was doing a complete study of the Russian revolution, Trotsky, Lenin, communism as we knew it. I was also reading about Zionism and Judaism. I realized that a lot of the communists were Jews and that Stalin tried to get rid of them. Then I learned more about antisemitism, and I started reading about Nazism. I knew plenty about the war. I was into making model planes, and then I started reading about the concentration camps. I read everything I could get my hands on. I don't think there is a book written on the Holocaust that I haven't read. By 1973 I had read them all. That's when it really hit home. It was about me. Even though my family never lived in a ghetto-type situation, I felt it was about me. . . . As I read about all these Sephardic Jews from Rome, Romania, Greece, and Hungary—all Spanish Jews, that was the spark. There wasn't a distinction between one group or one country, you're a Jew and it didn't matter if you were a practicing Jew, it didn't matter if your

> great grandmother was a Jew, anything could have sent you to the camps. That was a spark to me: the entire world tried to kill us. I say the entire world, because even the United States wouldn't open their doors.

For this descendant, the reality of the Holocaust and his own distant connection to the Sephardic Jews who died fostered the construction of a Jewish identity in which the boundaries between nationality and religion were blurred in his growing awareness of the effects of genocide on Jewish survival. As this respondent understood the magnitude of the Holocaust, his identity merged with that of the universal Jew whose history of persecution found its greatest expression in the concentration camps of World War II. Painful emotional responses such as these thus lie at the core of a developing Jewish ethnicity, since Jewish identity is formed around images, memories, and feelings of persecution that are internalized as personal as well as cultural history; and because there are few memorials to the Inquisition per se, it is the public remembrance of the Holocaust through which the descendants both see and experience their connection to the overwhelming reality of violent antisemitism.[14] As one descendant explained:

> I went to the Holocaust Museum in Washington, and I kept thinking, if there had been something like this for the Inquisition, if we had remembered the Inquisition in this way, the Holocaust might never have happened.

The connection among Jewish consciousness, suffering, and ancestral persecution is illustrative of the ways in which ethnicity and race are constructed under conditions of domination and oppression. In his 1940 essay on concepts of race, W. E. B. Du Bois spoke specifically to this aspect of racial identity formation.[15] Drawing on the memory of his fifteenth-century African ancestors, Du Bois wrote:

> Since the fifteenth century these ancestors of mine and their other ancestors have had a common history; have suffered a common disaster and have one long memory. The actual ties of heritage between the individuals of this group, vary with the ancestors that they have in common and many others: Europeans and Semites, perhaps Mongolians, certainly American Indians. But the physical bond is least and the badge of color relatively unimportant save as a badge; the real essence of this kinship is its social heritage of slavery; the discrimination and insult; and this heritage binds together not simply the children of Africa, but extends through yellow Asia and into the South Seas. It is this unity that draws me to Africa.[16]

In this passage from Du Bois's "Concepts of Race," the relationship between ethnic identification and a heritage of oppression is powerfully expressed, illuminating the deep ancestral ties that lie at the heart of a shared ethnic worldview.[17]

Knowledge of an ancestral past of persecution thus creates a trauma-based reality for those engaged in the recovery of Sephardic roots.[18] Through a heightened awareness of ethnic oppression, ancestral history becomes internalized as the descendant's own pain and suffering. These affective responses to hidden ancestry are then brought to bear in the narratives of ethnic recovery, reinforcing the emotional attachment between the descendant and her or his Jewish ethnicity.

## ETHNIC IDENTITY AND THE IDEALIZATION OF JEWISH CULTURE

As the above discussion reveals, an intense emotional awareness of historical oppression is a theme that emerges and reemerges throughout the descendant's self-identification as an ancestral Jew. At the same time, however, the descendants also express a certain pride in the survivorship of the Jewish people, particularly in the face of historical adversity. This is especially evident in their experiences at the Western Wall (see chapter 5), where the physical remains of the Temple engender a sense of spiritual triumph as well as sadness and loss. Thus, while religious persecution underlies the descendant's ethnic alignment with Jewish culture and community, associations with resistance, courage, and resilience also inform the descendant's connection to Jewish ancestry. The descendant's emotional attachment to the Jewish people therefore reflects the complex character of an ethnic alliance that embodies both the memory of tragic loss and the dignity of spiritual survival.

In addition to the strong emotional responses to victimization and survivorship, other cultural signifiers also contribute to the formation of social and psychological alliances between the descendants and the Jews as a distinct ethnic group. Among the most significant of these cultural signifiers is the image of the accomplished and cultured Jew in Western society. The descendants' idealized ideas about Jewish ethnicity are derived, for the most part, from popular impressions and stereotypes of Jewish culture that are heavily influenced by the notion of the Jews as a "model minority." According to this perspective, which is associated with the social theories of the 1960s, Jews represent the ideal type of ethnic group whose successful assimilation is evident in high educational achievement, strong family values, and economic success.[19] While such representations of Jewishness overlook the harsher realities of Jewish family life and economic struggle, the idealized image of Jewish culture has strongly influenced contemporary views of Jewish ethnicity in the United States. Thus, one respondent from northern New Mexico confided:

> I very much like the idea of being Jewish, because, you know, Jewish people are very, very, how should I say, very into the creative fields, very intelligent, very well read, whether or not they are highly educated. And it was a nice feeling to realize that I too was Jewish, because a lot of great people in our Western culture are Jewish.

A deep regard for Jewish culture in general characterized the narratives of the participants who made few distinctions between Ashkenazic and Sephardic ethnicity. Rather, in adopting a Jewish identity, the descendants reenvisioned their families within an idealized image of the "universal" Jewish home where an emphasis on education and the arts prevailed. In particular, the positive stereotype of the scholarly and cultured Jew held great significance for the descendants. A respondent from Texas gave this account of her family's distinctiveness:

> We did not have that much in common with other people I grew up with. Our assimilation with the Anglo culture happened very quickly. They [the family] knew that they had to become educated. My mother's family was very arrogant. There was a great deal of emphasis placed on education. Education is the most important thing, and I feel they kind of judge people by how many degrees they have. . . . So I asked myself, why is education so important to my mother's family? What is it about education that is so important? I think it may have something to do with our Jewish ancestry. When I was younger I wanted to be a scientist. I wanted to know what it was all about. Looking back now, I see how much I thought of Einstein as my mentor. When I took up painting in Europe, I remember the first thing I wanted to do was to paint Einstein. I still have the painting. It was the first thing I ever did. And I remember as I was painting Einstein how much my mother reminded me of Einstein.[20]

Another woman described the legacy of her Jewish ancestry in the following way:

> My parents encouraged music, classical music and an appreciation for literature—literature, education, and music—these were all cultural differences that distinguished my family, and I always thought it was class differences. But now that I know we have this Jewish history, I am thinking maybe that is the connection. Maybe it was because of our Jewish ancestry that these things are important to my family.

Many descendants construed this focus on education as a cultural inheritance from Jewish ancestry. One respondent who grew up in Denver thus describes his mother's emphasis on books and academic achievement:

> I remember how when we were kids, we always had a library at home. And my mother wanted me to be a lawyer so badly, because in Mexico and South America the lawyers were so important, more important than the doctors. And she would bring me books on law and business, and I would bring my friends over and they would say, "Boy, you have a nice library." I said, "Yeah, we do." None of my friends ever had libraries in their homes, and now I correlate that with my Jewish background. Most Jewish homes believe in education and have libraries.

Finally, a female descendant from Mexico spoke of her father's emphasis on education:

> My father pushed education, education, education and, you know, achievement, and work, hard work, and, I mean, all the principles of Judaism. It was such a Jewish home.

Particularly among North American descendants, the high value placed on Jewish cultural ancestry illuminates the sociopolitical forces that influence the self-concept of Latinas/os in the United States. Within the context of immigrant and racial stereotyping, Mexican culture in particular has been characterized as deficient and inferior. Denise Segura and Jennifer Pierce discuss this aspect of cultural socialization among Chicanas/os:

> Chicanas and Chicanos come to maturity as members of a racial and ethnic minority in a social and historical context in which their political, economic, and cultural uniqueness is constantly undermined, denigrated, and violated. Since the annexation of northern Mexico by the United States in 1848, Chicanas and Chicanos have experienced second-class citizenship both politically and economically. Chicanas and Chicanos have faced discrimination in employment, education, and political participation. They have been and continue to be concentrated among the poor and the working class in the United States. [21]

In keeping with Segura and Pierce's analysis, the narratives of the respondents speak to the racism that Mexican American descendants in this study have experienced. A descendant raised in Denver recounted the pervasiveness of racist discrimination in his own life:

> I have lived with racism all my life. As old as I am, racism just gets to be a part of everyday experience. Heck, I remember when as kids we'd be in

> old Denver and there'd be this little greasy spoon, and we'd walk in there, and this guy was the cook and he'd say, "Get out of here, you dirty Mexicans." I remember all that, and when you're young it hurts a lot, but after a while it doesn't faze you. My first year in medical school I was the only Hispanic out of ninety-six students. At the end of four years, maybe three other students would talk to me, and they were the Jewish students. And this was only ten years ago. And I was with these people every day for eight hours a day. We went to the same classes, the same labs, and after a while I got tired of trying to say hi to them when they wouldn't say hi to me. Finally, I thought, if people don't want to talk to you, they don't want to be friendly, as far as I'm concerned they are the ones missing out, not you.

One of the most destructive aspects of racism is the impact that such prejudice can have on the self-image of members of the targeted population who come to see themselves through the eyes of the dominant culture. Fanon was one of the first postcolonial theorists to address this psychological phenomenon, drawing on his own experience as an African Caribbean psychiatrist at the end of the French colonial era.[22] More than two decades later, Daniel Boyarin and Sander Gilman[23] expanded on Fanon's observations in their work on internalized antisemitism and the creation of what Boyarin refers to as the "colonized psyche," that is, the "internalized self contempt" that characterizes disempowered racial and ethnic minorities.[24]

The struggle to come terms with the sociopsychological ramifications of racism within the Mexican American community has been poignantly and powerfully articulated by the writer Cherrie Moraga in her autobiographical work, *Loving in the War Years*. The daughter of a Chicana mother and Anglo father, she describes how her "whiteness" offered her a privileged status within the family:

> No one ever quite told me this (that light was right), but I knew that being light was something valued in my family (who were all Chicano, with the exception of my father). In fact, everything about my upbringing (at least what occurred on a conscious level) attempted to bleach me of what color I did have. Although my mother was fluent in it, I was never taught much Spanish at home. I picked up what I did learn from school and from overheard snatches of conversation among my relatives and mother. She often called other lower-income Mexicans "*braceros*" or "wetbacks," referring to herself and family as "a different class of people." And yet, the real story was that my family, too, had been poor (some still are) and farm workers. My mother can remember this in her blood as if it were yesterday. But this is something she would like to forget (and rightfully), for to her, on a basic economic level, being Chicana meant being "less." It was through my mother's desire to protect her children from poverty

> and illiteracy that we became "Anglicized"; the more effectively we could pass in the white world, the better guaranteed our future.[25]

As Moraga's deeply personal account reveals, European culture and ancestry are highly valued within the Mexican American community, since whiteness and assimilation are understood to be fundamental to economic success and social acceptance within the United States. From a cross-cultural historical perspective, Moraga's observations of Mexican American assimilation can be compared to Jewish experience in Europe, colonized North Africa, and the United States. Just as Mexican Americans were forced to disengage from their ethnic culture to successfully assimilate, early-twentieth-century Jewish immigrants responded to similar pressures to Anglicize as they sought upward mobility through identification with white Protestant culture. According to both Karen Brodkin and Riv-Ellen Prell, first- and second-generation immigrant Jews altered their language, dress, speech patterns, and religious culture to reflect the white Protestant ideal of Americanization and to be accepted as whites within a racially stratified culture that discriminated against African Americans and Asian and Mexican immigrant populations.[26]

The critical theorist Albert Memmi explains Jewish identification with white Christian European culture as symptomatic of a colonized people whose own ethnic and religious heritage has been denigrated and undermined.[27] Memmi's insight on Jewish assimilationism derives from his analysis of Tunisian Jewry during the French colonial period. Memmi observed that, confronted with European racism, North African Jews tended to identify with the French colonizers rather than with Tunisian Muslims:

> The Jewish population identified as much with the colonizers as with the colonized. They were undeniably "natives," as they were then called, as near as possible to the Moslems in poverty, language, sensibilities, customs, taste in music, odors and cooking. However, unlike the Moslems, they passionately endeavored to identify themselves with the French. To them the West was the paragon of all civilization, all culture. The Jew turned his back happily on the East. He chose the French language, dressed in the Italian style and joyfully adopted every idiosyncrasy of the Europeans.[28]

The insights on assimilation, immigration, and colonization offered by Memmi, Moraga, Brodkin, and Prell help to explain the crypto-Jewish descendant's desired identification with an image of an idealized Jewish culture that is associated with European origins. As a manifestation of what Brodkin has termed the "whitening" of Jews in the United States, a number of these descendants have reinterpreted their European Spanish origins through a lens of Jewish ethnicity. In her provocative book *How Jews Became White Folks and What That Says About Race in America,* Brodkin argues that before World War II, European immigrants from outside northern Europe were not considered white but were viewed as "other" European ethnic groups of inferior racial heritage.[29] The construction of this ethnic/racial hierarchy began to change in the years immediately following the war when assimilation, economic advancement, and the persistence of racial distinctions between European ethnic groups and people of color recast European ethnics, including Jews, as white Europeans.[30] In the last two decades, as crypto-Jewish descendants have explored and adopted a Jewish cultural identity, it is primarily within the context of white European ethnicity that some individuals have come to understand their Sephardic ancestry. As pointed out in the earlier discussion of difference and isolation, the association of Jewishness with whiteness has led, in some instances, to a reification of the doctrine of "pure origins" among those descendants who equate Jewish ancestry with Spanish colonial heritage.

In contrast to this European emphasis, however, a sizable number of descendants have taken a more multicultural view of their Jewish lineage. These respondents, who identify as mestiza/o or as mixed-race Latinas/os, have voiced concerns about the preoccupation with European heritage and a white cultural bias within the contemporary descendant movement. One descendant worried about the promulgation of elitist attitudes within his own family:

> My daughter grew up in a Chicano neighborhood, a ghetto really, but my son doesn't know this world. I gave him a very Hispanic name for a purpose so that he would always know where he came from. He was going to private school for a while, and he started saying things like, "You know, Dad, some of my cousins are not that smart." And I didn't like that, and I told my wife, "I don't want our son thinking he is better than other Chicanos and start looking down on them." And so I enrolled him in public school.

Descendants from Texas and New Mexico also express a strong connection to Chicana/o ancestry and to Native American heritage, a multiethnic background in which they take a great deal of pride. Many of these respondents participated in the civil rights movements of the 1960s and 1970s and were heavily influenced by the politics of Mexican American identity, as one woman explained:

> I discovered I had a part in the Chicano movement in the late 1960s and early 1970s. How dare the "gringos" try to deprive us of our rights. We got in there and we hustled, because there is one thing about Hispanics, especially about people from our ancestry, we are never going to give the gringo the satisfaction of seeing you defeated—never. That drives you to the ultimate sacrifices, because you are not going to allow them to win! This is what I respect so much about the Chicanos in this country. They said, "Look, you have the freedom to be what you are. Claim it!"

With the recovery of Sephardic roots, some descendants have reframed their political values within a multiethnic perspective that has been broadened to include Jewish secularism as a moral basis for social activism.

## SECULARISM, ETHNICITY, AND JEWISH ETHICS

Throughout the development of Jewish thought and law, rabbinic teachings have stressed the relationship between social actions and religious practice in the observance of Judaism. This perspective on the religious Jew is illuminated in the writings of Hayim Halevy Donin, a rabbi and scholar whose 1972 book *To Be a Jew: A Guide to Jewish Observance in Contemporary Life* devotes a chapter to kindness, charity, and social action as religious values.[31] In his book, Donin draws on the prophetic discourse surrounding the term *tzedakeh,* a Hebrew term that, according to the prophet Isaiah, is meant to convey righteousness. As a Jewish value, the meaning of *tzedakeh* is traced to Genesis, where *tzedakeh* is described as a trait of Abraham that, when acted on by the Jews, will redeem the people of Israel.[32] In the current discourse on Jewish morality, *tzedakeh* has been variously construed as charity, support of the poor and disadvantaged, and/or a moral obligation to end the suffering and oppression of others.[33]

In recent times, a type of secular Judaism has developed out of these religious principles. Within the secularization movement, the definition of a "good Jew" has been expanded to include not only those who rigorously observe beliefs and practices but also those who engage in charitable acts and causes for social justice.[34] In her compelling autobiography, *Deborah, Golda, and Me,* the Jewish feminist author Letty Pogrebin distinguishes between secular Judaism and more traditional notions of Jewish religiosity:

> Having a Jewish identity is not merely about religious pride. It is about deciding each and every day what Jewishness *means* and how I will

> actualize it in my life. Being Jewish-identified doesn't only relate to how I worship, what I eat, whom I marry, or where I live. It finds more concrete expression in my ethical standards, the groups I join, where I give my charitable dollars, my particular way of supporting Israel, how I interact with non-Jews, and how I live my politics. . . .
>
> My identity politics, my way of living "Jewishly," positions me in the prophetic tradition which esteems justice, rather than in the rabbinic tradition which esteems order. [35]

As expressed by Pogrebin, Jewish secular identity is situated within a value system that emphasizes the ethics of social justice and the relationship between personal choice and political action. As such, her views resonate with those of modern crypto-Jewish descendants whose construction of Jewish ethnicity has moral and social overtones. The notion of charity, for example, was identified as a familial trait that originated in the Jewish ethic of social responsibility. Here a female descendant in her midfifties recalls her mother's generosity toward the poor:

> We had a rule in our house that anybody that came to the door was to be treated with kindness, even though the person might be a stranger. If he was hungry we were to feed that person, and my mother kept a plate under the sink, a place setting for any stranger that might come to the door and be hungry. . . . In my heart, I have a feeling that this is part of my mother's family's tradition, the Jewish tradition that a stranger is always to be welcomed and fed. It doesn't mean that you have to embrace him as one of you, but he is to be taken care of, his needs are to be taken care of.

In a somewhat different approach to Jewish ethics, a descendant who was raised in California attributed his growing awareness of interventionist politics to the adoption of a Jewish ethical perspective. Here he describes his reaction to the United States' involvement in Haiti:

> Before studying the ethical foundations of Jewish culture, I probably never would have thought about what's going on in Haiti right now, for example. We've invaded Haiti, for lack of a better word, you know. And I think, well, what would the great rabbis have said about invading another country under the conditions we find ourselves? Allegedly, we've gone into that country because the leaders of that country are abusing and murdering and violating everyone's rights to their own pursuit of happiness. So why are we there? So, right now I haven't seen any good reason why we're there. But if I think about it, if you just take it on an individual level you see someone over there who is being mistreated and being murdered and beaten. As an individual I have the right, the obligation, in fact, the responsibility to try to intervene to prevent any further injury to that person. So if you transfer that principle from an individual to a nation, does that rule still follow? So I wonder, what would be the Jewish

> response? So in that sense I feel a real connection to ethics that have already been written about and discussed.

In another narrative that pertains to a Jewish ethic of responsibility, a descendant from South America explained that, although religiously he does not consider himself a Jew, ethnically he expresses his Judaism through his connection to Jewish political and social values, especially those with a Marxist orientation:

> The more I learned about the Holocaust, also the prior persecutions of Jews in the Iberian peninsula, which I never realized was so intimately connected and a connection that of course fit with my anticapitalism, my antiimperialism, and my critique of the oppressive dimensions of Christianity and Catholicism—it's like everything started coming together—my leftism, my Marxism, and my Jewish roots of Marxism and socialism. . . . So feeling a part of a community of resistors and a community of remembrance and a critique of injustice suffered. . . . [I feel] the commitment not to do unto others the injustices we have suffered as a people.

In light of the descendants' tendency to idealize Jewish culture, it is significant that, while they have forged ethnic alliances along the lines of social ethics and values of social responsibility, such alignments exist in stark contrast to the antisemitic stereotypes that juxtapose the image of the socially conscious and charitable Jew against the representation of the Jew as materialistic and unethical in business. These conflicting and contradictory ideologies are problematic for the descendants, who seek to identify their Jewishness with social activism and compassion. Conspicuously absent from the high esteem with which Jewish culture is held by the descendants is a strong focus on economic success. Rather, the ideals of intellectualism and political justice are more heavily emphasized.[36]

The importance that the descendants place on Jewish social values and cultural achievement is perhaps best understood in relation to the adoption of a stigmatized identity. In emphasizing qualities such as intellectual abilities and social conscience, the descendants diminish the harsher and more negative Jewish stereotypes, thus strengthening the ties to the idealized Jewish community in which they seek membership. In bringing together the pain of the suffering Jewish victim and the accomplishments of the Jewish survivor and achiever, the crypto-Jewish descendants have constructed ethnic alliances in response to personal estrangement, social discrimination, and a deep sense of ethnic loss.

CONCLUSION

# Ethnic Loss and the Future of Crypto-Jewish Culture

Throughout this study of hidden ancestry and the recovery of Sephardic roots, accounts of loss and deprivation characterize descendant narratives as the respondents speak with regret of an unknown family history, a forgotten cultural past, or the absence of an ancestral religious tradition. Their expressions of loss highlight the effects of cultural destruction and forced assimilation on ethnic and racial communities that, although learning to adapt, nonetheless bear the consequences of a cultural genocide that leaves its own deep and lasting impression on the collective psyche of the once-colonized group.

In a self-conscious effort to reverse the effects of generations of denial and Christianization, the descendants of the crypto-Jews seek to embrace an outward ethnic identification that emphasizes rather than obscures their Jewish origins. At the same time, however, the creation of a more public Jewish identity is encumbered by the reality of the vast and irreversible cultural loss that accompanied the forced conversions and religious repression of medieval and premodern Spain and Portugal. Hoping to find their Jewishness in the remnants of Inquisitional Jewish history, the descendants are engaged in a struggle for ethnic recovery that illuminates the difficulties and emotional strains characterizing ethnic revivalism in postgenocide societies.

In these cultures of loss, feelings of anger among later generations give rise to a more politicized view of ethnic trauma and the destruction of an ancestral past. One descendant from Mexico thus spoke of the relationship between fear and the perpetuation of cultural annihilation:

> We have been cheated from that ancestry. We have been cheated from the culture, from the connection. It is so ingrained, and that is the fear we have of the unseen. . . . And you know why we have survived five hundred years? It is because we fought it successfully, haven't we? We have reclaimed our ancestry and our rightful place in the Jewish community.

Another descendant recalled with empathy her ancestors in New Mexico, as she imagined their fear of being discovered as exiled Jews in colonial Spain. In a self-published autobiography, she gives the following account of life in New Mexico, the "land of enchantment" that both protected and deprived those with a crypto-Jewish background:

> The windows to our past are still blurry and we still can't see through the tunnel that has few lights. Oh! Land of Enchantment you have closed your eyes for so many years, when are you going to let my people go? Haven't you done enough with your enchantment and superstitions?
>
> Let's start with our last names they all seem to be Sephardic names. Why have you kept this secret from your children? How else will we know who we are or where we are going if we don't truly know who we are. . . . Oh! Land of Enchantment you had five hundred years to take away our religion our language and our heritage. I must say you almost succeeded.[1]

As this descendant writes of her loss, she questioned why she had been chosen to end the silence and to carry on her family's Jewish heritage. For her, the discovery of her family's secret past carried with it a responsibility for the future, as she as well as other descendants considered the ethical and moral implications of remaining silent about and detached from their Jewish ancestry. The decision both to become Jewish and to end the silence surrounding Jewish ethnicity thus reflected a conscious moral choice on the part of respondents, a small number of whom came to believe that they alone had been chosen by God to reveal the family secret and to reclaim an ancestral Jewish heritage. A descendant from South America thus explained:

> I will have the heart to make this known to my family. But I feel very sad about some of my grandparents, aunts, and uncles. They died without knowing even when they knew they were different than everybody else. They were very spiritual, but they never had time to investigate the past, always working with the ranch, the cattle, or the selling of things. So it is my responsibility. I am the first in my family to come back, and I was the one chosen to tell the others. We are a very close family, and after I came back I held a meeting with 169 people and told them all.

This aspect of culture-bearing embodies the notion of a spiritual calling, the construction of the self as the preserver of a lost and threatened religious tradition. Such responses to suppressed Jewish roots are also found among children and grandchildren of Holocaust survivors, especially within those families that totally rejected Jewish religious practice in the aftermath of World War II. Psychological studies of Holocaust survivors found that in families in which the parents had lost faith in the Jewish religion, the next generation assumed the role of religious teacher and savior:[2]

> This process was particularly well illustrated in the case of Peter Y., whose parents had turned away from religion with the firm belief that it had lost its meaning for them. However, they gave their children a thorough religious education, so that Mr. Y eventually insisted forcefully that his parents adhere to the ritual. . . . It was Peter Y. who assumed the role of the lost rabbi in the family. . . . The belief that losses can be undone leads to a reversal of generations, as exemplified by Peter Y. who successfully imposed on his parents the religious practices that they had consciously abandoned; when he later started to waver in his beliefs, he felt guilty as if he were the first to abandon a tradition.[3]

The sense of personal obligation and responsibility reported by children of Holocaust survivors was also evident among crypto-Jewish descendants who took a somewhat mystical approach to their culture-bearing role. These descendants tended to view themselves as emissaries of God who were responsible for redressing the losses of past generations. A woman raised in Mexico thus believes that her recovery of Sephardic ancestry is part of God's plan:

> When every Jew in the world prays several times a day for the return to Jerusalem, for the rebuilding of the Temple, what are we asking for? I understand it. It means so much—it is so deep in my soul, and it is so alive in my head. To say, okay, you are it. You are going to be the guide. People are going to see you, they are going to hear you. God says, I am just going to use you as an instrument, because that's what the Jews are, all of us. We're instruments. I mean, we have no control over what we do, because all of it is for a reason, it's for a purpose.

Although other descendants were less passionate in their approach, a number of them indicated that they too saw themselves as culture bearers for a lost ethnic and religious heritage. Particularly among the respondents with children and grandchildren, the desire to create and sustain a connection to Jewish culture was especially strong, as the following account suggests:

> It is very important to have a sense of what has happened in the past and knowing what I know and what I feel, I think it is essential that I do this not only for myself but for my children and grandchildren, and, hopefully, it will continue.

Here and elsewhere descendants expressed the hope that their children might choose to become religious Jews as well. A female descendant thus reported that she provides a Jewish home for her children so that they might some day adopt the religion of their ancestors:

> I don't force them to do anything. They do it as they want to. But on Friday night, this table is Shabbat. We light the candles and I'll make a chicken and whatever they want, sometimes spaghetti too, but it's always very special, and then I go to the bakery and we get the challahs, and it's a special time. The children are with me Friday night, and they can't schedule anything from the time I get to the house at 6:00 until at least 9:00; that's family time. And the kids say, "Oh, Mom this dinner tastes so good," and I say, "It's because, you see, it's Shabbat. It is blessed." And periodically they go to services with me, but I don't consider that a necessity because I don't want Judaism to be imposed. I want them to decide for themselves.

A male respondent offered a similar perspective on his relationship with his twenty-year-old son:

> I told my kids about their Jewish background, and we started doing some holidays at home like Chanukah, but I want them to make the decision. In fact, my son, as he is growing up, is leaning more toward Judaism, and he did tell me he was thinking of converting. But I don't push him, because I want him to convert on his own.

The descendants who were raised in Mexico and Latin America were especially conscious of transmitting Jewish cultural history and religious training to their children. Here a mother of four who emigrated from Mexico expressed a sense of pride in the role she played in conveying Jewish values and rituals to her sons and daughters:

> Although in the United States we have succeeded in gaining material success, I think we are in a lot of denial about poverty and fascism and the rise of neo-Nazism. I never let the children forget who they are and where they come from. They have been raised going to synagogue now, and that is the most important thing I have accomplished. . . . One of the requirements and one of the things I did for the religion was to tell my daughters, I don't care who you marry as long as you have chosen a Jew, and you have to tell your children and train the children in their faith.

As illustrated by this narrative, the historical realities of forced conversion, exile, and secrecy together create a consciousness of loss and deprivation reflecting a diaspora worldview that has strengthened the descendants' commitment to preserving Jewish culture and tradition. While for most descendants the trend toward Jewish preservation reflects a willingness and desire to openly engage in Jewish practice and culture, public participation in religious institutions has remained somewhat difficult for a small number of respondents whose families are unsupportive of their shifting religious and ethnic identity. In one such case, a male descendant has reproduced the public/private split of earlier generations of crypto-Jewish descendants. In response to his spouse's objections to their children attending synagogue, the descendant has made his home a place of Jewish awareness and education:

> My wife is very upset about all of this. She says she married a Catholic. She'll tell me to take the boys to church. When I take them, I take a book and I read. I make them kneel down and stand up and do what they're supposed to do. That's their religion. I teach them Judaism at home. I tell them and explain about the historical side. I think in spirituality there is a historical content to everything, and to understand fully you need to know both sides of the story. That's what I teach them, and sometimes the priests get pretty upset because my sons tell them what I say about the Church and how they treated the Jews.

As this and other narratives of cultural persistence illustrate, culture-bearing among the modern descendant population has taken on a less gendered character for the last decade. In a shift from the historical evolution of crypto-Judaism, modern-day commitment to Jewish heritage and tradition is shared by Latino men and Latina women, both of whom have been influenced by the experiences of social isolation, the longing for community, and the moral issues of ethnic identification. That fathers as well as mothers support and encourage their children's Jewish identity is particularly evident in the following narrative of a father whose son had experienced rejection by a Jewish fraternity:

> When my son went to college he tried to get into a Jewish fraternity. That was the only frat he wanted, but the main guy didn't want him and they turned him down. He told me, "Dad, I don't think they wanted me because I am Hispanic." I said, "Don't worry about it, son. Because some of the other kids are really all right, and I'm sure they voted for you." It was just this one guy who didn't want him. I told him to try again next year. I said there is racism everywhere, and anti-Jewish[ness] too, and that he should just do the best he can and not let it bring him down.

It is clear from accounts such as these that the social and psychological effects of marginalization are deeply felt among descendants, who express a strong desire to belong and to seek out communities where they can feel at home, even when the ethnic "home" itself may be divided. This longing for community and social acceptance was perhaps best articulated by one descendant who became part of the small Sephardic community in Dallas:

> It's very interesting, the more I meet Sephardic families and see what they do with their kids and what they do at home and how they treat their spouses and their grandparents and how they pray and celebrate holidays—it's just amazing because I feel like it's home. I don't know how to explain it; there is a sense of belonging that is very soothing. When you talk about the psychological impact of knowing who you are, the concept of a marginal person, where you never really fit anywhere. You're looking for that merging of your personality and your ancestral mind.

In internalizing and reclaiming Jewish ancestry, the descendants are creating emotional, social, and spiritual alliances that establish desired links between a history of hidden ethnicity and a present-day association with Jewish culture and tradition. The reclamation of Jewish spirituality and the attending identification with Jewish ethnicity are indicative of a larger cultural trend in which the reinvention of the ethnic and religious self reflects the shifting socioreligious identities of post-Inquisition, postcolonial, and post-Holocaust societies. Through a commitment to cultural preservation and transmission, the descendants are contributing to the revival of a specifically Latina/o Jewish ethnicity that has come to define a new generation of Spanish-origin Jews who wish to sustain their ties to the past as they embrace a Jewish identity for the future.

Returning to the themes and insights that have been elaborated throughout this book, the study of modern crypto-Jewish descent provides an important lens through which to consider the ongoing effects of social stigma and alienation on marginalized populations in the United States and elsewhere. For Jewish culture in particular, the findings of my research offer a unique perspective through which to view the trauma of ethnic and religious violence as these forms of antisemitism affect the desire for secrecy and assimilation over multiple generations of descendants. Finally, this book has revealed the way in which women in endangered communities, specifically Latina women, have negotiated the demands for acculturation while creating opportunities for cultural preservation. Ultimately, it is through the ritual lives of women that the recovery of hidden ancestry has been made possible for descendants who believe that they and their families have suffered the losses created by ethnic and religious assimilation.

# Notes

## INTRODUCTION

1. See Martin A. Cohen and Abraham J. Peck, eds., *Sephardim in the Americas* (Tuscaloosa: University of Alabama Press, 1993); and Ruth B. Waxman and Bodoff Lippman, eds., "The Expulsion from Spain: A Symposium," parts 1 and 2, *Judaism* 41, nos. 162–63 (1992).

2. The term *Sephardic* is an Anglicized adjective that derives from the word *Sepharad,* the Hebrew term for Spain. It is used to describe the descendants of the medieval Spanish Jews, who created their own distinct culture within Muslim and Christian Spain that was characterized by, among other distinctions, the use of Ladino, a medieval Sephardic language. *Sephardim,* the plural form, refers to Spanish-origin Jews. Although in today's terminology, the word *Sephardic* has sometimes been used to designate Jews from the Middle East, the term *Mizrahi* is the more accurate descriptor for Jewish communities from North Africa and the Middle East who never emigrated to Spain or other parts of the world. Jews from Central and Eastern Europe, by comparison, are known as Ashkenazic or the Ashkenazim.

3. Before 1992 there had been previous media coverage of crypto-Jewish descendants. The commemoration acknowledgments, however, created a greater public awareness of this phenomenon. In 1988, National Public Radio broadcast the first of three programs on "The Hidden Jews of New Mexico." Two other programs followed in 1992 and 1995, which were directed by Nan Rubin and produced by Benjamin Shapiro.

4. The term *Latina/o,* designating both female and male, will be used throughout the study to describe the ethnicity of the descendant population. Some participants in the study self-identified as Chicano/a (Mexican American) and others as Hispanic (having Spanish ancestry). As applied here, the term *Latina/o* encompasses both these ethnic categories.

5. Historically, the term *Marrano* was used for crypto-Jews throughout Europe. Hence much of the historical literature on crypto-Judaism refers to secret Jews as Marranos and to the practice of crypto-Judaism as Marranism. Although the exact etymology of the word is unknown, an early-twentieth-century monograph by Arturo Finelli, *Marrano, storia di un vituperio* (Marrano, history of disgrace)(Geneva 1925), suggests that this term was a pejorative label that was derived from the word for swine. Although some descendants still self-identify as Marrano, because of the negative connotation of the label, other terms such as *anusim* (the Hebrew word for forced converts) or *conversos* (the Spanish word for converts) are generally preferred by modern descendants. The scholarship in the field has increasingly adopted the term *crypto-Jew* to refer to secret Jews, using the term *converso* only in relation to those Jews who truly converted to Christianity and retained no connection to Judaism. Throughout this study, the term *crypto-Jew* will be used to refer to converts who preserved some hidden aspects of Judaism in the centuries after the forced conversions in Spain and Portugal.

6. This is a period of time when Jewish culture and thought flourished in Andalusia—the tenth and eleventh centuries.

7. In the fifteenth and sixteenth centuries, the Ottoman Empire encouraged the exiled Iberian Jews to settle in Turkey. For a discussion of the Jewish expulsion and the Ottoman Empire, see Jane S. Gerber, *The Jews of Spain: A History of the Sephardic Experience* (New York: Free Press, 1992).

8. Yitzhak Baer, *A History of the Jews in Christian Spain,* 2 vols. (Philadelphia: Jewish Publication Society, 1966); David M. Gitlitz, *Secrecy and Deceit: The Religion of the Crypto-Jews* (Philadelphia: Jewish Publication Society, 1996).

9. Baer, *History of the Jews;* Gitlitz, *Secrecy and Deceit..*

10. Jose Faur, *In the Shadow of History: Jews and Conversos at the Dawn of Modernity* (Albany: State University of New York Press, 1992); Gitlitz, *Secrecy and Deceit.*

11. Baer, *History of the Jews,* 2: 324.

12. Baer, *History of the Jews,* vol. 2; Henry Charles Lea, *A History of the Inquisition of Spain,* vol. 1 (New York: Macmillan, 1906–8).

13. Baer, *History of the Jews,* vol. 2.

14. Baer, *History of the Jews,* 2: 327.

15. Lea, *History of the Inquisition,* 95.

16. Gitlitz, *Secrecy and Deceit,* 626.

17. Although large numbers of Jews did convert during this period, a portion of the Spanish Jews chose martyrdom or risked further persecution by their refusal to become Christians. It was the surviving population of Sephardic Jews that was ultimately expelled from Spain in 1492.

18. Gitlitz, *Secrecy and Deceit.*

19. Gitlitz, *Secrecy and Deceit.*

20. Yosef Haymin Yerushalmi, *From Spanish Court to Italian Ghetto: Isaac Cardoso: A Study in Seventeenth-Century Marranism and Jewish Apologetics* (New York: Columbia University Press, 1971); Benzion Netanyahu, *The Origins of the Inquisition in Fifteenth Century Spain* (New York: Random House, 1995).

21. Baer, *History of the Jews;* Gerber, *Jews of Spain.*

22. Gitlitz, *Secrecy and Deceit;* Eva Alexandra Uchmany, "The Crypto-Jews in New Spain During the First Years of Colonial Life, " *Proceedings of the Sixth World Congress of Jewish Studies* 2 (1977): 95–109, and "The Periodization of the History of the New Christians and Crypto-Jews in Spanish America," in *New Horizons in Sephardic Studies,* ed. Y. Stillman and G. Zucker (New York: State University of New York Press, 1993), 109–47.

23. Gitlitz, *Secrecy and Deceit.*

24. Officially, the Tribunal of the Holy Office was prohibited from prosecuting cases of Indian heresy. However, Native Americans were subject to the persecutions and punishments of the Inquisition through an alternative institution that was variously called the Office of Provisor of Nature, Tribunal of the Faith of Indians, Secular Inquisition Vicarage of the Indians, and Natives' Court. For a more complete discussion of Indians and the Inquisition, see Richard E. Greenleaf, *The Mexican Inquisition of the Sixteenth Century* (Albuquerque: University of New Mexico Press, 1969); and Roberto Moreno de los Arcos, "New Spain's Inquisition of Indians from the Sixteenth to the Nineteenth Century," in *Cultural Encounters: The Impact of the Inquisition in Spain and the New World,* ed. M. E. Perry and A. J. Cruz (Berkeley and Los Angeles: University of California Press, 1991), 23–36.

25. Seymour Liebman, *The Jews in New Spain: Faith, Flame, and the Inquisition* (Coral Gables, Fla.: University of Miami Press, 1970); Arnold Wiznitzer, "Crypto-Jews in Mexico During the Sixteenth Century," *American Jewish Historical Quarterly* 51 (1962): 168–214.

26. Gitlitz, *Secrecy and Deceit;* Stanley Mark Hordes, "The Inquisition and the Crypto-Jewish Community in Colonial Spain and New Mexico," in *Cultural Encounters,* ed. Perry and Cruz, 207–17.

27. Hordes, "The Inquisition and the Crypto-Jewish Community"; Robert Ferry, "The Blancas: Women, Honor, and the Jewish Community in Seventeenth-Century Mexico" (forthcoming).

28. Hordes, "The Inquisition and the Crypto-Jewish Community," 214.

29. David M. Gitlitz, "Nexos entre los CriptoJudios Coloniales y Contemporaneos," *Revista de Humanidades: Tecnológico de Monterrey (Mexico)* 5 (1998): 187–209.

30. Gitlitz, *Secrecy and Deceit;* Renee Levine Melammed, *Heretics or Daughters of Israel?: The Crypto-Jewish Women of Castile* (New York: Oxford University Press, 1999).

31. Samuel Schwarz, "The Crypto-Jews of Portugal," *Menorah Journal* 12 (1926): 138–49, 283–97, 325, reprinted in *Shofar: An Interdisciplinary Journal of Jewish Studies* 18, no. 1 (1999): 40–64.

32. The following represent the recent research on the existence of modern crypto-Judaism: Tomas Atencio, "Crypto-Jewish Remnants in Manito Society and Culture," *Jewish Folklore and Ethnology Review* 18, nos. 1–2 (1996): 59–67; David Augusto Canelo, *The Last Crypto Jews of Portugal* (Portland, Ore.: IJS, 1990); Schulamith C. Halevy, "Manifestations of Crypto-Judaism in the American Southwest," *Jewish Folklore and Ethnography Review* 18, nos. 1–2 (1996): 68–76, and "Jewish Practices Among the Anusim," *Shofar: An Inter-*

*disciplinary Journal of Jewish Studies* 18, no. 1 (1999): 80–99; Frances Hernandez, "The Secret Jews of the Southwest," in *Sephardim in the Americas,* ed. Cohen and Peck, 41–54; Seth Kunin, "Juggling Jewish Identities Among the Crypto-Jews of the American Southwest," *Religion* 31 (2001): 41–61; Carlos Montalvo Larralde, "Chicano Jews in South Texas" (Ph.d. diss., University of California at Los Angeles, 1978); David Nidel, "Modern Descendants of Conversos in New Mexico," *Western States Jewish History* 16, no. 3 (1984): 249–63; Roger Parks, "The Survival of Judeo-Spanish Cultural and Linguistic Traits Among Descendants of Crypto-Jews in New Mexico" (master's thesis, University of New Mexico, 1988); Dan Ross, *Acts of Faith: A Journey to the Fringes of Jewish Identity* (New York: St. Martin's Press, 1982); Richard Santos, "Chicanos of Jewish Descent in Texas," *Western States Jewish Historical Quarterly* 15, no. 4 (1983): 289–333; Henry Tobias, *A History of the Jews in New Mexico* (Albuquerque: University of New Mexico Press, 1990).

33. Intermarriage was reported by Mexican descendants living in Monterrey and among early-twentieth-century descendant populations in New Mexico. In these cases, descendants report that families knew of other families with crypto-Jewish backgrounds and that marriage among these families was encouraged.

34. In recent years a Marrano synagogue has been established in Brazil, and a Society for the Study of Marranismo was founded in São Paulo.

35. Gitlitz, "Nexos entre los CriptoJudios Coloniales y Contemporaneos"; Judith Neulander, "The Crypto-Jewish Canon: Choosing to be 'Chosen' in Millennial Tradition," *Jewish Folklore and Ethnology Review* 18, nos. 1–2 (1996): 19–59; David Mayer Gradwohl, "On Vestiges and Identities: Some Thoughts on the Controversy Concerning 'Crypto-Jews' in the American Southwest," *Jewish Folklore and Ethnology Review* 18, nos. 1–2 (1996): 83–84; Kunin, "Juggling Jewish Identities"; Seth Ward, "Converso Descendants in the U.S. Southwest: A Report on Research, Resources, and the Changing Search for Identity," in *Proceedings of the 1998 Conference of the European Association for Jewish Studies,* ed. A. Saenz-Badillos (Leiden: E. J. Brill, 1999), 677–86.

36. Karen McCarthy Brown, "On Feminist Methodology," *Journal of Feminist Studies in Religion* 1 (1985): 76–79; Ruth Behar and Deborah A. Gordon, eds., *Women Writing Culture* (Berkeley and Los Angeles: University of California Press, 1995); Shulamit Reinharz, with Lynn Davidman, *Feminist Methods in Social Research* (New York: Oxford University Press, 1992).

37. Reinharz, *Feminist Methods.*

38. Neulander, "Crypto-Jewish Canon."

39. An interesting parallel can be found among a portion of second- and third-generation Holocaust survivors who were raised as Christians and, after discovering their families' origins, have chosen to maintain a distance between themselves and their Jewish heritage. This phenomenon has become increasingly apparent not only in the post-Holocaust societies of Eastern Europe but also among some survivor families in the United States. In some instances, children of survivors have sought to end the secrecy surrounding their family's persecution, but their efforts to be more open have been met with resistance from those who lived through the horrors of the war. For an interesting and insightful

memoir on hidden Jewishness in post-Holocaust culture, see Helen Fremont, *After Long Silence* (New York: Delacorte Press, 1999).

## 1. SECRECY AND THE DANGERS OF JEWISHNESS

1. Kurt H. Wolff, *The Sociology of Simmel* (Glencoe, Ill.: Free Press, 1950), 330.

2. Wolff, *Sociology of Simmel*, 330.

3. Frantz Fanon, *Black Skin, White Masks: The Experiences of a Black Man in a White World*, trans. Charles Lam Markmann (New York: Grove Press, 1967); Jules Isaac, *The Teaching of Contempt: Christian Roots of Anti-Semitism*, trans. Helen Weaver (New York: Holt, Rinehart and Winston, 1964); Rosemary Radford Ruether, *Faith and Fratricide: The Theological Roots of Anti-Semitism* (New York: Seabury Press, 1974).

4. Isaac, *Teaching of Contempt;* Ruether, *Faith and Fratricide.*

5. Ruether, *Faith and Fratricide*, 117.

6. Ruether, *Faith and Fratricide*, 200.

7. Frederic Cople Jaher, *A Scapegoat in the New Wilderness: The Origins and Rise of Anti-Semitism in America* (Cambridge, Mass.: Harvard University Press, 1994); Sanford Shepard, "The Present State of the Ritual Crime in Spain," in *The Blood Libel Legend: A Casebook of Anti-Semitic Folklore*," ed. A. Dundes (Madison: University of Wisconsin Press, 1991), 162–77.

8. Claudine Fabre-Vassas, *The Singular Beast: Jews, Christians and the Pig*, trans. Carol Volk (New York: Columbia University Press, 1997), 131.

9. More that one hundred years after the La Guardia case ended, blood libel against the Jews was reintroduced into Spanish culture by the literary figure Lope de Vega. His seventeenth-century drama *El Niño Inocente de La Guardia* provided a dramaturgical representation of the La Guardia case that served to justify both the actions of the Inquisition and the Jewish expulsion from Spain during the same period. For a further discussion of Jews and blood libel, see Fabre-Vassas, *Singular Beast;* David M. Gitlitz, *Secrecy and Deceit: The Religion of the Crypto-Jews* (Philadelphia: Jewish Publication Society, 1996); and Shepard, "Present State of the Ritual Crime," ed. Dundes.

10. Gitlitz, *Secrecy and Deceit.*

11. Yitzhak Baer, *A History of the Jews in Christian Spain*, 2 vols. (Philadelphia: Jewish Publication Society, 1966).

12. Baer, *History of the Jews*, 288–89.

13. Ann Lewellyn Barstow, *Witchcraze* (San Francisco: HarperCollins, 1994); Gitlitz, *Secrecy and Deceit.*

14. Although the Toledo law was eventually repealed, similar laws were put into place in other regions of Spain throughout the fifteenth and sixteenth centuries. These laws regulated membership and employment in guilds, universities, military units, and religious orders. For a discussion of the blood statutes, see John Edwards, "The Beginnings of a Scientific Theory of Race," in *From Iberia to Diaspora: Studies in Sephardic History and Culture*, ed. Y. K. Stillman and N. A. Stillman (Boston: Brill, 1999), 179–96.

15. Jane S. Gerber, *The Jews of Spain: A History of the Sephardic Experience* (New York: Free Press, 1992), 127.

16. The last recorded case of the Inquisition in Mexico was in 1811. In that case, Padre Jose Maria Hildago y Costilla was charged with heresy, apprehended, and then shot. Among Hildago y Costilla's crimes were Judaizing and calling into question the veracity of the immaculate conception. See Richard E. Greenleaf, *The Mexican Inquisition of the Sixteenth Century* (Albuquerque: University of New Mexico Press, 1966).

17. David Sheinin and Lois Baer Barr, eds., *The Jewish Diaspora in Latin America: New Studies on History and Literature* (New York: Garland Publishing, 1996).

18. *Omega,* April 4, 1934, as cited in Laura Pérez Rosales, "Anticardenismo and Anti-semitism in Mexico, 1934–1940," in *Jewish Diaspora,* ed. Sheinin and Barr, 192.

19. Judith Laikin Elkin, "Colonial Origins of Contemporary Anti-Semitism in Latin America," in *Jewish Diaspora,* ed. Sheinin and Barr, 127.

20. Carlos Montalvo Larralde, "Chicano Jews in South Texas" (Ph.d. diss., University of California at Los Angeles, 1978).

21. Denise A. Segura and Jennifer L. Pierce, "Chicana/o Family Structure and Gender Personality: Chodorow, Familism, and Psychoanalytic Sociology Revisited," *Signs: Journal of Women in Culture and Society* 19, no. 1 (1993): 62–91.

22. For a discussion of passing as a strategy for stigmatized populations, see Erving Goffman, *Stigma: Notes on the Management of Spoiled Identity* (New York: Jason Aronson, 1974), 73–91.

23. Donna Meryl Goldstein, "Re-Imagining the Jew in Hungary: The Reconstruction of Ethnicity Through Political Affiliation," in *Rethinking Nationalism and Ethnicity: The Struggle for Meaning and Order in Europe,* ed. H. Wicker (New York: Oxford, 1997), 207–8.

24. Daniel Boyarin, "Epater L'embourgeoisement: Freud, Gender and the Decolonized Psyche," *diacritics* 24 (1994): 17–41; Sander Gilman, *Jewish Self-Hatred: Anti-Semitism and the Hidden Language of the Jews* (Baltimore: Johns Hopkins University Press, 1986); Dennis Klein, *Jewish Origins of the Psychoanalytic Movement* (Chicago: University of Chicago Press, 1985).

25. Gilman, *Jewish Self-Hatred,* 270.

26. Ashkenazic Jews are non-Spanish-origin Jews from Western and Eastern Europe.

27. Riv-Ellen Prell, *Fighting to Become Americans: Jews, Gender and the Anxiety of Assimilation* (Boston: Beacon Press, 1999).

28. Prell, *Fighting to Become Americans,* 53.

29. Prell, *Fighting to Become Americans;* Evelyn Torton Beck, "From 'Kike' to 'JAP': How Misogyny, Anti-Semitism, and Racism Construct the 'Jewish American Princess,'" in *Race, Class and Gender: An Anthology,* ed. M. L. Andersen and P. H. Collins (Belmont, Calif.: Wadsworth Publishing, 1992), 88–95.

30. Norman Kleeblatt, "'Passing' into Multiculturalism," in *Too Jewish?: Challenging Traditional Identities,* ed. N. Kleeblatt (New Brunswick, N.J.: Rut-

gers University Press, 1996), 1–38; Jay Geller, "The Godfather of Psychoanalysis: Circumcision, Antisemitism, Homosexuality, and Freud's 'Fighting Jew,'" *Journal of the American Academy of Religion* 67, no. 2 (1999): 355–85.

31. Kleeblatt, "'Passing' into Multiculturalism," 13.

32. From a somewhat different point of view, Jay Geller explains the nose as a signifier of Jewish ethnicity within the framework of psychoanalytic theory. Here the nose is identified with the penis. See Jay Geller, "'A Glance at the Nose': Freud's Inscription of Jewish Difference," *American Imago* 49, no. 4 (1992): 427–44, and "(G)nos(e)ology: The Cultural Construction of the Other," in *People of the Body: Jews and Judaism from an Embodied Perspective*, ed. H. Eilberg-Schwartz (Albany: State University of New York Press, 1992), 243–82.

33. Kleeblatt, "'Passing' into Multiculturalism."

34. Segura and Pierce, "Chicana/o Family Structure and Gender Personality," 62–91.

35. Philip Goodman, *The Hanukkah Anthology* (Philadelphia: Jewish Publication Society of America, 1976), 52.

36. Goodman, *Hanukkah Anthology,* 55.

37. The word *chuetas* (or *xuetas*) derives from a Catalan word *jueta,* meaning "little Jew." For a further explanation, see Fabre-Vassas, *Singular Beast,* 120–24.

38. Fabre-Vassas, *Singular Beast,* 120–21.

39. Fabre-Vassas, *Singular Beast,* 120–21.

40. This refers to a Jewish mourning custom wherein, after the death of an immediate family member, the mirrors in the home are covered.

41. David Gitlitz reports that a deathbed return to Judaism and requests for Jewish funeral rites were common among medieval converts who feared for their salvation, particularly if they had adopted the Christian belief of an afterlife. See Gitlitz, *Secrecy and Deceit.*

42. Maurice Halbwachs, *On Collective Memory,* trans. Lewis A. Coser (Chicago: University of Chicago Press, 1992).

43. Halbwachs, *On Collective Memory,* 59.

44. Emma Montoya, "New Mexico's Sephardim: Uncovering Jewish Roots," *La Herencia del Norte* (winter 1996): 9–12.

## 2. WOMEN AND THE PERSISTENCE OF CULTURE

1. Abigail Dyer and Richard Kagan, *Inquisitional Inquiries: Involuntary Autobiographies* (Baltimore: Johns Hopkins University Press, forthcoming). Dyer and Kagan cite the seventeenth-century case of Francisco de San Antonio, alias Abram Ruben, in whose possession was found a hidden Hebrew alphabet and who confessed to instructing other crypto-Jews in the "Law of Moses."

2. Renee Levine Melammed, "The Ultimate Challenge: Safeguarding the Crypto-Jewish Heritage," *Proceedings of the American Academy of Religion* 53 (1985): 91–109, "Sephardi Women in the Medieval and Early Modern Period," in *Jewish Women in Historical Perspective,* ed J. R. Raskin (Detroit: Wayne State University Press, 1991), 115–34, "Women in (Post-1492) Spanish Crypto-Jewish Society: Conversos and the Perpetuation and Preservation of Obser-

vances Associated with Judaism," *Judaism* 41 (1992): 156–68, *Heretics or Daughters of Israel?: The Crypto-Jewish Women of Castile* (New York: Oxford University Press, 1999); and Arnold Wiznitzer, "Crypto-Jews in Mexico During the Sixteenth Century," *American Jewish Historical Quarterly* 51 (1962): 168–214, and "Crypto-Jews in Mexico During the Seventeenth Century," *American Jewish Historical Quarterly* 51 (1962): 222–68.

3. Cecil Roth, *A History of the Marranos* (Philadelphia: Jewish Publication Society, 1932), 175.

4. I. S. Revah, "Les Marranes Portugais et l'Inquisition au XVIe Siecle," in *The Sephardic Heritage,* ed. R. D. Barnett (London: Vallentine, Mitchell, 1971), 520, as cited in Moshe Lazar, "Scorched Parchments and Tortured Memories: The 'Jewishness' of the Anussim (Crypto-Jews)," in *Cultural Encounters: The Impact of the Inquisition in Spain and the New World,* ed. M. E. Perry and A. J. Cruz (Berkeley and Los Angeles: University of California Press, 1991), 179; for an example of Inquisition testimony that supports Revah's views on women withholding their ritual practices from their husbands, see David M. Gitlitz, *Secrecy and Deceit: The Religion of the Crypto- Jews* (Philadelphia: Jewish Publication Society, 1996), 221.

5. Melammed, *Heretic or Daughters of Israel?*

6. Melammed, *Heretics or Daughters of Israel?,* 166.

7. Melammed, *Heretics or Daughters of Israel?,* 32.

8. Melammed, *Heretics or Daughters of Israel?,* 32.

9. Seymour Liebman, *The Jews in New Spain: Faith, Flame, and the Inquisition* (Coral Gables, Fla.: University of Miami Press, 1970); Wiznitzer, "Crypto-Jews in Mexico During the Sixteenth Century" and "Crypto-Jews in Mexico During the Seventeenth Century."

10. Luis de Carvajal Jr. is well known for his arrest and trials by the Inquisition in 1589 and from 1595 to 1596. He was a prolific writer, and before his execution by the Church, he wrote an autobiography and a last will and testament that provide insight into his spiritual and religious life and conscience. For a discussion of Carvajal's memoirs, see Donald Capps and Walter H. Capps, *The Religious Personality* (Belmont, Calif.: Wadsworth Publishing, 1970), 116–26.

11. Wiznitzer, "Crypto-Jews in Mexico During the Sixteenth Century," 184.

12. Wiznitzer, "Crypto-Jews in Mexico During the Sixteenth Century," 184.

13. Wiznitzer, "Crypto-Jews in Mexico During the Sixteenth Century," 184.

14. The Shema is the Jewish prayer that is part of every religious service and is also recited nightly by observant Jews. The prayer begins with the word *shema,* which means, "hear." The rest of the prayer translates from the Hebrew as, "Hear, O Israel, the Lord our God, the Lord is One." The prayer derives from Deuteronomy 6:4–9 and 11:13–21 and Numbers 15:37–41.

15. Liebman, *Jews in New Spain;* and Wiznitzer, "Crypto-Jews in Mexico During the Sixteenth Century."

16. The term *reconciled* refers to "returning" to the Church after the accused confessed to heresy. Doña Francisca and her children, like most others who were arrested by the Inquisition, eventually confessed and repented.

17. The auto-da-fé was a public ceremony in which the accused was sentenced and in which, if condemned to die, he or she would be put to death. The

secular authorities, who were charged with executing those who refused to confess and repent, offered the condemned a choice. If the prisoner agreed to publicly recant her or his Judaism, she or he would be allowed to die by the less painful method of strangulation before being burned at the stake. If the prisoner refused to recant, then she or he would be burned at the stake. Many of the condemned, including the members of the Carvajal family, thus chose to recant. In recanting, the prisoner would be forced to embrace the cross and recite a Catholic prayer before being put to death. For a more complete discussion of this aspect of Inquisition history, see Wiznitzer, "Crypto-Jews in Mexico During the Sixteenth Century."

18. Wiznitzer, "Crypto-Jews in Mexico During the Sixteenth Century," and "Crypto-Jews in Mexico During the Seventeenth Century."

19. Cyrus Adler, ed., *Trial of Gabriel de Granada by the Inquisition in Mexico 1642–1645,* trans. David Fergusson (Baltimore: Friedenwald, 1899), 12–13.

20. Robert Ferry's "The Blancas: Women, Honor, and the Jewish Community in Seventeenth Century Mexico" focuses specifically on the women of the Enriquez family who were arrested and tried during the 1640s.

21. Rachel Biale, *Women and Jewish Law: An Exploration of Women's Issues in Halakhic Sources* (New York: Schocken Books, 1984).

22. Ferry, "Blancas."

23. Gitlitz, *Secrecy and Deceit;* Melammed, *Heretics or Daughters of Israel?;* Liebman, *Jews in New Spain;* Roth, *History of the Marranos.*

24. Frances Hernandez, "The Secret Jews of the Southwest," in *Sephardim in the Americas,* ed. M. Cohen and A. Peck (Tuscaloosa: University of Alabama Press, 1993), 423.

25. David Augusto Canelo, *The Last Crypto-Jews of Portugal* (Portland, Ore.: IJS, 1990); Levine Melammed, *Heretics or Daughters of Israel?*

26. Canelo, *Last Crypto-Jews of Portugal,* 72.

27. Melammed, *Heretics or Daughters of Israel?*

28. James C. Scott, *Domination and the Arts of Resistance: Hidden Transcripts* (New Haven: Yale University Press, 1990).

29. Albert Raboteau, *Slave Religion: The "Invisible Institution" in the Antebellum South* (New York: Oxford University Press, 1978).

30. Other studies of ritual persistence identify the survival of Jewish mourning rites (dressing the deceased in a shroud, covering the mirrors in the home during the mourning period, and placing stones on the grave). For a discussion of these rites, see Schulamith Halevy, "Manifestations of Crypto-Judaism in the American Southwest," *Jewish Folklore and Ethnography Review* 18, nos. 1–2 (1996): 68–76; Hernandez, "Secret Jews of the Southwest"; and Richard Santos, "Chicanos of Jewish Descent in Texas," *Western States Jewish Historical Quarterly* 15, no. 4 (1983): 289–333. Among this study's population of descendants, five individuals reported the presence of these customs in their families. In addition, two respondents described what appear to be remnants of the observance of Sukkoth, originally a Jewish agricultural holiday that followed the Jewish New Year. During Sukkoth, a shelter is constructed with products from the earth such as branches and wood. Traditionally, families ate and even slept in the

sukkah booth over the seven-day period of observance. One respondent from South America described a fall festival, when her family would enter the woods and hold a harvest feast under a wooden structure each year.

31. Biale, *Women and Jewish Law.*

32. Leviticus 15:19.

33. Biale, *Women and Jewish Law,* 147.

34. Gitlitz, *Secrecy and Deceit;* Levine Melammed, *Heretics or Daughters of Israel?*

35. Haim Beinart, *Conversos on Trial: The Inquisition in Ciudad Real* (Jerusalem: Magnes, 1981).

36. Renee Levine (Melammed), "Women in Spanish Crypto-Judaism: 1492–1520" (Ph.D. diss., Brandeis University, 1982), 192.

37. Levine (Melammed), "Women in Spanish Crypto-Judaism," 193.

38. Levine (Melammed), "Women in Spanish Crypto-Judaism," 195.

39. Gitlitz, *Secrecy and Deceit,* 273.

40. Halevy, "Manifestations of Crypto-Judaism in the American Southwest."

41. Gitlitz, *Secrecy and Deceit,* 210.

42. Gitlitz, *Secrecy and Deceit;* Levine Melammed, *Heretics or Daughters of Israel?*; Liebman, *Jews in New Spain.*

43. Hernandez, "Secret Jews of the Southwest"; Santos, "Chicanos of Jewish Descent in Texas."

44. While some historians suggest that keeping milk and meat separate is characteristic of Spanish-origin Jews living in northern Mexico and the Southwest of the United States, others such as David Gitlitz maintain that there is little or no evidence that this dietary practice was observed by Sephardic Jews on the Iberian peninsula. Gitlitz therefore maintains that it is unlikely that this custom would have become part of Sephardic or crypto-Jewish culture in the Americas. For a discussion of the controversies surrounding remnant crypto-Jewish rituals, see David M. Gitlitz, "Nexos entre los CriptoJudios Coloniales y Contemporaneos," *Revista de Humanidades: Tecnológico de Monterrey (Mexico)* 5 (1998): 187–209.

45. It is of interest to note that at a seventeenth-century Inquisition trial in Mexico, Isabel de Rivera reported that Jews were prohibited from eating pork because the pig was a metamorphosed human being (see Wiznitner, "Crypto-Jews in Mexico During the Seventeenth Century"). This interpretation appears to derive from Christian parables that cast the Jew as the pig in fables of metamorphosis. One version of the story, from Claudine Fabre-Vassas, *The Singular Beast: Jews, Christians and the Pig,* trans. Carol Volk (New York: Columbia University Press, 1997), 93, goes as follows:

> The pig used to be a Jew. When the Lord walked the earth the Jews asked him one day to guess what was found beneath two tubs; under one was hidden a Jew and his children, under the other a sow and her piglets. Jesus responded by reversing them: "Here there is a sow and her piglets; there a Jew and her children." The Jews laughed at him for guessing wrong. But when they raised the tubs, the Jewess had become a sow with her piglets and the sow a Jewess with her children. Ever since then, Jews don't eat pork.

46. Mary Douglas, *Purity and Danger: An Analysis of Concepts of Pollution and Taboo* (New York: Routledge, 1966).

47. Yitzhak Baer, *A History of the Jews in Christian Spain,* vol. 2 (Philadelphia: Jewish Publication Society, 1966).

48. Baer, *History of the Jews in Christian Spain,* 137.

49. Baer, *History of the Jews in Christian Spain,* 132.

50. Leviticus 16:29–30.

51. Inquisition Archives, Testimony of Beatriz Enríquez, November 1642, translated by Robert Ferry.

52. Liebman, *Jews in New Spain,* 63

53. Canelo, *Last Crypto Jews of Portugal;* Liebman, *Jews in New Spain;* Roth, *History of the Marranos.*

54. Esther 7:2–4.

55. Gitlitz, *Secrecy and Deceit.*

56. Gitlitz, *Secrecy and Deceit.*

57. Roth reports that at least one young girl died as a result of a prolonged fast during the observance of this holy day period. See *History of the Marranos,* 188.

58. Crypto-Jews had access to the Apocrypha, which was included in the Christian Bible and held special importance for the converts. See Marc D. Angel, *Voices in Exile: A Study in Sephardic Intellectual History* (Hoboken, N.J.: KTAV Publishing House, 1991).

59. Apocrypha: 676–77.

60. Canelo, *Last Crypto-Jews of Portugal.*

61. Canelo, *Last Crypto-Jews of Portugal,* 79.

62. Liebman, *Jews in New Spain.*

63. Elizabeth Alvilda Petroff, ed., *Medieval Women's Visionary Literature* (New York: Oxford University Press, 1986); Randolph Bell, *Holy Anorexia* (Chicago: University of Chicago Press, 1985).

64. *New Catholic Encyclopedia,* vol. 9 (New York: McGraw-Hill, 1967).

65. Charles Stewart and Rosalind Shaw, eds., *Syncretism/Anti-Syncretism: The Politics of Religious Synthesis* (New York: Routledge, 1994); Anthony Stevens-Arroyo and Andres Perez y Mena, eds., *Enigmatic Powers: Syncretism with African and Indigenous People's Religions Among Latinos* (Decatur, Ga.: AETH Books, 1995).

66. Some ritual practices reported by descendants appear to have been influenced by contact with Ashkenazi Jewish customs in regions where descendant families lived alongside German Jewish immigrant communities The use of the dreidel (a spinning top) during Chanukah and the lighting of candles on successive nights, for example, are Ashkenazic rather than Sephardic in origin. Yet both these rituals have been reported as family customs by descendants in the southwestern United States. For a discussion of these cross-cultural patterns, see David Gitlitz, "Nexos entre los CriptoJudios Coloniales y Contemporaneos," 187–209.

67. David Nidel, "Modern Descendants of Conversos in New Mexico," *Western States Jewish History* 16, no. 3 (1984): 254.

68. Ada María Isasi-Díaz and Yolanda Tarango, *Hispanic Women: Pro-*

*phetic Voice in the Church* (Minneapolis: Fortress Press, 1992); Jeanette Rodriguez, *Our Lady of Guadalupe: Faith and Empowerment Among Mexican-American Women* (Austin: University of Texas, 1996); Anthony Stevens-Arroyo, "The Evolution of Marian Devotionalism Within Christianity and the Ibero-Mediterranean Polity," *Journal for the Scientific Study of Religion* 37, no. 1 (1998): 50–73.

69. Karen McCarthy Brown, *Mama Lola: A Vodou Priestess in Brooklyn* (Berkeley and Los Angeles: University of California Press, 1991), 220–21.

70. William G. McLoughlin, *The Cherokees and Christianity, 1794–1870: Essays on Acculturation and Cultural Persistence,* ed. Walter H. Conser Jr. (Athens: University of Georgia Press, 1994), 195.

71. This holiday was also referred to as La Fiesta de los Reyes, a derivation of the Spanish Feast of the Kings, which usually takes place in January.

72. Santos, "Chicanos of Jewish Descent in Texas."

73. In the Exodus story, God kills the firstborn son of the Egyptians as a punishment for the enslavement of the Jews. To distinguish the Jewish homes from those of the Egyptian houses, the Jews were told to mark their doors with blood so that God would "pass over" these families and spare their children.

74. Nidel, "Modern Descendants of Conversos in New Mexico," 261.

75. Susan S. Sered, *Women as Ritual Experts: The Religious Lives of Elderly Jewish Women in Jerusalem* (New York: Oxford University Press, 1992).

76. Sered, *Women as Ritual Experts,* 92.

## 3. THE SELF-IN-RELATION

1. Carol C. Gilligan, *In a Different Voice: Psychological Theory and Women's Development* (Cambridge, Mass.: Harvard University Press, 1982); Carol C. Gilligan, Nona P. Lyons, and Trudy J. Hanmer, eds., *Making Connections: The Relational Worlds of Adolescent Girls at Emma Willard School* (Cambridge, Mass.: Harvard University Press, 1990); Janet Liebman Jacobs, *Victimized Daughters: Incest and the Development of the Female Self* (New York: Routledge, 1994); Judith V. Jordan, Alexandra G. Kaplan, Jean Baker Miller, Irene P. Stiver, and Janet L. Surrey, eds., *Women's Growth in Connection: Writings from the Stone Center* (New York: Guilford Press, 1991).

2. Jean Baker Miller, "The Development of Women's Sense of Self," in *Women's Growth in Connection,* ed. Jordan et al., 14.

3. Clifford Geertz, "Religion as a Cultural System," in *Reader in Comparative Religion,* ed. W. L. Lessa and E. V. Vogt (New York: Harper and Row, 1972), 206.

4. Regina Lopez Caulboy, *This That and the Other* (Colorado Springs, Colo.: Caulboy, 1995), 106.

5. Sigmund Freud, *The Complete Works,* vol. 17 (London: Hogarth Press, 1917–19), 219–51.

6. Aryeh Kaplan, *Meditation and Kabbalah* (York Beach, Maine: Samuel Weiser, 1982).

7. Joseph Dan, "The Epic of a Millennium: Judeo-Spanish Culture's Confrontations," *Judaism: A Quarterly Journal* 41, no. 2 (1992): 113–29.

8. Arthur Green, "Religion and Mysticism: The Case of Judaism," in *Take Judaism, for Example: Studies Toward the Comparison of Religions,* ed. Jacob Neusner (Chicago: University of Chicago Press, 1983), 67–91; Gershom G. Scholem, *On the Kabbalah and Its Symbolism,* trans. Ralph Manheim (New York: Schocken Books, 1965); Elliot R. Wolfson, *Along the Path: Studies in Kabbalistic Myth, Symbolism, and Hermeneutics* (Albany: State University of New York Press, 1995).

9. As quoted in Kaplan, *Meditation and Kabbalah,* 155.

10. Abraham A. Neuman, *The Jews in Spain: Their Social, Political and Cultural Life During the Middle Ages,* vol. 2 (New York: Octagon Books, 1969).

11. Neuman, *Jews in Spain.*

12. Victor Perrera, *The Cross and the Pear Tree: A Sephardic Journey* (New York: Knopf, 1995), 142–43.

13. Evidence shows that women in Turkey have also carried on the spiritual healing traditions of Sephardic Judaism. For a fascinating discussion of women as healers in Istanbul today, see Isaac Jack Lévy and Rosemary Lévy Zumwalt, "Madame Sara: A Spirit Medium Between Two Worlds," in *From Iberia to Diaspora: Studies in Sephardic History and Culture,* ed. Y. K. Stillman and N. A. Stillman (Boston: Brill, 1999), 331–45.

14. *Curanderismo* derives from *curar,* the Spanish verb meaning "to heal."

15. Anthony Stevens-Arroyo and Ana Maria Diaz-Stevens, eds., *An Enduring Flame: Studies in Latino Popular Religiosity* (Decatur, Ga.: AETH Books, 1995); Ada María Isasi-Díaz and Yolanda Tarango, *Hispanic Women: Prophetic Voice in the Church* (Minneapolis: Fortress Press, 1992); Meredith B. McGuire, *Religion: The Social Context* (Belmont, Calif.: Wadsworth Publishing, 1981); Milagros Peña and Lisa M. Frehill, "Latina Religious Practice: Analyzing Cultural Dimensions in Measures of Religiosity," *Journal for the Scientific Study of Religion* 37, no. 4 (1998): 620–35.

16. Peña and Frehill, "Latina Religious Practice," 621.

17. Isasi-Díaz and Tarango, *Hispanic Women,* 40.

18. Marc D. Angel, *The Orphaned Adult: Confronting the Death of a Parent* (New York: Human Sciences Press, 1987); Colin Murray Parkes, *Bereavement: Studies of Grief in Adult Life* (New York: International Universities Press, 1972).

19. Nancy Chodorow, "Family Structure and Feminine Personality," in *Woman, Culture and Society,* ed. M. Z. Rosaldo and L. Lamphere (Stanford, Calif.: Stanford University Press, 1974), 50.

20. Denise A. Segura and Jennifer L. Pierce, "Chicana/o Family Structure and Gender Personality: Chodorow, Familism, and Psychoanalytic Sociology Revisited," *Signs: Journal of Women in Culture and Society* 19, no. 1 (1993): 62–91.

21. Segura and Pierce, "Chicana/o Family Structure," 79.

22. Chodorow, "Family Structure and Feminine Personality," 48.

## 4. SYNCRETISM AND FAITH BLENDING

1. Charles Stewart and Rosalind Shaw, eds., *Syncretism/Anti-Syncretism: The Politics of Religious Synthesis* (New York: Routledge, 1994), 1.

2. Birgit Meyer, "Beyond Syncretism: Translation and Diabolization in the Appropriation of Protestantism in Africa," in *Syncretism/Anti-Syncretism,* ed. Stewart and Shaw, 45–68.

3. David Gitlitz reports that partial conversion can also be found among a small number of sixteenth-century *conversos* who simultaneously believed in both Judaism and Christianity and who performed rituals and prayers that were derived from each tradition. According to Richard Popkin, Christopher Columbus may have been among those *conversos* who adhered to a mixed-faith belief system. Popkin argues that Columbus, who has been both "accused and recognized" as a crypto-Jew, held Jewish and Christian beliefs that were influenced by the prophetic religious culture of both traditions. For a further discussion, see David M. Gitlitz, *Secrecy and Deceit: The Religion of the Crypto-Jews* (Philadelphia: Jewish Publication Society, 1996); and Richard Popkin, "Jewish Christians and Christian Jews in Spain, 1492 and After," *Judaism Quarterly* 41, no. 3 (1992): 248–67.

4. Mary Crow Dog, with Richard Erdoes, *Lakota Woman* (New York: HarperCollins, 1990), 93–94.

5. The Torah is the Five Books of Moses that make up the Hebrew Bible.

6. Shoshanah Feher, *Passing Over Easter* (Los Angeles: Alta Mira, 1997); David A. Rausch, *Messianic Judaism: Its History, Theology and Polity* (New York: Edwin Mellen Press, 1982).

7. Daniel J. Lasker, "Jewish-Christian Polemics in Light of the Expulsion of the Jews from Spain," *Judaism* 41, no. 162 (1992): 148–55; Benzion Netanyahu, *The Origins of the Inquisition in Fifteenth Century Spain* (New York: Random House, 1995).

8. Abraham Gross, "The Expulsion and the Search for the Ten Tribes," *Judaism* 41, no. 2 (1992): 130–47; Lasker, "Jewish-Christian Polemics"; Netanyahu, *Origins of the Inquisition.*

9. Lasker, "Jewish-Christian Polemics."

10. Gross, "Expulsion and the Search for the Ten Tribes"; Lasker, "Jewish-Christian Polemics."

11. Gross, "Expulsion and the Search for the Ten Tribes."

12. Since her files have not survived, the data on this famous prophetess are derived from the trials of her followers. It appears that she was arrested, tried, and burned at the stake within a five-month period. See Yitzhak Baer, *A History of the Jews in Christian Spain,* vol. 2 (Philadelphia: Jewish Publication Society, 1966); and Renée Levine Melammed, *Heretics or Daughters of Israel?: The Crypto-Jewish Women of Castile* (New York: Oxford University Press, 1999).

13. Eva Alexandra Uchmany, "The Periodization of the History of the New Christians and Crypto-Jews in Spanish America," in *New Horizons in Sephardic Studies,* ed. Y. Stillman and G. Zucker (New York: State University of New York Press, 1993), 109–47.

14. Uchmany, "Periodization of the History of the New Christians; Arnold Wiznitzer, "Crypto-Jews in Mexico During the Seventeenth Century," *American Jewish Quarterly* 51 (1962): 222–68.

15. Wiznitzer, "Crypto-Jews in Mexico."

16. This is a fundamental Jewish prayer, a declaration of monotheism that is recited daily by religious Jews and on the Sabbath and holy day services.

17. Rausch, *Messianic Judaism.*

18. Charles W. Conn, *Like a Mighty Army: A History of the Church of God 1886–1976* (Cleveland, Tenn.: Pathway Press, 1977).

19. Conn, *Like a Mighty Army.*

20. Their interpretation of a spiritual circumcision comes from a passage in Jeremiah (9:25) that refers to the uncircumcised heart and the need for an inner commitment to God.

21. This case is based on the life of a descendant whose crypto-Jewish origins were first recorded in an ethnography that was completed by David Nidel as a senior thesis for the University of New Mexico in 1980 and that was later published as "Modern Descendants of Conversos in New Mexico," *Western States Jewish History* 16, no. 3 (1984): 249–22. In the last two decades, with the growing popularization of the crypto-Jewish phenomenon, this descendant was interviewed numerous times by the media. After being tape-recorded by an interviewer without his consent, he withdrew from the public eye. When I contacted him in 1996, with the recommendation of a mutual acquaintance, he agreed to let me interview him after I explained that I was not a journalist but a researcher at the University of Colorado. For two days, he spoke of his family history and the difficult and painful experiences that he had undergone since first "coming out" as a crypto-Jew in the 1970s. Although Nidel's study and my own follow-up research are incorporated where applicable throughout this book, the discussion of syncretism involves a more in-depth treatment of this descendant's narrative.

22. Interview transcript from David Nidel's 1980 senior thesis, University of New Mexico. This information was rerecorded during my interview with this descendant in 1996.

23. In Judaism, the term for God is designated by these Hebrew letters, which are translated in Hebrew as *Adonai.*

24. Rosemary Radford Ruether, *Mary: The Feminine Face of the Church* (Philadelphia: Westminster Press, 1977).

25. Ana Maria Diaz-Stevens, "The Saving Grace: The Matriarchal Core of Latino Catholicism," *Latino Studies Journal* 4, no. 3 (1993): 60–78; Jeanette Rodriguez, *Our Lady of Guadalupe: Faith and Empowerment Among Mexican-American Women* (Austin: University of Texas Press, 1994).

26. Rodriguez, *Our Lady of Guadalupe,* 1.

27. Rodriguez, *Our Lady of Guadalupe,* 1.

28. In kabbalistic Judaism, the term *Hokhmah* is masculinized and refers to the creative principle of wisdom. In the Kabbalah the feminine principle is *Binah,* which is translated as "understanding" or "intelligence." See June Singer, *Androgyny* (New York: Anchor Books, 1977); and Z'ev ben Shimon Halevi, *The Work of the Kabbalist* (York Beach, Maine: Samuel Weiser, 1985).

29. Ana Maria Rizzuto, *The Birth of the Living God: A Psychoanalytic Study* (Chicago: University of Chicago Press, 1979).

30. The origins of the southwestern Penitentes are unknown. Various theo-

ries suggest that the brotherhood may have originated with the penitential confraternities in Spain and been influenced by Franciscan and mystical Spanish Catholicism. For a more extensive discussion of these theories, see Marta Weigle, *Brothers of Light, Brothers of Blood: The Penitentes of the Southwest* (Albuquerque: University of New Mexico Press, 1976).

31. Women were generally not part of the brotherhood societies but formed auxiliary organizations that were responsible for domestic support. Women also participated in the Holy Week processions and performed penances.

32. It may be of interest to note that both Gitlitz (*Secrecy and Deceit*) and Seymour Liebman (*The Jews in New Spain: Faith, Flame, and the Inquisition* [Coral Gables, Fla.: University of Miami Press, 1970]) report evidence of scarification among seventeenth-century crypto-Jews in Mexico. These rituals involved cutting the flesh of both men and women, after which the flesh was eaten. The following testimony from a trial in 1647 described how a young boy was witness to his father's scarring of a woman. According to the trial record, his father:

> stripped her naked to the waist and told her that he wanted to make a mark on her left shoulder as a sign that she was a Jewess. And binding her eyes with a towel from Rouen, and tying her hands at the wrist with a handkerchief, he saw him cut with a knife from her left shoulder a piece of flesh . . . the size of a half *real* coin, which bled profusely and gave her great pain. And Duarte de Leon put certain powders into the wound and bandaged it, and dressed her again, and took the piece of flesh and roasted it in the coals of a little brazier and ate it. (Gitlitz, 206)

33. In Jewish law and tradition, midrash is a form of rabbinic interpretation that may involve the use of stories or homilies to explain the meaning of law or to provide a moral lesson.

## 5. CONVERSION AND REKINDLING

1. Marc D. Angel, *Seeking Good, Speaking Peace: Collected Essays of Rabbi Marc D. Angel* (Hoboken, N.J.: KTAV Publishing House, 1994); Michael Asheri, *Living Jewish: The Lore and the Law of the Practicing Jew* (New York: Everest House, 1978).

2. Since 1983 the Reform Movement has recognized patrilineal descent. A child born of a non-Jewish mother and Jewish father will be considered a Jew, provided he or she was brought up as a Jew.

3. Asheri, *Living Jewish;* Arthur A. Cohen and Paul Mendes Flohr, eds., *Contemporary Jewish Religious Thought: Original Essays on Critical Concepts, Movements, and Beliefs* (New York: Scribner, 1987).

4. Deuteronomy 7:2–4.

5. Asheri, *Living Jewish.*

6. J. H. Hertz, ed., *The Pentateuch and Haftorahs: Hebrew Text, English Translation and Commentary* (London: Soncino Press, 1969), 775.

7. For a discussion of fathers and their control over daughters in Jewish biblical and Talmudic law, see Judith Romney Wegner, *Chattel or Person?: The Status of Women in the Mishnah* (New York: Oxford University Press, 1988).

8. Dan Ross, *Acts of Faith: A Journey to the Fringes of Jewish Identity* (New York: St. Martin's Press, 1982).

9. Halakah is the body of Jewish law that governs Jewish practice and belief.

10. Angel, *Seeking Good, Speaking Peace,* 277.

11. Richard M. Goodman, *Genetic Disorders Among the Jewish People* (Baltimore: Johns Hopkins University Press, 1979).

12. The Lubavitchers are a modern Hasidic Orthodox sect that proselytizes.

13. The Orthodox position is grounded in the belief that a person undergoing a non-Orthodox conversion will not be required to make a formal promise to observe all 613 commandments in the Torah, the full *Kabbat mitzvot* (acceptance of the commandments). See Walter Homolka, Walter Jacob, and Esther Seidel, eds., *Not By Birth Alone: Conversion to Judaism* (London: Cassell, 1997).

14. Jochanan H. A. Wijnhoven, "Convert and Conversion," in *Contemporary Jewish Religious Thought,* ed. Cohen and Flor, 100–106.

15. As quoted in Jonathan Wittenberg, "The Significance of Motivation in the Halachah Conversion," in *Not By Birth Alone,* ed. Homolka, Jacob, and Seidel, 91.

16. The ark is the sanctified structure in the synagogue that houses the Torah.

17. For a discussion of the Sephardim in the Americas, see Martin A. Cohen and Abraham Peck, eds., *Sephardim in the Americas: Studies in Culture and History* (Tuscaloosa: University of Alabama Press, 1993).

18. Aviva Ben-Ur, "Sephardim or Oriental Jews?: The Ethnic/Racial Debate Between the 'Grandees' and the 'Turkish Jews,' in the Early 20th Century New York City" (paper presented at the annual meeting of the Society for the Scientific Study of Religion, Boston, 1999); Joseph M. Papo, "The Sephardim in North America in the Twentieth Century," in *Sephardim in the Americas,* ed. Cohen and Peck, 267–308.

19. Debra Regina Crespin and Sarah Jacobus, "Sephardi and Mizrahi Women Write About Their Lives: Editors' Introduction," *Bridges: A Journal for Jewish Feminists and Our Friends* 7, no. 1 (1988): 7.

20. The concept of "imagined community" is taken from Benedict Anderson, *Imagined Communities: Reflections on the Origin and Spread of Nationalism* (London: Verso, 1983).

21. Wijnhoven, "Convert and Conversion," 101.

22. Adin Steinsaltz, *Teshuvah: A Guide for the Newly Observant Jew* (New York: Free Press, 1987), 3.

23. This prayer is derived from Deuteronomy 6:4–9 and other verses and is recited at every religious service and in daily prayers. The English translation for the prayer is "Hear, O Israel, the Lord is our God, the Lord is One."

24. David M. Gitlitz, *Secrecy and Deceit: The Religion of the Crypto-Jews* (Philadelphia: Jewish Publication Society, 1996).

25. Jewish feminist discourse has tended to view the tradition of family purity as demeaning to women, whose bodies are deemed impure and polluting by this aspect of Jewish law. For a feminist discussion of the monthly ritual of the *mikveh,* see Rachel Adler, "In Your Blood, Live: Re-visions of a Theology

of Purity," *Tikkun* 8 (1993): 38–41; Rachel Biale, *Women and Jewish Law: An Exploration of Women's Halakhic Sources* (New York: Schocken Books, 1984); and Laura Levitt and Sue Ann Wasserman, "Mikveh Ceremony for Laura (1989)," in *Four Centuries of Jewish Women's Spirituality,* ed. Ellen Umansky and Diane Ashton (Boston: Beacon Press, 1992), 321–26.

26. Ultra-Orthodox men also use the *mikveh* before the Sabbath and before holy days.

27. Depending on the presiding rabbi, the convert may or may not be required to perform a ritual of immersion as part of her or his conversion to Judaism. A *mikveh,* however, is required in all Orthodox conversions.

28. Yebamot 22a, as cited in Dirk Herweg and Rachel Monika Herweg, "Over Land and Sea for a Proselyte?: Conversion in Antiquity and the Talmudic Period," in *Not By Birth Alone,* ed. Homolka, Jacob, and Seidel, 17.

29. Steinsaltz, *Teshuvah,* 153.

30. Linda Begley Soroff, *The Maintenance and Transmission of Ethnic Identity: A Study of Four Ethnic Groups of Religious Jews in Israel* (New York: University Press of America, 1995).

31. Lisa Anteby's research on Ethiopian Jewish immigrant women in Israel suggests that language has exacerbated the conflicts with the Israeli rabbinate. According to Anteby, Amharic, the language of Ethiopian Jews, distinguishes between flowing and stagnant water. The ritual baths in Israel are viewed as stagnant by the Ethiopians and therefore as unsuitable for purification. For a more detailed discussion of the experience of Ethiopian Jews in Israel, see Lisa Anteby, "'There's Blood in the House': Negotiating Female Rituals of Purity Among Ethiopian Jews of Israel," in *Women and Water: Menstruation in Jewish Law and Life,* ed. Rahel R. Wasserfall (Hanover, Mass., and London: Brandeis University Press, 1999), 166–86; and Soroff, *Maintenance and Transmission of Ethnic Identity.*

32. Popular writings by non-Orthodox Jewish women in the United States who have visited the *mikveh* for the first time also stress themes of relationship and connection. See Shira Dicker, "Mikveh," *Tikkun* 7 (1992): 62–64; Lis Harris, *Holy Days: The World of a Hasidic Family* (New York: Summit Books, 1985); and Lisa Shiffman, *Generation J* (San Francisco: HarperCollins, 1999), chap. 7.

33. Amitiyah Elayne Hyman, "Womanist Ritual," in *Women and Religious Ritual,* ed. Lesley A. Northup (Washington, D.C.: Pastoral Press), 174–75.

34. William James, *The Varieties of Religious Experience* (Cambridge, Mass.: Harvard University Press, 1985).

35. Wade Clark Roof and Sarah McFarland Taylor, "The Force of Emotion: James's Reorientation of Religion and the Contemporary Rediscovery of the Body, Spirituality, and the 'Feeling Self,'" in *The Struggle For Life: A Companion to William James's The Varieties of Religious Experience,* ed. Donald Capps and Janet L. Jacobs (Newton, Kans.: Society for the Scientific Study of Religion and Princeton Theological Seminary, 1995), 205.

36. For a discussion of the role of the body in biblical Judaism, see Howard Eilberg-Schwartz, *The Savage in Judaism: An Anthropology of Israelite Religion and Ancient Judaism* (Bloomington: University of Indiana Press, 1990); and

Michael Wyschogrod, *The Body of Faith: Judaism as Corporeal Election* (New York: Seabury Press, 1983).

37. Since 691, the Temple Mount has also been a sacred area for Muslims. On the remains of the Temple site stands the El Aqsa mosque, among the most holy of Muslim shrines. The Dome of the Rock, another significant Islamic religious site, is adjacent to the mosque. The shared sacred space remains a strong source of contention between Muslims and Jews living in the Middle East.

38. In 2000, Israel's High Court of Justice ended an eleven-year legal battle over women's right to pray at the Western Wall. The court ruled that women be allowed to hold prayer services with the Torah and to wear prayer shawls. This ruling was in opposition to the Orthodox position. For a discussion of women and the Wall before this ruling, see Letty Cottin Pogrebin, *Deborah, Golda, and Me: Being Female and Jewish in America* (New York: Doubleday, 1991).

39. The Western Wall is also known as the Wailing Wall because of the lamentations over loss that have historically been associated with this ritual space.

40. Vera Schwarcz, *Bridge Across Broken Time: Chinese and Jewish Cultural Memory* (New Haven: Yale University Press, 1998).

41. Schwarcz, *Bridge Across Broken Time,* 59, 65.

42. Z. Harry Gutstein, *Passover Haggadah,* trans. Nathan Goldberg (New York: KTAV Publishing House, 1966), 23–24.

43. Aviva Cantor, "An Egalitarian Hagada," *Lilith* 9 (1982): 16.

44. Jules Harlow, ed., *Mahzor for Rosh Hashanah and Yom Kippur: A Prayer Book for the Days of Awe* (New York: Rabbinical Assembly, 1988), 691.

## 6. JEWISH ANCESTRY AND ETHNIC IDENTITY

1. Richard Alba, *Ethnic Identity: The Transformation of White America* (New Haven: Yale University Press, 1990), 1–2.

2. Alba, *Ethnic Identity,* 1–2.

3. Kurt H. Wolff, ed. and trans., *The Sociology of Georg Simmel* (Glencoe, Ill.: Free Press, 1950), 402–8.

4. Tomas Atencio, "Crypto-Jewish Remnants in Manito Society and Culture," *Jewish Folklore and Ethnology Review* 18, nos. 1–2 (1996): 59–67.

5. Simone de Beauvoir, *The Second Sex* (New York: Vintage Books, 1974).

6. de Beauvoir, *Second Sex,* xix–xx.

7. Frantz Fanon, *Black Skin, White Masks: The Experiences of a Black Man in a White World,* trans. Charles Lam Markmann (New York: Grove Press, 1967), 111–12.

8. Erving Goffman, *Stigma: Notes on the Management of Spoiled Identity* (New York: Jason Aronson, 1974), 4.

9. Atencio, "Crypto-Jewish Remnants."

10. Simon Herman, *Jewish Identity: A Social Psychological Perspective* (Beverly Hills, Calif.: Sage Publications, 1987), 45.

11. Herbert J. Gans, "Symbolic Ethnicity: The Future of Ethnic Groups and Cultures in America," *Ethnic and Racial Studies* 2 (1979): 11.

12. Seymour Liebman, *The Jews in New Spain: Faith, Flame, and the Inquisition* (Coral Gables, Fla.: University of Miami Press, 1970).

13. Emile Durkheim, *The Elementary Forms of Religious Life* (New York: Macmillan, 1915).

14. Between 1996 and 1997, a number of commemorations and memorials were held in Portugal and in the United States during the five-hundred-year anniversary of the expulsion of the Jews from Portugal. In Portugal, the commemoration included a government-sponsored day of atonement and the dedication of a synagogue in Belmonte, where a surviving crypto-Jewish community resides. In the United States, a memorial service was held for the Carvajal family in Dallas, Texas, who were executed for Judaizing four hundred years earlier; and in New York, the Sephardic House and Congregation Shearith Israel (the Spanish Portuguese synagogue) held a weekend commemoration focusing on exile and the Inquisition. While these events represent a growing awareness of the Inquisition's violence against the Jews, for the most part, the persecutions of the Inquisition are rarely remembered in public memorials.

15. Eric J. Sundquist, ed., *The Oxford W. E. B. Du Bois Reader* (New York: Oxford University Press, 1996).

16. Sundquist, *Oxford W. E. B. Du Bois Reader,* 87.

17. Sundquist, *Oxford W. E. B. Du Bois Reader,* 87.

18. Judith Lewis Herman, *Trauma and Recovery* (New York: Basic Books, 1992).

19. Karen Brodkin, *How Jews Became White Folks and What That Says About Race in America* (New Brunskwick, N.J.: Rutgers University Press, 2000).

20. It is of interest to note that this descendant saw a physical resemblance between her mother and Einstein. During her interview, she took out a photograph of her ninety-year-old mother that she compared to a picture of the elderly Einstein. In both images she saw a facial structure and facial features that she described as ethnically similar. The notion of a Jewish "phenotype" thus contributed to the construction of ethnicity among a small number of descendants who described both themselves and other family members as "looking Jewish." One respondent remarked, "When I was a teenager I lived with a Jewish woman, and she wondered if my parents were maybe Jewish. I passed beautifully. And I remember my mother joking about us looking Jewish, you know. So that notion has been there for quite a ways back." For a discussion of physical appearance and ethnic identity, see Mary Waters, *Ethnic Options: Choosing Identities in America* (Berkeley and Los Angeles: University of California Press, 1990).

21. Denis A. Segura and Jennifer L. Pierce, "Chicana/o Family Structure and Gender Personality: Chodorow, Familism, and Psychoanalytic Sociology Revisited,"*Signs: Journal of Women in Culture and Society* 19, no. 1 (1993): 70.

22. Fanon, *Black Skin, White Masks.*

23. Daniel Boyarin, "Epater L'embourgeoisement: Freud, Gender and the Decolonized Psyche," *diacritics* 24 (1994): 17–41; Sander Gilman, *Jewish Self-Hatred: Anti-Semitism and the Hidden Language of the Jews* (Baltimore: Johns

Hopkins University Press, 1986), *Freud, Race and Gender* (Princeton: Princeton University Press, 1993), and *Love + Marriage = Death and Other Essays on Representing Difference* (Stanford, Calif.: Stanford University Press, 1998).

24. Boyarin, "Epater."

25. Cherríe Moraga, *Loving in the War Years* (Boston: South End Press, 1983), 51.

26. Brodkin, *How Jews Became White Folks;* Riv-Ellen Prell, *Fighting to Become Americans: Jews, Gender and the Anxiety of Assimilation* (Boston: Beacon Press, 1999).

27. Albert Memmi, *The Colonizer and the Colonized* (Boston: Beacon Press, 1967).

28. Memmi, *Colonizer and the Colonized,* xiv.

29. Brodkin, *How Jews Became White Folks;* Brodkin's thesis is supported by the work of both Linda Gordon and Angela Davis, who cite especially the early-twentieth-century presidential policies of Theodore Roosevelt. In the face of the large immigration movement from southern and eastern Europe, Roosevelt warned that unless native-born white women ended their "willful sterility," the nation would succumb to "race suicide." For a further discussion of this historical period, see Angela Davis, *Women, Race and Class* (New York: Random House, 1981); and Linda Gordon, *Women's Body, Women's Right; A Social History of Birth Control in America* (New York: Grossman, 1976).

30. Brodkin, *How Jews Became White Folks.*

31. Hayim Halevy Donin, *To Be a Jew: A Guide to Jewish Observance in Contemporary Life* (New York: Basic Books, 1972).

32. Donin, *To Be a Jew.*

33. Jerome S. Legge Jr., "Understanding American Judaism: Revisiting the Concept of 'Social Justice,'" in *Jews in America: A Contemporary Reader,* ed. R. R. Farber and C. I. Waxman (Hanover, Mass.: Brandeis University Press, 1999), 201–11.

34. Legge, "Understanding American Judaism."

35. Letty Cottin Pogrebin, *Deborah, Golda, and Me: Being Female and Jewish in America* (New York: Doubleday, 1991), 162–63.

36. Although a handful of respondents did associate Jewish ethnicity with success in business, the descendants did not dwell on this stereotype in their discussions of Jewish identity.

## CONCLUSION

1. Regina Lopez Caulboy, *This That and the Other* (Colorado Springs, Colo.: Caulboy, 1995), 113–16.

2. M. M. Oliner, "Hysterical Features Among Children of Survivors," in *Generations of the Holocaust,* ed. M. S. Bergmann and M. E. Jucovy (New York: Basic Books, 1982), 267–85.

3. Oliner, "Hysterical Features Among Children," 277, 281.

# Selected Bibliography

Adler, Cyrus, ed. *Trial of Gabriel de Granada by the Inquisition in Mexico 1642–1645*. Translated by David Fergusson. Baltimore: Friedenwald, 1899.

Adler, Rachel. "In Your Blood, Live: Re-visions of a Theology of Purity." *Tikkun* 8 (1993): 38–41.

Alba, Richard. *Ethnic Identity: The Transformation of White America*. New Haven: Yale University Press, 1990.

Anderson, Benedict. *Imagined Communities: Reflections on the Origin and Spread of Nationalism*. London: Verso, 1983.

Angel, Marc D. *The Orphaned Adult: Confronting the Death of a Parent*. New York: Human Sciences Press, 1987.

———. *Seeking Good, Speaking Peace: Collected Essays of Rabbi Marc D. Angel*. Hoboken, N.J.: KTAV Publishing House, 1994.

———. *Voices in Exile: A Study in Sephardic Intellectual History*. Hoboken, N.J.: KTAV Publishing House, 1991.

Anteby, Lisa. "'There's Blood in the House': Negotiating Female Rituals of Purity Among Ethiopian Jews of Israel." In *Women and Water: Menstruation in Jewish Law and Life,* edited by R. Wasserfall. Hanover, Mass., and London: Brandeis University Press, 1999.

Asheri, Michael. *Living Jewish: The Lore and the Law of the Practicing Jew*. New York: Everest House, 1978.

Atencio, Tomas. "Crypto-Jewish Remnants in Manito Society and Culture." *Jewish Folklore and Ethnology Review* 18, nos. 1–2 (1996): 59–67.

Baer, Yitzhak. *A History of the Jews in Christian Spain*. 2 vols. Philadelphia: Jewish Publication Society, 1966.

Barstow, Ann Lewellyn. *Witchcraze*. San Francisco: HarperCollins, 1994.

Beck, Evelyn Torton. "From 'Kike' to 'JAP': How Misogyny, Anti-Semitism, and Racism Construct the 'Jewish American Princess.'" In *Race, Class and*

*Gender: An Anthology,* edited by M. L. Andersen and P. H. Collins. Belmont, Calif.: Wadsworth Publishing, 1992.

Behar, Ruth, and Deborah A. Gordon, eds. *Women Writing Culture.* Berkeley and Los Angeles: University of California Press, 1995.

Beinart, Haim. *Conversos on Trial: The Inquisition in Ciudad Real.* Jerusalem: Magnes, 1981.

Bell, Randolph. *Holy Anorexia.* Chicago: University of Chicago Press, 1985.

Ben-Ur, Aviva. "Sephardim or Oriental Jews?: The Ethnic/Racial Debate Between the 'Grandees' and the 'Turkish Jews' in the Early 20th Century New York City." Paper presented at the annual meeting of the Society for the Scientific Study of Religion, Boston, 1999.

Biale, Rachel. *Women and Jewish Law: An Exploration of Women's Issues in Halakhic Sources.* New York: Schocken Books, 1984.

Boyarin, Daniel. "Epater L'embourgeoisement: Freud, Gender and the Decolonized Psyche." *diacritics* 24 (1994): 17–41.

Brodkin, Karen. *How Jews Became White Folks and What That Says About Race in America.* New Brunswick, N.J.: Rutgers University Press, 2000.

Brown, Karen McCarthy. *Mama Lola: A Vodou Priestess in Brooklyn.* Berkeley and Los Angeles: University of California Press, 1991.

———. "On Feminist Methodology." *Journal of Feminist Studies in Religion* 1 (1985): 76–79.

Canelo, David Augusto. *The Last Crypto Jews of Portugal.* Portland, Ore.: IJS, 1990.

Cantor, Aviva. "An Egalitarian Hagada." *Lilith* 9 (1982): 10–24.

Capps, Donald, and Walter H. Capps. *The Religious Personality.* Belmont, Calif.: Wadsworth Publishing, 1970.

Chodorow, Nancy. "Family Structure and Feminine Personality." In *Woman, Culture and Society,* edited by M. Z. Rosaldo and L. Lamphere. Stanford, Calif.: Stanford University Press, 1974.

Cohen, Arthur A., and Paul Mendes Flohr, eds. *Contemporary Jewish Religious Thought: Original Essays on Critical Concepts, Movements, and Beliefs.* New York: Scribner, 1987.

Cohen, Martin A., and Abraham J. Peck, eds. *Sephardim in the Americas: Studies in Culture and History.* Tuscaloosa: University of Alabama Press, 1993.

Conn, Charles W. *Like a Mighty Army: A History of the Church of God, 1886–1976.* Cleveland, Tenn: Pathway Press, 1977.

Crespin, Debra Regina, and Sarah Jacobus. "Sephardi and Mizrahi Women Write About Their Lives: Editors' Introduction." *Bridges: A Journal for Jewish Feminists and Our Friends* 7, no. 1 (1988): 7.

Crow Dog, Mary, with Richard Erdoes. *Lakota Woman.* New York: HarperCollins, 1990.

Dan, Joseph. "The Epic of a Millennium: Judeo-Spanish Culture's Confrontations." *Judaism: A Quarterly Journal* 41, no. 2 (1992): 113–29.

Davis, Angela. *Women, Race and Class.* New York: Random House, 1981.

de Beauvoir, Simone. *The Second Sex.* New York: Vintage Books, 1974.

Diaz-Stevens, Ana Maria. "The Saving Grace: The Matriarchal Core of Latino Catholicism." *Latino Studies Journal* 4, no. 3 (1993): 60–78.

Dicker, Shira. "Mikveh." *Tikkun* 7 (1992): 62–64.
Donin, Hayim Halevy. *To Be a Jew: A Guide to Jewish Observance in Contemporary Life*. New York: Basic Books, 1972.
Douglas, Mary. *Purity and Danger: An Analysis of the Concepts of Pollution and Taboo*. New York: Praeger, 1966.
Durkheim, Emile. *The Elementary Forms of Religious Life*. New York: Macmillan, 1915.
Dyer, Abigail, and Richard Kagan. *Inquisitional Inquiries: Involuntary Autobiographies*. Baltimore: Johns Hopkins University Press, forthcoming.
Edwards, John. "The Beginnings of a Scientific Theory of Race." In *From Iberia to Diaspora: Studies in Sephardic History and Culture*, edited by Y. K. Stillman and N. A. Stillman. Boston: Brill, 1999.
Eilberg-Schwartz, Howard. *The Savage in Judaism: An Anthropology of Israelite Religion and Ancient Judaism*. Bloomington: University of Indiana Press, 1990.
Elkin, Judith Laikin. "Colonial Origins of Contemporary Anti-Semitism in Latin America." In *The Jewish Diaspora in Latin America*, edited by D. Sheinin and L. B. Barr. New York: Garland Publishing, 1996.
Fabre-Vassas, Claudine. *The Singular Beast: Jews, Christians and the Pig*. Translated by Carol Volk. New York: Columbia University Press, 1997.
Fanon, Frantz. *Black Skin, White Masks: The Experiences of a Black Man in a White World*. Translated by Charles Lam Markmann. New York: Grove Press, 1967.
Faur, José. *In the Shadow of History: Jews and Conversos at the Dawn of Modernity*. Albany: State University of New York Press, 1992.
Feher, Shoshanah. *Passing Over Easter*. Los Angeles: Alta Mira, 1997.
Ferry, Robert. "The Blancas: Women, Honor and the Jewish Community in Seventeenth Century Mexico" (forthcoming).
Fremont, Helen. *After Long Silence*. New York: Delacorte Press, 1999.
Freud, Sigmund. *The Complete Works*, vol. 17. London: Hogarth Press, 1917–19.
Gans, Herbert J. "Symbolic Ethnicity: The Future of Ethnic Groups and Cultures in America." *Ethnic and Racial Studies* 2 (1979): 11.
Geertz, Clifford. "Religion as a Cultural System." In *Reader in Comparative Religion*, edited by W. L. Lessa and E. V. Vogt. New York: Harper and Row, 1972.
Geller, Jay. "'A Glance at the Nose': Freud's Inscription of Jewish Difference." *American Imago* 49, no. 4 (1992): 427–44.
———. "(G)nos(e)ology: The Cultural Construction of the Other." In *People of the Body: Jews and Judaism from an Embodied Perspective*, edited by H. Eilberg-Schwartz. Albany: State University of New York Press, 1992.
———. "The Godfather of Psychoanalysis: Circumcision, Antisemitism, Homosexuality, and Freud's 'Fighting Jew.'" *Journal of the American Academy of Religion* 67, no. 2 (1999): 355–85.
Gerber, Jane S. *The Jews of Spain: A History of the Sephardic Experience*. New York: Free Press, 1992.

Gilligan, Carol. *In a Different Voice: Psychological Theory and Women's Development.* Cambridge, Mass.: Harvard University Press, 1982.

Gilligan, Carol, Nona P. Lyons, and Trudy J. Hanmer, eds. *Making Connections: The Relational Worlds of Adolescent Girls at Emma Willard School.* Cambridge, Mass.: Harvard University Press, 1990.

Gilman, Sander. *Freud, Race and Gender.* Princeton: Princeton University Press, 1993.

———. *Jewish Self-Hatred: Anti-Semitism and the Hidden Language of the Jews.* Baltimore: Johns Hopkins University Press, 1986.

———. *Love + Marriage = Death and Other Essays on Representing Difference.* Stanford, Calif.: Stanford University Press, 1998.

Gitlitz, David M. "Nexos entre los CriptoJudios Coloniales y Contemporaneos." *Revista de Humanidades: Tecnológico de Monterrey (Mexico)* 5 (1998): 187–209.

———. *Secrecy and Deceit: The Religion of the Crypto-Jews.* Philadelphia: Jewish Publication Society, 1996.

Goffman, Erving. *Stigma: Notes on the Management of Spoiled Identity.* New York: Jason Aronson, 1974.

Goldstein, Donna Meryl. "Re-Imagining the Jew in Hungary: The Reconstruction of Ethnicity Through Political Affiliation." In *Rethinking Nationalism and Ethnicity: The Struggle for Meaning and Order in Europe,* edited by H. Wicker. New York: Oxford, 1997.

Goodman, Philip. *The Hanukkah Anthology.* Philadelphia: Jewish Publication Society of America, 1976.

Goodman, Richard M. *Genetic Disorders Among the Jewish People.* Baltimore: Johns Hopkins University Press, 1979.

Gordon, Linda. *Women's Body, Women's Right: A Social History of Birth Control in America.* New York: Grossman, 1976.

Gradwohl, David Mayer. "On Vestiges and Identities: Some Thoughts on the Controversy Concerning 'Crypto-Jews' in the American Southwest." *Jewish Folklore and Ethnology Review* 18, nos. 1–2 (1996): 83–84.

Green, Arthur. "Religion and Mysticism: The Case of Judaism." In *Take Judaism, for Example: Studies Toward the Comparison of Religions,* edited by Jacob Neusner. Chicago: University of Chicago Press, 1983.

Greenleaf, Richard E. *The Mexican Inquisition of the Sixteenth Century.* Albuquerque: University of New Mexico Press, 1969.

Gross, Abraham. "The Expulsion and the Search for the Ten Tribes." *Judaism* 41, no. 2 (1992): 130–47.

Halbwachs, Maurice. *On Collective Memory.* Translated by Lewis A. Coser. Chicago: University of Chicago Press, 1992.

Halevi, Z'ev ben Shimon. *The Work of the Kabbalist.* York Beach, Maine: Samuel Weiser, 1985.

Halevy, Schulamith C. "Jewish Practices Among the Anusim." *Shofar: An Interdisciplinary Journal of Jewish Studies* 18, no. 1 (1999): 88–99.

———. "Manifestations of Crypto-Judaism in the American Southwest." *Jewish Folklore and Ethnography Review* 18, nos. 1–2 (1996): 68–76.

Harris, Lis. *Holy Days: The World of a Hasidic Family*. New York: Summit Books, 1985.
Herman, Judith Lewis. *Trauma and Recovery*. New York: Basic Books, 1992.
Herman, Simon. *Jewish Identity: A Social Psychological Perspective*. Beverly Hills, Calif.: Sage Publications, 1987.
Hernandez, Frances. "The Secret Jews of the Southwest." In *Sephardim in the Americas*, edited by M. Cohen and A. Peck. Tuscaloosa: University of Alabama Press, 1993.
Herweg, Dirk, and Rachel Monika Herweg. "Over Land and Sea for a Proselyte?: Conversion in Antiquity and the Talmudic Period." In *Not By Birth Alone: Conversion to Judaism*, edited by Walter Homolka, Walter Jacob, and Esther Seidel. London: Cassell, 1997.
Hordes, Stanley Mark. "The Inquisition and the Crypto-Jewish Community in Colonial Spain and New Mexico." In *Cultural Encounters: The Impact of the Inquisition in Spain and the New World*, edited by M. E. and A. J. Cruz. Berkeley and Los Angeles: University of California Press, 1991.
Hyman, Amitiyah Elayne. "Womanist Ritual." In *Women and Religious Ritual*, edited by Lesley A. Northup. Washington, D.C.: Pastoral Press, 1993.
Isaac, Jules. *The Teaching of Contempt: Christian Roots of Anti-Semitism*. Translated by Helen Weaver. New York: Holt, Rinehart and Winston, 1964.
Isasi-Díaz, Ada María, and Yolanda Tarango. *Hispanic Women: Prophetic Voice in the Church*. Minneapolis: Fortress Press, 1992.
Jacobs, Janet Liebman. *Victimized Daughters: Incest and the Development of the Female Self*. New York: Routledge, 1994.
Jaher, Frederic Cople. *A Scapegoat in the New Wilderness: The Origins and Rise of Anti-Semitism in America*. Cambridge, Mass.: Harvard University Press, 1994.
James, William. *The Varieties of Religious Experience*. Cambridge, Mass.: Harvard University Press, 1985.
Jordan, Judith V., Alexandra G. Kaplan, Jean Baker Miller, Irene P. Stiver, and Janet L. Surrey, eds. *Women's Growth in Connection: Writings from the Stone Center*. New York: Guilford Press, 1991.
Kaplan, Aryeh. *Meditation and Kabbalah*. York Beach, Maine: Samuel Weiser, 1982.
Kleeblatt, Norman. "'Passing' into Multiculturalism." In *Too Jewish?: Challenging Traditional Identities*, edited by N. Kleeblatt. New Brunswick, N.J.: Rutgers University Press, 1996.
Klein, Dennis. *Jewish Origins of the Psychoanalytic Movement*. Chicago: University of Chicago Press, 1985.
Kunin, Seth. "Juggling Identities among the Crypto-Jews of the American Southwest." *Religion* 31 (2001): 41–61.
Larralde, Carlos Montalvo. "Chicano Jews in South Texas." Ph.D diss., University of California at Los Angeles, 1978.
Lasker, Daniel J. "Jewish-Christian Polemics in Light of the Expulsion of the Jews From Spain." *Judaism* 41, no. 162 (1992): 148–55.
Lazar, Moshe. "Scorched Parchments and Tortured Memories: 'The Jewishness'

of the *Anussim* (Cyrpto-Jews)." In *Cultural Encounters: The Impact of the Inquisition in Spain and the New World,* edited by M. E. Perry and A. J. Cruz. Berkeley and Los Angeles: University of California Press, 1991.

Lea, Henry Charles. *A History of the Inquisition of Spain.* New York: Macmillan, 1906–8.

Legge, Jerome S. Jr. "Understanding American Judaism: Revisiting the Concept of 'Social Justice.'" In *Jews in America: A Contemporary Reader,* edited by R. R. Farber and C. I. Waxman. Hanover, Mass.: Brandeis University Press, 1999.

Levine Melammed, Renée. *Heretics or Daughters of Israel?: The Crypto-Jewish Women of Castile.* New York: Oxford University Press, 1999.

———. "Sephardi Women in the Medieval and Early Modern Period." In *Jewish Women in Historical Perspective,* edited by J. R. Raskin. Detroit: Wayne State University Press, 1991.

———. "The Ultimate Challenge: Safeguarding the Crypto-Jewish Heritage." *Proceedings of the American Academy of Religion* 53 (1985): 91–109.

———. "Women in (Post 1492) Spanish Crypto-Jewish Society: Conversos and the Perpetuation and Preservation of Observances Associated with Judaism." *Judaism* 41 (1992): 156–68.

———. "Women in Spanish Crypto-Judaism: 1492–1520." Ph.D. diss., Brandeis University, 1982.

Levitt, Laura, and Sue Ann Wasserman. "Mikveh Ceremony for Laura (1989)." In *Four Centuries of Jewish Women's Spirituality,* ed. Ellen Umansky and Diane Ashton. Boston: Beacon Press, 1992.

Lévy, Isaac Jack, and Rosemary Lévy Aumwalt. "Madame Sara: A Spirit Medium Between Two Worlds." In *From Iberia to Diaspora: Studies in Sephardic History and Culture,* edited by Y. K. Stillman and N. A. Stillman. Boston: Brill, 1999.

Liebman, Seymour. *The Jews in New Spain: Faith, Flame, and the Inquisition.* Coral Gables, Fla.: University of Miami Press, 1970.

McGuire, Meredith B. *Religion: The Social Context.* Belmont, Calif.: Wadsworth Publishing, 1981.

McLoughlin, William G. *The Cherokees and Christianity, 1794–1870: Essays on Acculturation and Cultural Persistence,* edited by Walter H. Conser Jr. Athens: University of Georgia Press, 1994.

Memmi, Albert. *The Colonizer and the Colonized.* Boston: Beacon Press, 1967.

Meyer, Birgit. "Beyond Syncretism: Translation and Diabolization in the Appropriation of Protestantism in Africa." In *Syncretism/Anti-Syncretism: The Politics of Religious Synthesis,* edited by Charles Stewart and Rosalind Shaw. New York: Routledge, 1994.

Montoya, Emma. "New Mexico's Sephardim: Uncovering Jewish Roots." *La Herencia del Norte* (winter 1996): 9–12.

Moraga, Cherríe. *Loving in the War Years.* Boston: South End Press, 1983.

Moreno de los Arcos, Roberto. "New Spain's Inquisition of Indians from the Sixteenth to the Nineteenth Century." In *Cultural Encounters: The Impact of the Inquisition in Spain and the New World,* edited by M. E. Perry and A. J. Cruz. Berkeley and Los Angeles: University of California Press, 1991.

Netanyahu, Benzion. *The Origins of the Inquisition in Fifteenth Century Spain.* New York: Random House, 1995.

Neulander, Judith. "The Crypto-Jewish Canon: Choosing to Be Chosen in Millennial Tradition." *Jewish Folklore and Ethnology Review* 18, nos. 1–2 (1996): 19–59.

Neuman, Abraham A. *The Jews in Spain: Their Social, Political and Cultural Life During the Middle Ages,* vol. 2. New York: Octagon Books, 1969.

Nidel, David. "Modern Descendants of Conversos in New Mexico." *Western States Jewish History* 16, no. 3 (1984).

Oliner, M. M. "Hysterical Features Among Children of Survivors." In *Generations of the Holocaust,* edited by M. S. Bergamnn and M. E. Jucovy. New York: Basic Books, 1982.

Papo, Joseph M. "The Sephardim in North America in the Twentieth Century." In *Sephardim in the Americas,* edited by M.A. Cohen and A. J. Peck. Tuscaloosa: University of Alabama Press, 1993.

Parkes, Colin Murray. *Bereavement: Studies of Grief in Adult Life.* New York: International Universities Press, 1972.

Parks, Roger. "The Survival of Judeo-Spanish Cultural and Linguistic Traits Among Descendants of Crypto-Jews in New Mexico." Master's thesis, University of New Mexico, 1988.

Peña, Milagros, and Lisa M. Frehill. "Latina Religious Practice: Analyzing Cultural Dimensions in Measures of Religiosity." *Journal for the Scientific Study of Religion* 37, no. 4 (1998): 620–35.

Perrera, Victor. *The Cross and the Pear Tree: A Sephardic Journey.* New York: Knopf, 1995.

Petroff, Elizabeth Alvilda, ed. *Medieval Women's Visionary Literature.* New York: Oxford University Press, 1986.

Pogrebin, Letty Cottin. *Deborah, Golda, and Me: Being Female and Jewish in America.* New York: Doubleday, 1991.

Popkin, Richard. "Jewish Christians and Christian Jews in Spain, 1492 and After." *Judaism* 41, no. 3 (1992): 248–67.

Prell, Riv-Ellen. *Fighting to Become Americans: Jews, Gender, and the Anxiety of Assimilation.* Boston: Beacon Press, 1999.

Raboteau, Albert. *Slave Religion: The "Invisible Institution" in the Antebellum South.* New York: Oxford University Press, 1978.

Rausch, David A. *Messianic Judaism: Its History, Theology and Polity.* New York: Edwin Mellen Press, 1982.

Reinharz, Shulamit, with Lynn Davidman. *Feminist Methods in Social Research.* New York: Oxford University Press, 1992.

Revah, I. S. "Les Marranes Portugais et l'Inquisition au XVIe Siecle." In *The Sephardic Heritage,* edited by R. D. Barnett. London: Vallentine, Mitchell, 1971.

Rizzuto, Ana Maria. *The Birth of the Living God: A Psychoanalytic Study.* Chicago: University of Chicago Press, 1979.

Rodriquez, Jeanette. *Our Lady of Guadalupe: Faith and Empowerment Among Mexican-American Women.* Austin: University of Texas Press, 1994.

Roof, Wade Clark, and Sarah McFarland Taylor. "The Force of Emotion:

James's Reorientation of Religion and the Contemporary Rediscovery of the Body, Spirituality, and the 'Feeling Self.'" In *The Struggle for Life: A Companion to William James's The Varieties of Religious Experience,* edited by Donald Capps and Janet L. Jacobs. Newton, Kans.: Society for the Scientific Study of Religion and Princeton Theological Seminary, 1995.

Rosales, Laura Pérez. "Anticardenismo and Anti-Semitism in Mexico, 1934–1940." In *The Jewsih Diaspora in Latin America,* edited by D. Sheinin and L. B. Barr. New York: Garland Publishing, 1996.

Ross, Dan. *Acts of Faith: A Journey to the Fringes of Jewish Identity.* New York: St. Martin's Press, 1982.

Roth, Cecil. *A History of the Marranos.* Philadelphia: Jewish Publication Society, 1932.

Ruether, Rosemary Radford. *Faith and Fratricide: The Theological Roots of Anti-Semitism.* New York: Seabury Press, 1974.

———. *Mary: The Feminine Face of the Church.* Philadelphia: Westminster Press, 1977.

Santos, Richard. "Chicanos of Jewish Descent in Texas." *Western States Jewish Historical Quarterly* 15, no. 4 (1983): 289–333.

Scholem, Gershom G. *On the Kabbalah and Its Symbolism.* Translated by Ralph Manheim. New York: Schocken Books, 1965.

Schwarcz, Vera. *Bridge Across Broken Time: Chinese and Jewish Cultural Memory.* New Haven: Yale University Press, 1998.

Schwartz, Samuel. "The Crypto-Jews of Portugal." *Menorah Journal* 12 (1926): 138–49, 283–97, 325.

Scott, James C. *Domination and the Arts of Resistance: Hidden Transcripts.* New Haven: Yale University Press, 1990.

Segura, Denise A., and Jennifer L. Pierce. "Chicana/o Family Structure and Gender Personality: Chodorow, Familism, and Psychoanalytic Sociology Revisited." *Signs: Journal of Women in Culture and Society* 19, no. 1 (1993): 62–91.

Sered, Susan S. *Women as Ritual Experts: The Religious Lives of Elderly Jewish Women in Jerusalem.* New York: Oxford University Press, 1992.

Shepard, Sanford. "The Present State of the Ritual Crime in Spain." In *The Blood Libel Legend: A Casebook of Anti-Semitic Folklore,* edited by A. Dundes. Madison: University of Wisconsin Press, 1991.

Shiffman, Lisa. *Generation J.* San Francisco: HarperCollins, 1999.

Singer, June. *Androgyny.* New York: Anchor Books, 1977.

Soroff, Linda Begley. *The Maintenance and Transmission of Ethnic Identity: A Study of Four Ethnic Groups of Religious Jews in Israel.* New York: University Press of America, 1995.

Steinsaltz, Adin. *Teshuvah: A Guide for the Newly Observant Jew.* New York: Free Press, 1987.

Stevens-Arroyo, Anthony. "The Evolution of Marian Devotionalism Within Christianity and the Ibero-Mediterranean Polity." *Journal for the Scientific Study of Religion* 37, no. 1 (1998): 50–73.

Stevens-Arroyo, Anthony, and Ana Maria Diaz-Stevens, eds. *An Enduring*

*Flame: Studies in Latino Popular Religiosity*. Decatur, Ga.: AETH Books, 1995.
Stevens-Arroyo, Anthony, and Andres Perez y Mena, eds. *Enigmatic Powers: Syncretism with African and Indigenous People's Religions Among Latinos*. Decatur, Ga.: AETH Books, 1996.
Stewart, Charles, and Rosalind Shaw, eds. *Syncretism/Anti-Syncretism: The Politics of Religious Synthesis*. New York: Routledge, 1994.
Sundquist, Eric J., ed. *The Oxford W. E. B Du Bois Reader*. New York: Oxford University Press, 1996.
Tobias, Henry. *A History of the Jews in New Mexico*. Albuquerque: University of New Mexico Press, 1990.
Uchmany, Eva Alexandra. "The Crypto-Jews in New Spain During the First Years of Colonial Life." *Proceedings of the Sixth World Congress of Jewish Studies*, 2 (1977): 95–109.
———. "The Periodization of the History of the New Christians and Crypto-Jews in Spanish America." In *New Horizons in Sephardic Studies*, edited by Y. Stillman and G. Zucker. New York: State University of New York Press, 1993.
Ward, Seth. "Converso Descendants in the U.S. Southwest: A Report on Research, Resources, and the Changing Search for Identity." In *Proceedings of the 1998 Conference of the European Association for Jewish Studies*, edited by A. Saenz-Badillos. Leiden: E. J. Brill, 1999.
Waters, Mary. *Ethnic Options: Choosing Identities in America*. Berkeley and Los Angeles: University of California Press, 1990.
Wegner, Judith Romney. *Chattel or Person?: The Status of Women in the Mishnah*. New York: Oxford University Press, 1988.
Weigle, Marta. *Brothers of Light, Brothers of Blood: The Penitentes of the Southwest*. Albuquerque: University of New Mexico Press, 1976.
Wijnhoven, Jochanan H. A. "Convert and Conversion." In *Contemporary Jewish Religious Thought: Original Essays on Critical Concepts, Movements and Beliefs*, edited by A. A. Cohen and P. M. Flohr. New York: Scribner, 1987.
Wiznitzer, Arnold. "Crypto-Jews in Mexico During the Seventeenth Century." *American Jewish Historical Quarterly* 51 (1962): 222–68.
———. "Crypto-Jews in Mexico During the Sixteenth Century." *American Jewish Historical Quarterly* 51 (1962): 168–214.
Wolff, Kurt H., ed. and trans. *The Sociology of Georg Simmel*. Glencoe, Ill.: Free Press, 1950.
Wolfson, Elliot R. *Along the Path: Studies in Kabbalistic Myth, Symbolism, and Hermeneutics*. Albany: State University of New York Press, 1995.
Wyschogrod, Michael. *The Body of Faith: Judaism as Corporeal Election*. New York: Seabury Press, 1983.
Yerushalmi, Yosef Haymin. *From Spanish Court to Italian Ghetto: Isaac Cardoso: A Study in Seventeenth-Century Marranism and Jewish Apologetics*. New York: Columbia University Press, 1971.

# Index

Compositor: Binghamton Valley Composition
Text: 10/13 Sabon
Display: Sabon
Printer and Binder: Thomson-Shore, Inc.